D0907721

A Guide to
Basic Econometric
Techniques

A Guide to Basic Econometric Techniques

Second Edition

Elia Kacapyr

M.E.Sharpe
Armonk, New York
London, England

Copyright © 2014 by M.E. Sharpe, Inc.

All rights reserved. No part of this book may be reproduced in any form
without written permission from the publisher, M.E. Sharpe, Inc.,
80 Business Park Drive, Armonk, New York 10504.

Library of Congress Cataloging-in-Publication Data

Kacapyr, Elia, 1956-
  [Introductory econometrics for undergraduates]
  A guide to basic econometric techniques / by Elia Kacapyr. – Second edition.
      pages cm
  Revised edition of the author's Introductory econometrics for undergraduates.
  Includes bibliographical references and index.
  ISBN 978-0-7656-4477-0 (alk. paper) 1. Econometrics. I. Title.
  HB139.K26 2014
  330.01'5195—dc23   2013043917

Printed in the United States of America

The paper used in this publication meets the minimum requirements of
American National Standard for Information Sciences
Permanence of Paper for Printed Library Materials,
ANSI Z 39.48-1984.

IBT (p)   10   9   8   7   6   5   4   3   2   1

Contents

Note on Supplementary Materials for Students and Instructors

All of the input data required for solving the end-of-chapter problems in this text beginning in Chapter 5 are available at www.mesharpe-student.com.

The data files are in Excel format, which allows them to be imported into a variety of statistical software packages including Eviews and gretl.

Eviews by IHS was used to solve the problems in the book, but any package will do. Free shareware is available (such as gretl) that can do all the problems in this text. Excel by Microsoft can be used to run regressions, but it does not calculate all the residual statistics needed in later chapters.

Adopting instructors may obtain a full complement of ancillary materials from the Publisher at www.mesharpe-instructor.com.

Preface

Econometrics can be a real eye-opener for students as they come to understand that many of the theories they have learned can be questioned and tested using real-world data. This Second Edition of *A Guide to Basic Econometric Techniques* serves as a universal supplement for all introductory econometrics courses. Whether used by undergraduates or students in advanced programs or by practitioners, this student-friendly book provides an introduction to econometrics and economic forecasting, with an emphasis on the proper application and interpretation of regression results.

"Student-friendly" does not mean superficial or easy. It means that the explanations of essential concepts are concise, yet clearly illustrated step by step. For instance, the derivation of the ordinary least-squares estimators is shown with simple algebra once the chain rule is applied. Skip this derivation if you are interested only in applications.

Most of the concepts are demonstrated with interesting examples, and students apply what they have learned by solving problems at the back of each chapter. Seven full-length exams, enabling students to gauge their mastery of these concepts, are provided throughout the book.

The solutions to the odd-numbered problems and to the questions in the exams are presented in the back of the book. The data sets required to solve the end-of-chapter problems can be found at M.E. Sharpe's student Web site (www.mesharpe-student.com). These data sets can be used with a wide variety of statistical software packages.

In addition, instructors have access to PowerPoint slides and problem-solving and testing materials. This supplemental material can be found at the password-protected M.E. Sharpe Web site for instructors (www.mesharpe-instructor.com).

A course with terms like "heteroskedasticity," "first-order Markov scheme," and "pseudoautocorrelation" can seem intimidating, but it does not have to be. The typical junior or senior economics major can master these topics and many more by reading this textbook and working on the problems at the end of each chapter; they can confirm their newfound understanding of fundamental concepts of econometrics by completing the exams. Add a good instructor to the mix and the material should come to life.

EK
Ithaca, NY

Chapter 1

The Nature of Econometrics

What is Econometrics?

The Econometric Methodology

Many Applications

Terms

Chapter 1 Problems

1.1 What is Econometrics?

Literally, econometrics means "economic measurement." Therefore, gathering data and generating economic statistics such as gross domestic product and the consumer price index could be considered econometrics. In practice econometrics is about testing economic hypotheses with statistical techniques. Respected econometricians have given us a variety of definitions. One favorite, perhaps because of its brevity, is from Henri Theil: "Econometrics is concerned with the empirical determination of economic laws" (Theil 1971, p. 1).

1.2 The Econometric Methodology

You might remember the "scientific method" from a middle school science class. The first step is to state clearly the hypothesis to be tested. Econometric methodology is a specific form of that. Let's work through an example inspired by Keynes' Law of Consumption:

"The fundamental psychological law, upon which we are entitled to depend with great confidence both *a priori* from our knowledge of human nature and from the detailed facts of experience, is that men are disposed, as a rule and on average, to increase their consumption as their income increases, but not by as much as the increase in income" (Keynes 1936, p. 96).

The steps of the econometric methodology can be applied to this law.

1) State the theory, law, or hypothesis

It is impossible to state Keynes' law more eloquently than the master economist himself. However, it may be stated more succinctly: When income goes up, consumer spending goes up, but not by as much.

2) Specify the econometric model

This step requires writing the idea in mathematical form. One of the simplest forms is slope-intercept. Again, from middle school you may remember $y = mx + b$. We will replace the y with CONS (consumer spending) and the x with INC (consumer income):

$$CONS = m \, (INC) + b$$

The tradition in econometrics is to replace the b with β_0 and the m with β_1 and write the same equation this way:

$$CONS = \beta_0 + \beta_1 \, INC + u$$

The u is known as the error term, disturbance, or residual. (You will soon come to see that everything in econometrics has at least two names.) This formulation assumes the relationship between CONS and INC is linear (in slope-intercept form). The error term is explicit recognition that the relationship is not exact.

Notice that Keynes' law implies that $0 < \beta_1 < 1$. That way if INC increases by 1 dollar, CONS will increase by β_1 dollars.

3) Collect the data

Now we need data on CONS and INC so that we can see if CONS does indeed go up when INC increases, but not by as much. Several alternatives present themselves. The Bureau of Labor Statistics annually surveys households concerning their income and expenditures. We could get CONS and INC for each household in 2011. This is cross-sectional data.

Household	CONS	INC
1	$76,234	$83,234
2	$22,346	$23,457
3	$56,873	$57,876
4	$44,829	$35,987
...	...	...

Another possibility is to use the macroeconomic from the Bureau of Economic Analysis. Here we have CONS and INC for the entire nation over the years. The data are per capita and adjusted for inflation. This is time-series data.

Year	CONS per capita	INC per capita
...	...	...
2008	$30,248	$33,229
2009	$29,339	$32,016
2010	$29,687	$32,335
2011	$30,217	$32,527

Finally, we could pool both cross-sectional and time-series data. If we surveyed the same households over the years, then we would have panel data.

Year	Household	CONS	INC
2002	1	$76,234	$83,234
2003	1	$77,703	$82,316
2002	2	$22,346	$23,457
2003	2	$29,294	$34,970
...	...	...	...

In any case, we would have a vector of data on CONS and a vector of data on INC. Using the time-series data from 1960 to 2011 we can graph the numbers.

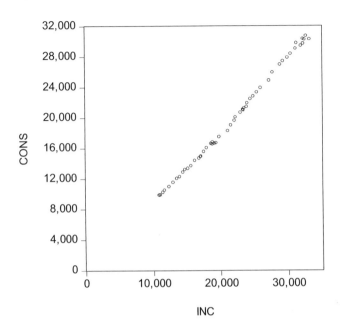

Each dot on the scattergram represents the CONS/INC combination for a particular year.

4) Estimate the parameters of the model

In this step we find values for β_0 and β_1. There are many possibilities. The "eyeball" technique involves drawing a straight line freehand in the scattergram above. If we use graph paper we can read off β_0 -- it is the vertical intercept. β_1 is the slope of the line.

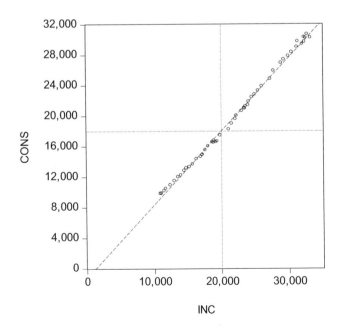

If we extend the line back to the vertical axis, it appears as if it may intersect at around (-1000). The slope of this line, as calculated from the graph, is less than one because when INC is 20,000, CONS is 18,000, making for a slope of 0.95 (= rise/run = 0 to 18,000/1 to 20,000 = 18,000/19,000). Therefore, we have CONS = -1,000 + 0.9 INC + u.

One problem with the eyeball technique is that different eyeballs may yield different lines. We need a more scientific approach. Indeed, much of the next chapter will be concerned with developing such a technique -- ordinary least-squares.

5) Test the theory, law, or hypothesis

If we use ordinary least-squares to estimate β_0 and β_1, we get

CONS = -1216 + 0.96 INC + u

Not much different than the eyeball technique in this case. These results verify Keynes' law of consumption because β_1 = 0.96, which is greater than zero but less than 1. The equation above makes it clear that if INC increased by $1, then CONS would be expected to increase by $0.96. Indeed, the 0.96 is an estimate of the marginal propensity to consume in the United States. If given an extra dollar, the typical American will increase consumption by 96 cents.

Statisticians are very loath to "accept" theories. In this case, we are not willing to say that our analysis has verified Keynes' law of consumption. Instead, we say our analysis has "not rejected" the theory. If we were to conduct the analysis with data from another country or time period, or if we used cross-sectional data instead of time-series data, we would obtain different results. The new results could produce a β_1 that is greater than one or less than zero, which would reject Keynes' theory.

6) Forecast with the model

We can use our results to make predictions. For example, in 2010 INC = $32,335. We would expect CONS = -1216 + 0.96 INC = -1216 +.96 * $32,335 = $29,871. The actual value of CONS in 2010 is $29,871. The forecast error is $29,687 - $29,871 = -$184. Our econometric equation predicts a value that is $184 over the actual value for CONS in 2010. In the model, CONS = -1216 + 0.96 INC + u, the -$184 is represented by u.

1.3 Many Applications

The econometric methodology outlined above has been applied to an incredible array of theories and hypotheses. The popular book *Freakonomics* (Levitt and Dubner 2009) details some of the more exotic applications: Did legalization of abortion lower the crime rate? Is a backyard swimming pool more dangerous to little children than a gun? Do street level drug dealers make less than the minimum wage?

Some of these issues do not appear to be within the realm of economics, but they are. Remember, economics is about how people make choices to maximize their satisfaction. All of the applications in Freakonomics concern people responding to incentives.

Many disciplines have adapted the econometric methodology to their own specific fields. Thus we have biometrics, psychometrics, and sociometrics. Sabermetrics is the analysis of baseball with this very same methodology. No matter what field we are in, the object is to test hypotheses with statistical techniques.

Terms

Cross-sectional data – Information on many units at a point in time.

Econometrics – The empirical determination of economic laws, theories, and hypotheses.

Error term (residual or disturbance) – This variable is attached to the end of an econometric model. It captures the difference between the observed value of the Y-variable and the value predicted by the econometric model.

Ordinary least-squares – A technique for estimating the structural parameters of an econometric model. This technique minimizes Σe_i^2.

Panel data – Information on more than one unit over time. It is a combination of cross-sectional and time-series data.

Time-series data – Information on one unit over time.

Chapter 1 Problems

1. The hours of study (per weekday) and GPA of three students are given below:

hours	GPA
2	2
4	3
2	3

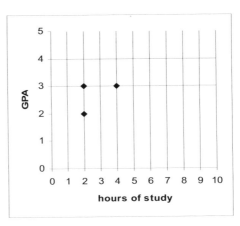

A) Draw a line through these dots so that the sum of the vertical distances from the dots to the line equals zero. When the dot lies above the line the distance is positive. When the dot lies below the line the distance is negative. Can you draw another line that meets this criterion?

B) Now draw a line through the dots so that the sum of the absolute value of the vertical distances between the dots and the line is minimized. Can you draw another line that meets this criterion?

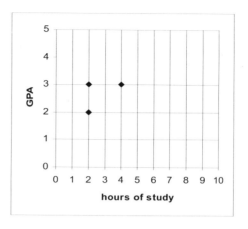

2. The SAT scores and GPA of three students are given below:

SAT	GPA
800	2
1000	2
1000	3

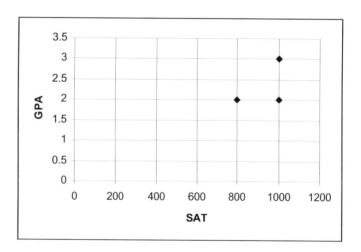

A) Draw two lines through these dots so that the sum of the vertical distances from the dots to the line equals zero. When the dot lies above the line the distance is positive. When the dot lies below the line the distance is negative.

B) Now draw two lines through the dots so that the sum of the absolute value of the vertical distances between the dots and the line is minimized.

SAT	GPA
800	2
1000	2
1000	3

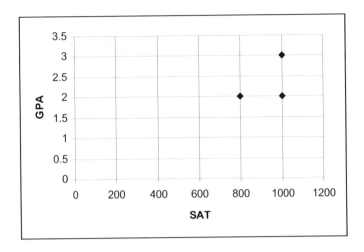

3. Suppose we estimate the following regression: CONS = -1218 + 0.97 INC + u

A) What is the predicted value of CONS in 1960 given INC = $9,735 in 1960?

B) Actual CONS in 1960 equals $8,837. Give several reasons why the forecast may be off from the actual.

4. Suppose we estimate the following regression: CONS = -1218 + 0.97 INC + u

A) What is the predicted value of CONS in 2005 given INC = $27,340 in 2005?

B) Actual CONS in 2005 equals $26,476. Give several reasons why the forecast may be off from the actual.

5. A) Specify an econometric model to test the theory that an increase in the money supply has no effect on real GDP.

B) What does this theory imply about the value of β_1?

6. A) Specify an econometric model to test the theory that an increase in the interest rate on automobile loans will lower car sales.

B) What does this theory imply about the value of β_1?

7. A professor gathers data on student performance in college and the number of alcoholic drinks students consume to determine if alcohol consumption affects performance in college. Can this research be classified as econometrics? Explain why or why not.

8. Data are collected on rainfall and temperature in the Bordeaux region of France to determine if weather can be used to predict the quality of the wine produced in a particular year. Can this research be classified as econometrics? Explain why or why not.

Chapter 2

Simple Regression Analysis

The Basic Idea

Notation

The Ordinary Least-Squares Technique

Deriving the Ordinary Least-Squares Estimators

An Example of Regression Analysis

The Stochastic Error Term

Example: Economic Performance and Corruption

Terms

Chapter 2 Problems

Appendix: Algebra of Summation Signs

2.1 The Basic Idea

Suppose we have a hypothesis that X affects Y negatively -- that is, whenever X increases, this causes Y to decrease. The econometric model to test this hypothesis might be: $Y = \beta_0 + \beta_1 X + u$. If the hypothesis is true, then β_1 should be negative.

Now we collect data on Y and X. Here are the data and a scattergram of them:

X	Y
1514.567	11.20333
1560.333	11.57667
1593.433	12.83000
1620.733	13.16333
1664.600	13.98333
1694.067	14.92000
1737.767	14.61667
1777.133	15.01000
1815.133	14.51000
1849.000	13.75333
1891.133	11.87667
1994.133	11.84333
2045.000	11.57000
2076.933	12.34333
2114.700	12.41000
...	...

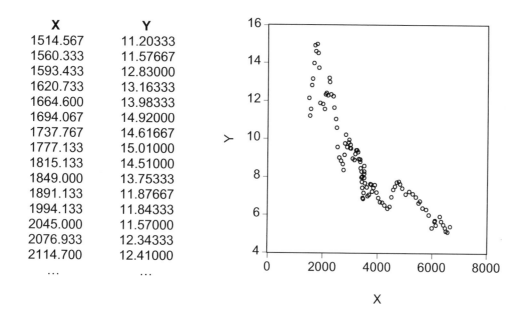

We need to fit a straight line through the points on the scattergram. We discussed the "eyeball" technique in Chapter 1. Another possibility is to take the point furthest to the left and the point furthest to the right and draw a line connecting them, ignoring all the other points. Both of these techniques are simple and easy to apply, but lack rigor.

The preferred technique is to fit a line so that the sum of the vertical distances from the points to the line squared is minimized -- that is, fit a line such that Σu^2 is minimized. Later we will be in a position to see why this technique is preferred.

2.2 Notation

Even though it may appear fussy, notation is important in econometrics. All of the subscripts, carets, and bars we will use symbolize concepts. If your notation is incorrect it implies that your understanding of the underlying concepts may be faulty.

To test the notion that X affects Y negatively, we have written the following econometric model: $Y = \beta_0 + \beta_1 X + u$. Nothing is wrong with this notation. However, we may add subscripts to indicate that this is the "i*th*" of n observations on X and Y:

$$Y_i = \beta_0 + \beta_1 X_i + u_i$$

The term u_i indicates that there will be n error terms. Y_i is known as the "dependent variable" or "y-variable." X_i is called the "independent variable" or the "x-variable." β_0 and β_1 are referred to as "estimators" or "structural parameters." We do not know their values, but can estimate them. The entire equation is called the "econometric model," "structural equation," or "regression function." Again, everything in econometrics goes by at least two names.

If we obtain all the data on Y_i and X_i, error-free, then we can use some technique, such as the "eyeball" technique, to estimate β_0 and β_1. However, in most instances we will only be able to obtain a sample of the observations on Y_i and X_i, and those numbers will undoubtedly have some errors in them. Since we only have an error-ridden sample of the true Y_i and X_i, we will not obtain the true values of β_0 and β_1. To indicate this situation we place carets (^) over the values that are mere estimates of the true values.

$$Y_i = \hat{\beta}_0 + \hat{\beta}_1 X_i + e_i$$

In addition, the u_i's turn into e_i's because we will not obtain the true error terms without the true β_0 and β_1. $Y_i = \beta_0 + \beta_1 X_i + u_i$ is called the "population regression function." Only God knows the true values of β_0 and β_1 because only she has access to all the error-free data on Y_i and X_i.

$Y_i = \hat{\beta}_0 + \hat{\beta}_1 X_i + e_i$ is known as the "sample regression function" because we mortals are working with a sample of the entire population of data on X_i and Y_i. We put carets (sometimes called hats) over β_0 and β_1 to indicate that these are merely estimates of their true values. The e_i's are estimates of the u_i's.

Another notational complication arises when we want to refer to the predicted value of Y. To obtain this value for any given i, we plug in for X_i:

$$E(Y_i|X_i) = \hat{Y}_i = \hat{\beta}_0 + \hat{\beta}_1 X_i$$

We no longer add on the e_i because that would give the actual value of Y_i and we want the predicted value ($\hat{Y}_i$). The caret appears over the Y_i because it is an estimated value, not the actual value. $\hat{Y}_i$ can be written $E(Y_i|X_i)$. This latter notation is read "the expected value of Y_i given X_i."

2.3 The Ordinary Least-Squares Technique

We want to obtain values of $\hat{\beta}_0$ and $\hat{\beta}_1$ such that Σe_i^2 is minimized. Another way to envision this task is that we want to fit a line between the observations on a scattergram so that the distances from the points to the line squared are minimized. This technique has many advantages over the "eyeball" technique and the "first dot/last dot" method of fitting a line. $\hat{\beta}_0$ is the vertical intercept of our line and $\hat{\beta}_1$ is its slope. When we fit a line with this criterion in mind it is called "ordinary least-squares."

There are many reasons for choosing to calculate $\hat{\beta}_0$ and $\hat{\beta}_1$ so that Σe_i^2 is minimized. Certainly this criterion is more rigorous than the "eyeball" technique and does not waste as much data as the first dot/last dot method. Later we will see that the estimators that result from ordinary least-squares have many desirable qualities. At this point one or two advantages will be mentioned.

The ordinary least-squares line is unique. Only one line will minimize Σe_i^2. This is not true of some other criteria such as calculating $\hat{\beta}_0$ and $\hat{\beta}_1$ so that $\Sigma e_i = 0$. It turns out that there are an infinite number of lines that would fit this latter criterion in any given situation. The ordinary least-squares line not only minimizes Σe_i^2, but also is one of the infinite lines that have $\Sigma e_i = 0$.

Another possibility is to fit the line so that $\Sigma |e_i|$ is minimized. In most cases this will yield a unique line. Unfortunately, the resulting estimates of $\hat{\beta}_0$ and $\hat{\beta}_1$ will not have the desirable statistical properties of the ordinary least-squares estimates.

The ordinary least-squares technique is easy to implement. In order to fit a line such that Σe_i^2 is minimized, all one needs to do is calculate

$$\hat{\beta}_0 = \overline{Y} - \hat{\beta}_1 \overline{X}$$

and

$$\hat{\beta}_1 = \frac{\Sigma(X_i - \overline{X})Y_i}{\Sigma(X_i - \overline{X})^2}$$

In these formulas $\overline{Y}$ and $\overline{X}$ refer to the means of Y and X, respectively. $\hat{\beta}_0$ is the vertical intercept and $\hat{\beta}_1$ is the slope of a line that minimizes Σe_i^2. The formulas for each of these estimators are derived below. First let's do an example.

Suppose we want to test the hypothesis that grade point average (GPA) is affected by the amount of time a student spends studying (HOURS). An econometric model of this hypothesis would be:

$$GPA_i = \hat{\beta}_0 + \hat{\beta}_1 \, HOURS_i + e_i$$

To keep the calculations to a minimum we consider only three students:

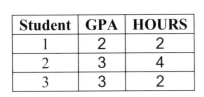

Student	GPA	HOURS
1	2	2
2	3	4
3	3	2

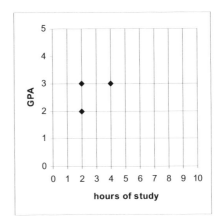

First calculate the numerator of the equation:

$$\hat{\beta}_1 = \frac{\Sigma(X_i - \overline{X})Y_i}{\Sigma(X_i - \overline{X})^2} :$$

$$\Sigma(X_i - \overline{X})Y_i = (2 - 2.667)(2) + (4 - 2.667)(3) + (2 - 2.667)(3) = 0.667$$

Now the denominator of the equation:

$$\Sigma(X_i - \overline{X})^2 = (2 - 2.667)^2 + (4 - 2.667)^2 + (2 - 2.667)^2 = 2.667$$

So that we have:

$$\hat{\beta}_1 = \frac{\Sigma(X_i - \overline{X})Y_i}{\Sigma(X_i - \overline{X})^2} = \frac{0.667}{2.667} = 0.25$$

Now we can plug into the equation $\hat{\beta}_0 = \overline{Y} - \hat{\beta}_1\overline{X}$:

$$\hat{\beta}_0 = \overline{Y} - \hat{\beta}_1\overline{X} = 2.667 - 0.25(2.667) = 2.0$$

And we may report the regression results as:

$$GPA_i = 2.0 + 0.25 \ HOURS_i + e_i$$

The structural parameters can be interpreted as follows:

$\hat{\beta}_0 = 2.0$ – A student who reports 0 study hours is expected to have a GPA equal to 2.0.

$\hat{\beta}_1 = 0.25$ – If HOURS increases by 1 unit, then GPA is expected to increase by 0.25 units.

$\hat{\beta}_0$ is the vertical intercept and $\hat{\beta}_1$ is the slope of our regression line:

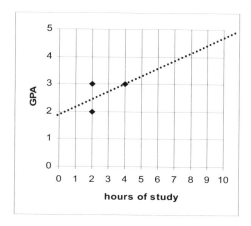

The three error terms can be calculated by re-writing our results:

$$GPA_i = 2.0 + 0.25\ HOURS_i + e_i \qquad as:$$

$$e_i = GPA_i - 2.0 - 0.25\ HOURS_i$$

Then $e_1 = 2 - 2.0 - 0.25(2) = -0.5$
$e_2 = 4 - 2.0 - 0.25(3) = 0.0$
$e_3 = 2 - 2.0 - 0.25(3) = 0.5$

As mentioned previously, $\Sigma e_i = 0$. The $\Sigma e_i^2 = -0.5^2 + 0.0^2 + 0.5^2 = 0.5$. How do we know that there is not another line that yields a lower Σe_i^2? Because $\hat{\beta}_0$ and $\hat{\beta}_1$ were derived so that they would minimize Σe_i^2. The derivation makes it clear that our line is unique.

2.4 Deriving the Ordinary Least-Squares Estimators

We have $Y_i = \hat{\beta}_0 + \hat{\beta}_1 X_i + e_i$

We want to minimize $\sum e_i^2$; that is minimize $\sum(Y_i - \hat{\beta}_0 - \hat{\beta}_1 X_i)^2$

To find the equations for $\hat{\beta}_0$ and $\hat{\beta}_1$ that minimize this expression, take the partial derivative with respect to $\hat{\beta}_0$ and set it equal to zero:

$$\frac{\partial \Sigma(Y_i - \hat{\beta}_0 - \hat{\beta}_1 X_i)^2}{\partial \hat{\beta}_0} = 2\Sigma(Y_i - \hat{\beta}_0 - \hat{\beta}_1 X_i)(-1) = 0$$

Dividing both sides of this equation by -2 leaves $\Sigma(Y_i - \hat{\beta}_0 - \hat{\beta}_1 X_i) = 0$

Now distribute the summation sign: $\Sigma Y_i - n\hat{\beta}_0 - \hat{\beta}_1 \Sigma X_i = 0$; n is number of observations i.

Moving the second and third terms to the other side gives: $\Sigma Y_i = n\hat{\beta}_0 + \hat{\beta}_1 \Sigma X_i$

The result is known as a "normal equation."

We repeat the process only this time with respect to $\hat{\beta}_1$. Begin by taking the partial derivative of the expression we wish to minimize with respect to $\hat{\beta}_1$ and set it equal to zero:

$$\frac{\partial \Sigma(Y_i - \hat{\beta}_0 - \hat{\beta}_1 X_i)^2}{\partial \hat{\beta}_1} = 2\Sigma(Y_i - \hat{\beta}_0 - \hat{\beta}_1 X_i)(-X_i) = 0$$

Dividing both sides of this equation by -2 leaves $\Sigma(Y_i - \hat{\beta}_0 - \hat{\beta}_1 X_i)(X_i) = 0$

Now distribute X_i and the summation sign: $\Sigma Y_i X_i - \hat{\beta}_0 \Sigma X_i - \hat{\beta}_1 \Sigma X_i^2 = 0$

Moving the second and third terms to the other side gives: $\Sigma Y_i X_i = \hat{\beta}_0 \Sigma X_i + \hat{\beta}_1 \Sigma X_i^2$

The result is known as a "normal equation."

We have two normal equations and two unknowns, $\hat{\beta}_0$ and $\hat{\beta}_1$. The first normal equation can be solved for $\hat{\beta}_0$:

$$\Sigma Y_i = n\hat{\beta}_0 + \hat{\beta}_1 \Sigma X_i$$
$$n\hat{\beta}_0 = \Sigma Y_i - \hat{\beta}_1 \Sigma X_i$$

$$\hat{\beta}_0 = \frac{\Sigma Y_i - \hat{\beta}_1 \Sigma X_i}{n} = \bar{Y} - \hat{\beta}_1 \bar{X}$$

This result can be substituted into the second normal equation, which is then solved for $\hat{\beta}_1$:

$$\Sigma Y_i X_i = \hat{\beta}_0 \Sigma X_i + \hat{\beta}_1 \Sigma X_i^2$$

$$\Sigma Y_i X_i = (\bar{Y} - \hat{\beta}_1 \bar{X})\Sigma X_i + \hat{\beta}_1 \Sigma X_i^2$$

Distribute the ΣX_i: $\Sigma Y_i X_i = \bar{Y}\Sigma X_i - \hat{\beta}_1 \bar{X}\Sigma X_i + \hat{\beta}_1 \Sigma X_i^{\,2}$

Now factor the last two terms on the right: $\Sigma Y_i X_i = \bar{Y}\Sigma X_i + \hat{\beta}_1(\Sigma X_i^{\,2} - \bar{X}\Sigma X_i)$

Rearrange the terms: $\hat{\beta}_1(\Sigma X_i^{\,2} - \bar{X}\Sigma X_i) = \Sigma Y_i X_i - \bar{Y}\Sigma X_i$

To isolate $\hat{\beta}_1$, divide both sides by $(\Sigma X_i^{\,2} - \bar{X}\Sigma X_i)$: $\hat{\beta}_1 = \dfrac{\Sigma Y_i X_i - \bar{Y}\Sigma X_i}{\Sigma X_i^{\,2} - \bar{X}\Sigma X_i}$

A more convenient expression for $\hat{\beta}_1$ is:

$$\hat{\beta}_1 = \frac{\Sigma(X_i - \bar{X})Y_i}{\Sigma(X_i - \bar{X})^2} \quad \text{which is equivalent to } \hat{\beta}_1 = \frac{\Sigma Y_i X_i - \bar{Y}\Sigma X_i}{\Sigma X_i^{\,2} - \bar{X}\Sigma X_i}$$

The proof of this equivalence comes up in the problems at the end of this chapter. More importantly, any time we want to fit a line so that Σe_i^2 is minimized, we only need calculate the intercept and slope of that line with our two formulas.

2.5 An Example of Regression Analysis

Let's do an example. Given the data below on Y and X, calculate $\hat{\beta}_0$ and $\hat{\beta}_1$ in $Y_i = \hat{\beta}_0 + \hat{\beta}_1 X_i + e_i$

Y	X
11.20	5.40
-27.10	6.70
33.40	7.10
0.02	8.80

First calculate $\hat{\beta}_1 = \dfrac{\Sigma(X_i - \bar{X})Y_i}{\Sigma(X_i - \bar{X})^2}$. Begin with the numerator:

Subtract $\bar{X}$ from the first X_i : 5.40 -7.00 = -1.60
Subtract $\bar{X}$ from the second X_i : 6.70 -7.00 = -0.30
Subtract $\bar{X}$ from the third X_i : 7.10 -7.00 = 0.10
Subtract $\bar{X}$ from the fourth X_i : 8.80 -7.00 = 1.80

Now multiply each of these results by the respective Y_i:

-1.60 x 11.20 = -17.92
-0.30 x -27.10 = 8.13

0.10 x 33.40 = 3.34
1.80 x 0.02 = 0.04

The last operation in the numerator is to sum up these four products to get -6.41.

$$\hat{\beta}_1 = \frac{-6.41}{\Sigma(X_i - \overline{X})^2}$$

In the denominator, we once again subtract each $\overline{X}$ from X_i. This time each result is squared:

$-1.60^2 = 2.56$
$-0.03^2 = 0.09$
$0.10^2 = 0.01$
$1.80^2 = 3.24$

The last operation in the denominator is to sum up these four squares to get 5.90.

$$\hat{\beta}_1 = \frac{-6.41}{5.90} = -1.09$$

Once we calculate $\hat{\beta}_1$ to equal -1.09, it is a simple matter to obtain

$$\hat{\beta}_0 = \overline{Y} - \hat{\beta}_1\overline{X} = 4.38 - (-1.09)(7.00) = 11.99$$

The slope of our regression is -1.09 and the vertical intercept is 11.99.

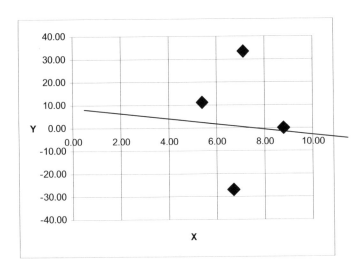

2.6 The Stochastic Error Term

Notice that our regression line does not pass through any of the four observations. The distance of each observation from the regression line is the error term or e_i.

$$e_i = Y_i - \hat{Y}_i = Y_i - (\hat{\beta}_0 + \hat{\beta}_1 X_i) = 11.20 - (11.99 + (-1.09 \times 5.40)) = 5.08$$

The first observation lies 5.08 units above the regression line. The other error terms are calculated in a similar manner.

$$e_i = Y_i - \hat{Y}_i = Y_i - (\hat{\beta}_0 + \hat{\beta}_1 X_i) = -27.10 - (11.99 + (-1.09 \times 6.70)) = -31.81$$
$$e_i = Y_i - \hat{Y}_i = Y_i - (\hat{\beta}_0 + \hat{\beta}_1 X_i) = 33.40 - (11.99 + (-1.09 \times 7.10)) = 29.13$$
$$e_i = Y_i - \hat{Y}_i = Y_i - (\hat{\beta}_0 + \hat{\beta}_1 X_i) = 0.02 - (11.99 + (-1.09 \times 8.80)) = -2.40$$

Notice that the four error terms sum to zero. The distances of the error terms above the line exactly equal the distances of the error terms below the line. Although we fit our line such that Σe_i^2 is minimized, it turns out that $\Sigma e_i = 0$ as well.

Also notice that the regression line passes through $(\overline{Y}, \overline{X}) = (4.38, 7.00)$. If we plug 7.00 into the regression line, we get: $\hat{Y}_i = 11.99 + -1.09(7.00) = 4.38$

2.7 Example: Economic Performance and Corruption

To test the hypothesis that corruption negatively affects a nation's economic performance, we propose the following econometric model:

$$GDP_i = \hat{\beta}_0 + \hat{\beta}_1 COR_i + e_i$$

COR measures corruption in a nation on a scale of 0 (least) to 10 (most) and GDP measures output in dollars per capita. We have cross-sectional data from four nations:

Nation	COR	GDP
Brazil	5.9	6100
Bulgaria	6.7	4100
Chile	3.1	12500
China	6.6	3600

Applying our formulas we obtain:

$$\hat{\beta}_1 = \frac{\Sigma(X_i - \overline{X})Y_i}{\Sigma(X_i - \overline{X})^2} = \frac{-20652.5}{8.55} = -2416.20$$

$$\hat{\beta}_0 = \overline{Y} - \hat{\beta}_1\overline{X} = 6575.00 - (-2416.20)(5.58) = 20045.33$$

We do indeed obtain a negative value for $\hat{\beta}_1$ indicating that COR and GDP are negatively related. More specifically, $\hat{\beta}_1 = -2416.20$ may be interpreted as follows: When COR increases by 1 unit, GDP is expected to decrease by 2416.20 units.

$\hat{\beta}_0 = 20045.33$ is interpreted as follows: when COR = 0, GDP is expected to equal 20045.33 units. This strict interpretation of $\hat{\beta}_0$ often results in nonsense, as we shall see going forward.

The four error terms of this model are calculated to be:

$$e_i = Y_i - \hat{Y}_i = Y_i - (\hat{\beta}_0 + \hat{\beta}_1 X_i) = 6100 - (20045.33 + (-2416.20 \times 5.9)) = 310.27$$

$$e_i = Y_i - \hat{Y}_i = Y_i - (\hat{\beta}_0 + \hat{\beta}_1 X_i) = 4100 - (20045.33 + (-2416.20 \times 6.7)) = 243.23$$

$$e_i = Y_i - \hat{Y}_i = Y_i - (\hat{\beta}_0 + \hat{\beta}_1 X_i) = 012500 - (20045.33 + (-2416.20 \times 3.1)) = -55.10$$

$$e_i = Y_i - \hat{Y}_i = Y_i - (\hat{\beta}_0 + \hat{\beta}_1 X_i) = 3600 - (20045.33 + (-2416.20 \times 6.6)) = -498.39$$

Proportionally speaking, these errors are rather small. What causes the errors to be large or small? The error term is the result of four categories of factors:

1) important variables excluded – There are many variables that affect GDP per capita in a given nation. Money supply and fiscal policy come to mind. Leaving these important factors out of our econometric analysis results in larger errors.

2) randomness – Even if no important variables are omitted from consideration, we can still make large errors when the dependent variable is erratic. For example, it is extremely difficult to predict daily changes in stock prices. They have a large random component. This will lead to larger errors in a regression analysis.

3) measurement error – If errors were made when measuring COR or GDP, then larger errors will result. COR and GDP are figures that are estimated. To the extent that these estimates are poor, we can expect larger error terms.

4) minor variables excluded – Undoubtedly, many minor factors impact GDP in a given nation. Hopefully, these often immeasurable forces will cancel each other out. To the extent that they do not, larger regression errors will result.

Terms

Dependent variable (Y-variable) – In an econometric model, this variable appears to the left of the equality sign. It is affected by the independent variable.

Econometric model (structural equation or regression equation) – A mathematical expression that captures the essence of the cause-and-effect relationship between two variables.

Error term (residual or disturbance) – This variable is attached to the end of an econometric model. It captures the difference between the observed value of the Y-variable and the value predicted by the econometric model.

Independent variable (X-variable) – In an econometric model, this variable appears to the right of the equality sign. It is affected by the dependent variable.

Normal equation – An equation that comes up in the derivation of the formulas for the ordinary least-squares estimators.

Ordinary least-squares – A technique for estimating the structural parameters of an econometric model. This technique minimizes Σe_i^2.

Population regression function – An econometric model estimated with error-free data that includes the entire population of interest.

Sample regression function – An econometric model estimated from sample data.

Stochastic variable – A variable that can take on different values depending on the sample data. $\hat{\beta}_0$ and $\hat{\beta}_1$ are stochastic variables, as are the e_i's.

Structural parameter – In an econometric model, $\hat{\beta}_0$ and $\hat{\beta}_1$ are the structural parameters.

Chapter 2   Problems

1. Which of the following is (are) NOT correct?

A) $Y_i = \beta_0 + \beta_1 X_i + e_i$
B) $\hat{Y}_i = \beta_0 + \beta_1 X_i + e_i$
C) $Y_i = \beta_0 + \beta_1 X_i + u_i$

D) $Y_i = \hat{\beta}_0 + \hat{\beta}_1 X_i + e_i$
E) $\hat{Y}_i = \hat{\beta}_0 + \hat{\beta}_1 X_i + e_i$
F) $Y_i = \hat{\beta}_0 + \hat{\beta}_1 X_i + u_i$

G) $Y_i = \beta_0 + \beta_1 X_i$
H) $\hat{Y}_i = \beta_0 + \beta_1 X_i + u_i$
I) $E(Yi|Xi) = \hat{\beta}_0 + \hat{\beta}_1 X_i + e_i$

2. Which of the following is (are) NOT correct?

A) $Y_i = \beta_0 + \beta_1 X_i + u_i$
B) $\hat{Y}_i = \beta_0 + \beta_1 X_i + u_i$
C) $Y_i = \beta_0 + \beta_1 X_i + e_i$

D) $Y_i = \hat{\beta}_0 + \hat{\beta}_1 X_i + u_i$
E) $\hat{Y}_i = \hat{\beta}_0 + \hat{\beta}_1 X_i + u_i$
F) $Y_i = \hat{\beta}_0 + \hat{\beta}_1 X_i + e_i$

G) $Y_i = \beta_0 + \beta_1 X_i$
H) $\hat{Y}_i = \beta_0 + \beta_1 X_i + e_i$
I) $E(Yi|Xi) = \beta_0 + \beta_1 X_i + u_i$

3. The savings and number of children of four families are given below:

sav	child
0.03	2
0.874	2
0.374	0
1.2	1

A) Calculate the values of $\hat{\beta}_0$ and $\hat{\beta}_1$ so that Σe_i^2 is minimized for

$sav_i = \hat{\beta}_0 + \hat{\beta}_1 \ child_i + e_i$

B) Interpret the values you obtained.
C) Sketch your line in the graph.

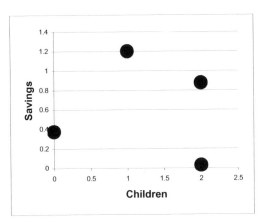

4. The hours of preparation and math SAT scores of four students are given below:

prep	SAT
1	300
3	400
1	400
3	500

A) Calculate the values of $\hat{\beta}_0$ and $\hat{\beta}_1$ so that Σe_i^2 is minimized for

Math $SAT_i = \hat{\beta}_0 + \hat{\beta}_1 \ prep_i + e_i$

B) Interpret the values you obtained.
C) Sketch your line in the graph.

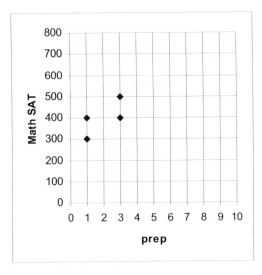

5. A) Calculate the values of the structural parameters for a regression of X on Y given:

Y	X
1.8	2
1.7	5
1.5	-2
0.6	5
25.4	6

B) Show that the $\Sigma e_i = 0$ in this case.

6. A) Calculate the values of the structural parameters for a regression of X on Y given:

Y	X
1.8	1.2
1.7	-8.4
1.5	4.8
0.6	3.5
25.4	2.2

B) Show that the $\Sigma e_i = 0$ in this case.

7. Prove $\dfrac{\Sigma Y_i X_i - \bar{Y}\Sigma X_i}{\Sigma X_i^2 - \bar{X}\Sigma X_i} = \dfrac{\Sigma(X_i - \bar{X})(Y_i - \bar{Y})}{\Sigma(X_i - \bar{X})^2}$

8. Prove $\dfrac{\Sigma(X_i - \bar{X})(Y_i - \bar{Y})}{\Sigma(X_i - \bar{X})^2} = \dfrac{\Sigma(X_i - \bar{X})Y_i}{\Sigma(X_i - \bar{X})^2}$

9. Prove that $\Sigma e_i X_i = 0$ for the ordinary least-squares regression line.

10. Prove that $\Sigma e_i = 0$ for the ordinary least-squares regression line.

APPENDIX to Chapter 2   Algebra of Summation Signs

Most students have had little experience doing algebra when summation signs (Σ) are involved. It turns out that only a few rules are required to get through all the derivations and proofs in this book.

FOILing: Suppose we want to expand the following expression: $\Sigma(X_i - \bar{X})(Y_i - \bar{Y})$. We can FOIL it out. FOIL stands for First; Outer; Inner; Last.

$$\Sigma(X_i - \bar{X})(Y_i - \bar{Y}) = \Sigma(X_i Y_i - X_i \bar{Y} - \bar{X}Y_i + \bar{X}\bar{Y})$$

Distribution: Suppose we wish to distribute the summation sign through the parentheses in the following expression: $\Sigma(X_i Y_i - X_i \bar{Y} - \bar{X}Y_i + \bar{X}\bar{Y})$

Just bring the summation sign before each of the four terms:
$$\Sigma X_i Y_i - \Sigma X_i \bar{Y} - \Sigma \bar{X}Y_i + \Sigma \bar{X}\bar{Y}$$

The first term ($\Sigma X_i Y_i$) cannot be simplified further. It instructs us to take each X_i and multiply it by the corresponding Y_i and then sum up those i products.

The second term ($\Sigma X_i \overline{Y}$) may be re-written as $\overline{Y}\Sigma X_i$. This is because a constant ($\overline{Y}$ is the mean of the Y_i's) can be pulled out and placed before the summation sign.

Similarly, the third term ($\Sigma \overline{X} Y_i$) becomes $\overline{X}\Sigma Y_i$.

The fourth term ($\Sigma \overline{XY}$) makes no sense. It asks us to sum up the product of two constants ($\overline{XY}$). There is nothing to sum up. In cases like this, when the summation sign is placed before a constant or constants alone, it turns into an "n". So the fourth term becomes $n\overline{XY}$.

In summary, the summation sign may be distributed through the parentheses in $\Sigma(X_i Y_i - X_i \overline{Y} - \overline{X} Y_i + \overline{XY})$ to obtain $\Sigma X_i Y_i - \overline{Y}\Sigma X_i - \overline{X}\Sigma Y_i + n\overline{XY}$

Substitution: The expression $\Sigma X_i Y_i - \overline{Y}\Sigma X_i - \overline{X}\Sigma Y_i + n\overline{XY}$ can be simplified further by making some substitutions. ΣX_i is equal to $n\overline{X}$. Using this substitution, the second term in our expression becomes $\overline{Y} n \overline{X}$. The third term becomes $\overline{X} n \overline{Y}$. So now we have:

$$\Sigma X_i Y_i - \overline{Y} n \overline{X} - \overline{X} n \overline{Y} + n\overline{XY}$$

Cancellation: Notice that the last three terms in the expression $\Sigma X_i Y_i - \overline{Y} n \overline{X} - \overline{X} n \overline{Y} + n\overline{XY}$ are equivalent. One of the two negative terms will cancel the fourth term, which is positive, and we are left with $\Sigma X_i Y_i - \overline{Y} n \overline{X}$.

Chapter 3

Residual Statistics

Measures of Goodness-of-Fit

The Standard Errors of $\hat{\beta}_0$ and $\hat{\beta}_1$

Repeated Sampling

Terms

Chapter 3 Problems

Test Yourself on Chapters 1, 2, and 3

3.1 Measures of Goodness-of-Fit

The regression from the last example in Chapter 2 appears to have rather small error terms.

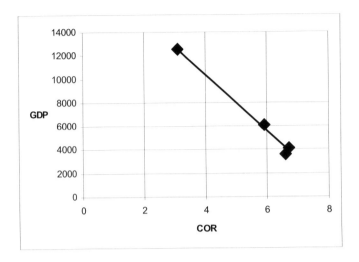

However the example from section 2.5 appears to have larger errors.

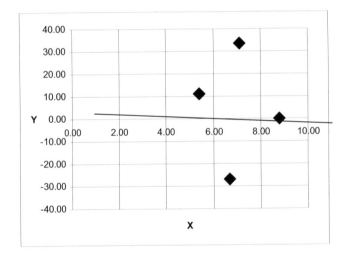

But these diagrams can be deceptive because of the scaling. Indeed the largest error in the second diagram is –31.81, while the smallest error in the top diagram is –55.10. But proportionally, the errors in the first diagram are smaller.

It would be useful to have a statistic that would help us discern when we have small errors (a good fit) or large errors (a poor fit). There are several popular statistics for this purpose. We will discuss two of them.

$$\textbf{Standard Error of the Regression (SER)} = \hat{\sigma} = \sqrt{\frac{\Sigma e_i^{\,2}}{n-2}}$$

This statistic represents the typical distance of an observation from the regression line. The SER is useful only when compared to the dependent variable. If the SER of a given regression equals 0.487, we have no way of assessing if this is large or small. A good rule of thumb is if the SER is less than half of the mean of the absolute value of the dependent variable, then the fit is adequate.

For the first diagram, the SER = 451.03; for the second, SER = 30.75. Even though it doesn't look like it when comparing the graphs, the errors in the first diagram are larger. However, relative to the magnitude of the dependent variable, the errors in the first diagram are proportionally smaller.

The first diagram represents an adequate fit since the SER < ½ the absolute value of the mean of GDP, which is 6575.00. The interpretation here is that the typical distance of an observation from the regression line is 451.03. This is a rather small error given that the dependent variable has a mean of 6575.00.

The second diagram represents a poor fit since the SER > ½ the absolute value of the mean of Y, which is 4.38. The interpretation in this case is that the typical distance of an observation from the regression line is 30.75. However, 30.75 is a rather large error given that the dependent variable is centered on 4.38.

The second measure of goodness-of-fit is the coefficient of determination.

$$\textbf{Coefficient of Determination (r}^2\textbf{)} = 1 - \frac{\Sigma e_i^{\,2}}{\Sigma(Y_i - \bar{Y})^2}$$

The coefficient of determination (or r-squared) is the most popular measure of goodness-of-fit. It ranges between 0 and 1, where 1 is a perfect fit and zero is a horizontal regression through random observations.

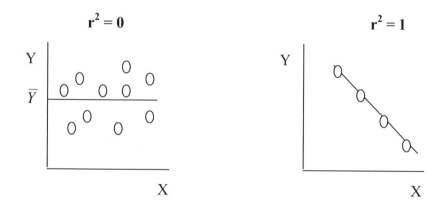

Going back to the two drawings at the beginning of this section, the first has an r^2 = 0.99. The interpretation is 99 percent of the variation in GDP is explained by COR. The second drawing has an r^2 = 0.004; only 0.4 percent of the variation in Y is explained by X.

Both the SER and r^2 indicate the same results: The regression between COR and GDP has an adequate or very good fit, while the regression of Y on X has a poor fit.

3.2 The Standard Errors of $\hat{\beta}_0$ and $\hat{\beta}_1$

$\hat{\beta}_0$ and $\hat{\beta}_1$ vary in repeated sampling. If we were to get data on Y and X and run a regression, we would obtain estimates of $\hat{\beta}_0$ and $\hat{\beta}_1$. If we were to obtain a new sample of data on Y and X and re-run the regression, it would be highly unlikely that we would obtain the exact same values for $\hat{\beta}_0$ and $\hat{\beta}_1$. Can we expect the new values of $\hat{\beta}_0$ and $\hat{\beta}_1$ to be close to the original estimates? That depends. The standard error of $\hat{\beta}_0$ is an estimate of how much $\hat{\beta}_0$ typically varies in repeated sampling.

$$\text{Standard Error of } \hat{\beta}_0 = \text{SE}(\hat{\beta}_0) = \sqrt{\frac{\hat{\sigma}^2 \Sigma X_i^2}{n\Sigma(X_i - \overline{X})^2}} \quad ; \text{ where } \hat{\sigma}^2 = \frac{\Sigma e i^2}{n-2} = \text{SER}^2$$

Similarly, the standard error of $\hat{\beta}_1$ is an estimate of how much $\hat{\beta}_1$ typically varies in repeated sampling.

$$\text{Standard Error of } \hat{\beta}_1 = \text{SE}(\hat{\beta}_1) = \sqrt{\frac{\hat{\sigma}^2}{\sum(X_i - \overline{X})^2}}$$

Going back to our example of corruption's impact on economic growth, we can now more fully report the results:

$$
\begin{aligned}
&\text{GDP}_i = 20045.33 - 2416.20\ \text{COR}_i + e_i \\
&\qquad\quad (889.14)\quad (154.27) \quad \leftarrow \text{standard errors} \\[6pt]
&\text{SER} = 451.03 \quad \overline{\text{GDP}} = 6575.00 \quad r^2 = 0.99 \quad n = 4 \\[6pt]
&\text{COR measures corruption in a nation on a scale of 0 (least) to 10 (most)} \\
&\text{GDP measures output in dollars per capita.}
\end{aligned}
$$

These results indicate that $\hat{\beta}_0$ is estimated to be 20045.33. However, if we ran the regression repeatedly with new data each time, we would expect $\hat{\beta}_0$ to vary by 889.14 on average. This does not mean that $\hat{\beta}_0$ cannot come out to be zero in one of the regressions, but that would surprise us since $\hat{\beta}_0$ typically varies by 889.14 in repeated sampling and its estimated value is 20,045.33.

$\hat{\beta}_1$ is estimated to be -2416.20 with a standard error of 154.27. The regression has an SER equal to 451.03 indicating an adequate fit since the SER $< \frac{1}{2}$ the mean of GDP. r^2 is equal to 0.99, which means 99 percent of the variation in GDP is explained by COR. Finally, $n = 4$ says four data points were used to estimate all these statistics.

3.3 Repeated Sampling

The concept of repeated sampling will be used extensively going forward. It is the hypothetical notion that the structural parameters, $\hat{\beta}_0$ and $\hat{\beta}_1$, could be estimated tens of thousands of times using fresh data each time. The values obtained each time would be different. That's what is meant by the term "stochastic": $\hat{\beta}_0$ and $\hat{\beta}_1$ vary in repeated sampling.

Terms

Coefficient of determination (r^2) – A statistic that measures how well a regression line fits the data.

Repeated sampling –Estimating the structural parameters of a regression over and over with fresh data each time.

Standard error of an estimator – A statistic that estimates the amount a structural parameter will vary on average in repeated sampling.

Standard error of the regression (SER) – A statistic that represents the typical distance of an observation from the regression line.

Chapter 3   Problems

1.A) Calculate the values of the structural parameters for a regression of X on Y given:

Y	X
1.8	2
1.7	5
1.5	-2
0.6	5
25.4	6

   B) Interpret the value you obtained for the intercept.
   C) Interpret the value you obtained for the slope coefficient.
   D) Calculate r^2 for this regression.
   E) Interpret the value of r^2 for this regression.
   F) Calculate the SER for this regression.
   G) Interpret the value of the SER for this regression.

H) Calculate the standard error of the intercept term.
I) Interpret the standard error of the intercept term.
J) Calculate the standard error of the slope coefficient.
K) Interpret the standard error of the slope coefficient.

2. A) Calculate the values of the structural parameters for a regression of X on Y given:

Y	X
1.8	1.2
1.7	−8.4
1.5	4.8
0.6	3.5
25.4	2.2

B) Interpret the value you obtained for the intercept.
C) Interpret the value you obtained for the slope coefficient.
D) Calculate r^2 for this regression.
E) Interpret the value of r^2 for this regression.
F) Calculate the SER for this regression.
G) Interpret the value of the SER for this regression.
H) Calculate the standard error of the intercept term.
I) Interpret the standard error of the intercept term.
J) Calculate the standard error of the slope coefficient.
K) Interpret the standard error of the slope coefficient.

3. Given the following: $GDP_i = \hat{\beta}_0 + \hat{\beta}_1 COR_i + e_i$

Nation	COR	GDP
Ukraine	7.4	2200
UK	1.4	21200
USA	2.5	31500
Vietnam	7.4	1770

Where COR measures corruption in a nation on a scale of 0 (least) to 10 (most) and GDP measures output in dollars per capita.

A) Calculate the values of the structural parameters for the regression above.
B) Interpret the values of the structural parameters.
C) Calculate r^2 for this regression.
D) Interpret the value of r^2 for this regression.
E) Calculate the SER for this regression.
F) Interpret the value of the SER for this regression.
G) Does this regression have a good fit? Explain.
H) Calculate the standard error of the intercept term.
I) Interpret the standard error of the intercept term.
J) Would you be surprised if the intercept term equaled 26776.70 if you re-ran this regression with data on four different countries? Explain.

4. Given the following: $GDP_i = \hat{\beta}_0 + \hat{\beta}_1 COR_i + e_i$

Nation	COR	GDP
Bulgaria	6.7	4100
Canada	0.8	22400
Chile	3.1	12500
China	6.6	3600

Where COR measures corruption in a nation on a scale of 0 (least) to 10 (most) and GDP measures output in dollars per capita.

A) Calculate the values of the structural parameters for the regression above.
B) Interpret the values of the structural parameters.
C) Calculate r^2 for this regression.
D) Interpret the value of r^2 for this regression.
E) Calculate the SER for this regression.
F) Interpret the value of the SER for this regression.
G) Does this regression have a good fit? Explain.
H) Calculate the standard error of the slope coefficient.
I) Interpret the standard error of the slope coefficient.
J) Would you be surprised if the slope coefficient equaled –3342.80 if you re-ran this regression with data on four different countries? Explain.

Test Yourself on Chapters 1, 2, and 3

1. Given

Yi	Xi
11.2	5.4
–27.1	6.7
33.4	7.1
0.02	–8.8

A) Calculate the values for the structural parameters of $Y_i = \hat{\beta}_0 + \hat{\beta}_1 X_i + e_i$
   (Show your work, making the details of your calculations apparent.)
B) Interpret the values you obtained for $\hat{\beta}_0$ and $\hat{\beta}_1$ above.
C) According to the SER, is the fit of the regression adequate? Explain.
D) What percent of the variation in Y is explained by X in this regression?
E) Suppose we ran this regression again with a new set of observations on Y and X. Would you be surprised if $\hat{\beta}_1$ turned out to be –2.0? Explain why or why not.

2. Answer the following questions:

A) Distinguish between the population regression function and the sample regression function.
B) Distinguish between cross-sectional and time-series data.
C) What is a normal equation?
D) Explain why a perfectly vertical regression line is impossible.

3. Which of the following is (are) NOT correct?

A) $Y_i = \beta_0 + \beta_1 X_i$ D) $Y_i = \hat{\beta}_0 + \hat{\beta}_1 X_i + e_i$ G) $E(Y_i|X_i) = \beta_0 + \beta_1 X_i$

B) $\hat{Y}_i = \beta_0 + \beta_1 X_i$ E) $\hat{Y}_i = \hat{\beta}_0 + \hat{\beta}_1 X_i + e_i$ H) $\hat{Y}_i = \beta_0 + \beta_1 X_i + u_i$

C) $Y_i = \beta_0 + \beta_1 X_i + u_i$ F) $Y_i = \hat{\beta}_0 + \hat{\beta}_1 X_i + u_i$ I) $E(Y_i|X_i) = \hat{\beta}_0 + \hat{\beta}_1 X_i + e_i$

4. Answer True or False:

A) Sabermetrics is the application of statistical analysis to war.
B) Unless all the observations lie on a straight line, it is impossible to fit a line such that $\Sigma |e_i| = 0$.
C) When a line is fit to observations on a scattergram so that Σe_i^2 is minimized, then $\Sigma e_i = 0$.
D) When a line is fit to observations on a scattergram so that Σe_i^2 is minimized, then sometimes more than one line meets this criteria.
E) $\Sigma(X_i - \bar{X})(Y_i - \bar{Y}) = \bar{X}\Sigma Y_i - \bar{Y}\Sigma X_i$
F) $\Sigma(X_i - \bar{X}) = 0$
G) A large SER and low r^2 can be the result of the Y- variable being very random.
H) If $r^2 = 0$, then β_1 must $= 0$.
I) If $r^2 = 1$, then β_1 must $= 1$.
J) If SER $= 0$, then r^2 must $= 1$.

Chapter 4

Hypothesis Testing

4.1 Hypothesis Testing

Once we calculate $\hat{\beta}_0$ and $\hat{\beta}_1$, we can make statistical inferences about the true β_0 and β_1. For instance, suppose we calculate $\hat{\beta}_0 = 0.12$. Is that close enough to zero to suggest that the true $\beta_0 = 0$? The answer depends on the standard error of $\hat{\beta}_0$. Suppose the SE($\hat{\beta}_0$) = 0.03. Then we know that if we run the regression many times with different samples it is unlikely that $\hat{\beta}_0$ will turn out to be zero or negative in many instances. Therefore, even though $\hat{\beta}_0 = 0.12$ seems quite close to zero, it is too far away from zero to suggest that the true $\beta_0 = 0$.

However, we cannot say with certainty that $\beta_0 \neq 0$. No one knows for certain. Instead, we will use a hypothesis testing procedure that allows us to be specific about how certain we are that $\beta_0 = 0$. That procedure is outlined in the box below.

The 5-step hypothesis testing procedure
1. State the null and alternative hypotheses
2. Choose the level of significance
3. State the decision rule
4. Get the numbers
5. Reject or do not reject the null hypothesis

We will use the regression results below to demonstrate various hypothesis tests. Thirty students in an econometrics class were asked about their grade point average (GPA) and study time (ST).

$GPA_i = 2.87 - 0.02\ ST_i + e_i$
       (0.21) (0.06) $\leftarrow$ standard errors

$SER = 0.45$ $\overline{GPA} = 2.81$ $r^2 = 0.004$ $n = 30$

GPA_i is grade point average of the ith student.
ST_i is average daily study time of the ith student.

Here is a strict interpretation of the regression results:

$\hat{\beta}_0 = 2.87$ A student with zero study time is expected to have a GPA = 2.87.

$\hat{\beta}_1 = -0.02$ A 1 unit increase in study time is expected to lower GPA by 0.02 units.

SER = 0.45   The typical distance of an observation from the regression line is 0.45 units.

$\overline{GPA} = 2.81$ The average GPA of the 30 students is 2.81. The fit of the model is adequate since SER < ½ GPA bar.

$r^2 = 0.004$ 0.4 percent of the variation in GPA is explained by study time.

n = 30   The regression was estimated with a sample of 30 students.

4.2 Test of Significance

A test of significance is used to determine if an estimator is probably equal to zero or not. Let's perform a test of significance on $\hat{\beta}_1 = -0.02$ using the 5-step procedure:

<u>1. State the null and alternative hypotheses</u>
The hypothesis we wish to test is the null hypothesis. The alternative hypothesis is the implication if the null hypothesis is rejected.

$$Ho: \beta_1 = 0 \quad Ha: \beta_1 \neq 0$$

Notice that both the null and alternative hypotheses involve β_1, not $\hat{\beta}_1$. We know $\hat{\beta}_1 \neq 0$. Given that $\hat{\beta}_1 = -0.02$, can we infer that the true β_1 might equal 0?

<u>2. Choose the level of significance</u>
The level of significance is sometimes called the "critical level" of the test. It represents the probability that the test will result in a TYPE I error. A TYPE I error is when a true null hypothesis is rejected. The tradition in econometrics is to use 5 or 10 percent for the critical level. Let's make it our tradition to use 5 percent.

5%

To demonstrate the difference between TYPE I and TYPE II errors, consider the judicial system in the United States. Any defendant is considered innocent until proven guilty. That is, the null hypothesis is that the defendant is not guilty.

Ho: Defendant is Not Guilty   Ha: Defendant is Guilty

Suppose the defendant is in truth innocent and the jury finds her guilty. This would be a TYPE I error since a true null is rejected. If a guilty defendant is found innocent by the jury, this is a TYPE II error. Here, a false null hypothesis is not being rejected.

In Truth →	Defendant Is Guilty	Defendant Is Not Guilty
Jury Finds ↓		
Defendant Guilty	**Proper Verdict**	**TYPE I Error**
Defendant Not Guilty	**TYPE II Error**	**Proper Verdict**

Econometricians, like jurists, abhor TYPE I errors. Our judicial process has all sorts of mechanisms to ensure that an innocent defendant will be found not guilty. Miranda rights and the right to an attorney are two examples of these mechanisms.

Econometricians prevent against TYPE I errors by setting very low critical levels for hypothesis tests. A 5 percent chance of committing a TYPE I error is the norm and 10 percent is typically the highest most econometricians are willing to risk in hypothesis testing.

Unfortunately, there is only one way to ensure that no TYPE I errors will occur: Do not reject any null hypotheses. Declare every defendant not guilty. But then we would make the maximum number of TYPE II errors. There is an inverse relationship between the probability of TYPE I and TYPE II errors.

In econometrics we set the critical level of hypothesis tests at 5 percent because we want to protect against the possibility of making a TYPE I error. This means we will be making more TYPE II errors than if we had set the critical level higher. However, like jurists who are unsure in a particular case, we would rather let a guilty defendant go free than convict an innocent person.

Graphically, the t-distribution for a given number of degrees of freedom shows the probability of obtaining any t-ratio when Ho is true.

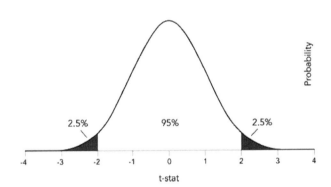

In the graph above, the probability of obtaining a t-ratio greater than 2 is 2.5 percent. This is represented by the area under the t-distribution to the right of t-stat = 2. Similarly, the probability of obtaining a t-ratio less than -2 is 2.5 percent. If we were to reject Ho when |t-ratio| > 2, then there is 5 percent chance we will be rejecting a true null hypothesis. That is to say, there is a 5 percent chance we will make a TYPE I error. This is what it means to set the critical level of a hypothesis test at 5 percent.

3. State the decision rule

The decision rule is used to test the hypothesis. You simply must know which rule to use for each test. After we do a few tests it will become apparent which rules should be used in which circumstances. For a test of significance, the decision rule is:

If $|\text{t-ratio}| > t^c$, then reject Ho

The t-ratio is defined as:

$$t - ratio = \frac{\hat{\beta_1} - \beta_{Ho}}{SE(\hat{\beta_1})} \; ; \; \text{where } \beta_{Ho} \text{ is the value of } \beta_1 \text{ stated in the hull hypothesis.}$$

t^c is the critical t-ratio found in a t-table such as the one in the back of this book. To look up t^c, three pieces of information are needed:

1) The degrees of freedom of the test = $n - k = 30 - 2 = 28$
2) The critical level of the test = 5%
3) The fact that a test of significance is 2-sided

This last bit of information is referring to the fact that the alternate hypothesis is $\hat{\beta_1} \neq 0$. $\hat{\beta_1}$ may differ from zero in two ways -- by being greater than zero or by being less than zero. The ability to distinguish between 1-sided and 2-sided tests will become apparent as we do more examples.

4. Get the numbers

Here we calculate the t-ratio and look up t^c.

$$t - ratio = \frac{\hat{\beta_1} - \beta_{Ho}}{SE(\hat{\beta_1})} = \frac{-0.02 - 0}{0.06} = -0.33$$

From the table in the back of the book, $t^c = 2.048$. Critical values for the t-distribution and other distributions are available online as well. One can also use Excel to find critical values.

5. Reject or do not reject the null hypothesis

Since $|\text{t-ratio}| < t^c$, we cannot reject Ho. This implies that β_1 is not significantly different from zero. Do Not Reject Ho: β_1 is not statistically different from zero. Let's think about that for a second. If $\beta_1 = 0$, then no matter how much study time (ST) increases, GPA will not be affected. In other words, study time is an insignificant factor in determining a student's GPA. Do you believe this result? Why or why not?

Here is the summary of the entire 5-step procedure for this particular test of significance.

Test of significance
1. Ho: $\beta_1 = 0$ Ha: $\beta_1 \neq 0$
2. 5%
3. If $\left| \text{t-ratio} \right| > t^c$, then reject Ho
4. $0.33 < 2.048$ (d.f. = n - k = $30 - 2 = 28$)
5. Do Not Reject Ho; β_1 is not statistically different from zero.

4.3 Confidence Intervals

A confidence interval is a range of values within which the true value of an estimated parameter is likely to fall. To form a 95 percent confidence interval around the coefficient on ST ($\hat{\beta}_1 = -0.02$) in our example:

95% CI for $\hat{\beta}_1 = -0.02$: $\hat{\beta}_1$ +/- se($\hat{\beta}_1$)(t^c)

$$-0.02 \text{ +/- } 0.06 \, (2.048) \quad \rightarrow \quad -0.14 \text{ to } 0.10$$

If we construct an infinite number of such intervals, 95 percent of them will contain the true β_1. Notice that the interval spans zero. This corresponds with our test of significance at the 5 percent critical level that indicated that $\hat{\beta}_1$ is not statistically different from zero.

A 90 percent confidence interval is similarly constructed:

90% CI for $\hat{\beta}_1$: -0.02 +/- 0.06 (**1.701**) $\rightarrow$ -0.12 to 0.08

If we construct an infinite number of such intervals, 90 percent of them will contain the true β_1. Notice that the 90% confidence interval is smaller than the 95% confidence interval. This makes sense. To be more confident, we need a wider interval. A 100% confidence interval would run from negative infinity to positive infinity.

4.4 Negative Sign Test

A negative sign test is different from a test of significance in that we are solely interested in the estimator being less than zero. A negative sign test is more specific in that Ha is $\beta_1 < 0$, not $\beta_1 \neq 0$. $\hat{\beta}_1 = -0.02$ in our example. Let's test if this is significantly less than zero.

---

1) Ho: $\beta_1 = 0$ Ha: $\beta_1 < 0$
2) 5%
3) If t-ratio $< -t^c$, then reject Ho
4) $-.33 > -1.701$ (d.f. = n- k = 30 – 2 =28)
5) Do Not Reject Ho; β_1 is not significantly negative

Notice the differences between this test and the test of significance:

1) Ha is now $\beta_1 < 0$, not Ha: $\beta_1 \neq 0$.
2) The decision rule is If t-ratio $< -t^c$, then reject Ho, not If $|$ t-ratio $| >$ tc, then reject Ho. Still, the t-ratio is calculated with the same formula.
3) The degrees of freedom are the same; however, this is a one-tailed test, so we obtain a different t^c.

The conclusion of our negative sign test is that β_1 is not significantly negative.

4.5 Positive Sign Test

A positive sign test is different from a test of significance in that we are not interested in the estimator being different from zero, but greater than zero. $\hat{\beta}_0 = 2.87$ in our example. Let's test if this is significantly greater than zero. Here is the 5-step procedure:

1) Ho: $\beta_0 = 0$ Ha: $\beta_0 > 0$
2) 5%
3) If t-ratio $> t^c$, then reject Ho
4) 13.67 > 1.701 (d.f. = n- k = 30 – 2 =28)
5) Reject Ho; β_0 is significantly positive

We reject Ho, which implies that β_0 is significantly positive.

4.6 A Review of the Decision Rules

After doing a test of significance and two sign tests, you have learned three decision rules. It is easy to remember which decision rule to use in each instance because the rules are aligned with the alternate hypotheses.

Review of decision rules

If Ha has a $\neq$: if |t-ratio| $> t^c$, reject Ho
If Ha has a $>$: if t-ratio $> t^c$, reject Ho
If Ha has a $<$: if t-ratio $< -t^c$, reject Ho
(The latter two are one-tailed tests.)

4.7 Specific Value Test

A specific value test is used to determine if an estimator equals some pre-specified value, not zero. Specific value tests can be one- or two-tailed. It depends on how they are set up. For instance, we might ask if β_0, which is estimated by $\hat{\beta}_0 = 2.87$ in our example, is significantly less than 3. This is a one-tailed test since the alternate hypothesis is Ha: $\beta_0 < 3$.

Be careful in calculating the t-ratio since $\beta_{Ho} \neq 0$ in this test:

$$t - ratio = \frac{\hat{\beta}_0 - \beta_{Ho}}{SE(\hat{\beta}_0)} = \frac{2.87 - 3}{0.21} = -0.62$$

Here is the entire test:

1) Ho: $\beta_0 = 3$ Ha: $\beta_0 < 3$
2) 5%
3) If t-ratio $< -t^c$, then reject Ho
4) -0.62 > -1.701 (d.f. = n- k = 30 – 2 =28)
5) Do Not Reject Ho; β_0 is not significantly less than 3

We do not reject Ho, which implies β_0 is not significantly less than 3.

4.8 Test for r = 0

r is the correlation coefficient between two variables. It ranges between plus and minus 1.

$$r = \frac{\Sigma(X_i - \overline{X})(Y_i - \overline{Y})}{\sqrt{\Sigma(X_i - \overline{X})^2 (Y_i - \overline{Y})^2}}$$

When r = 1, it implies that the two variables are perfectly linearly correlated. For instance, every time X increases by 7, Y increases by 3. When r = -1, the two variables are perfectly inversely correlated. Every time X increases by 7, Y decreases by 3. When r = 0, it implies that the variables are not at all linearly related.

The correlation coefficient between GPA and ST in our example equals -0.061. Is this value close enough to zero to say that there is no correlation between GPA and ST?

The t-ratio for this test is calculated as follows:

$$t - ratio = \frac{r\sqrt{n-2}}{\sqrt{(1-r^2)}} = \frac{-.061\sqrt{30-2}}{\sqrt{1-.0037}} = \frac{-.323}{.998} = -.324$$

1) Ho: r = 0   Ha: r ≠ 0
2) 5%
3) If $\left| \text{t-ratio} \right| > t^c$, then reject Ho
4) $0.324 < 2.048$ (d.f. = n - 2 = 30 – 2 = 28)
5) Do Not Reject Ho ; r is not statistically different from zero.

We do not reject Ho, which implies that r is not statistically different from zero. Notice that all of the hypothesis tests we have learned to this point include a statistic called "t-ratio" and sometimes referred to as "t-statistic". Also notice that this statistic is calculated differently for some of the tests. This can be confusing. The test of significance, positive sign test, and negative sign test all use the same formula to calculate the t-ratio. However, the specific value test and the test for r = 0 use different formulas for the t-ratio.

The next hypothesis test uses an F-statistic.

4.9 Test for $r^2 = 0$

If the coefficient of determination (r^2) equals zero, it implies that the explanatory variable explains none of the variation in the dependent variable. In our example, $r^2 = 0.004$. Is this close enough to suggest the true r^2 equals zero?

This is the first hypothesis test we have encountered where the test statistic is distributed as an F-statistic. F-statistics can only be positive so they are always one-sided tests. Here is the 5-step procedure:

1) Ho: $r^2 = 0$ Ha: $r^2 > 0$
2) 5%
3) If $F > F^c$, then reject Ho
4) $0.104 < 4.20$ (d.f. = k-1 in the numerator and n-k in the denominator)
5) Do Not Reject Ho; r^2 is not statistically greater than zero.

The F is calculated with either of the formulas below:

$$F = \frac{\Sigma(Y_i - \overline{Y})^2 / (k-1)}{\Sigma e_i^2 / (n-k)} \quad \text{or} \quad F = \frac{r^2 / (k-1)}{(1 - r^2)/(n-k)}$$

F^c is found in a table such as the one in the back of this book. To look up F^c, find where the degrees of freedom in the numerator (k-1 = 1) intersect with the degrees of freedom in the denominator (n-k = 30-2 = 28). F^c also can be found online or with Excel.

In this example we do not reject Ho: r^2 is not statistically greater than zero. Study time does not account for any of the variation in GPA across these 30 students.

4.10 Probability Values

A probability value is the lowest level of significance that can be used in a hypothesis test while still rejecting Ho. As such, P-values (as they are commonly known) provide a quick method for determining the results of a hypothesis test: If the P-value is less than .05, then the result of the hypothesis test will be to reject Ho.

Consider the GPA regression we have used throughout this chapter. The P-value on the coefficient on ST for a test of significance is equal to 0.73. Since this is greater than the critical level of the test (0.05), the test of significance will result in "do not reject Ho". That is, we can immediately see that ST is insignificant at the 5 percent critical level since the P-value is greater than 0.05.

Indeed, even if we set the critical level of this test of significance at 72 percent we would still say "do not reject Ho". Only when the critical level surpasses 73 percent would we say "reject Ho" and conclude that ST is significant. However, critical levels above 10 percent are not acceptable in hypothesis testing.

The P-value is the area under the t-distribution that would have to be considered in order to reject Ho for a given t-ratio and degrees of freedom.

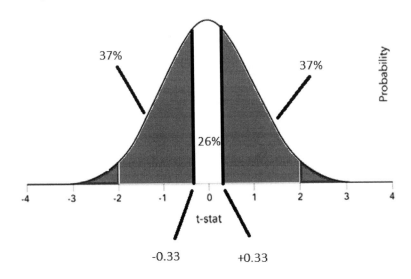

A critical level of 74 percent, 37 plus 37 percent, is required to reject Ho in this case.

Terms

Confidence interval – A range of values within which the true value of an estimated parameter is likely to fall.

Correlation coefficient (r) – A statistic ranging between –1 and 1 that measures the degree to which two variables are linearly related.

Critical level (level of significance) – The probability of making a TYPE I error in a hypothesis test.

F-ratio (F-statistic) – Any statistic that follows the F-distribution.

Probability value – The lowest level of significance that can be used in a hypothesis test while still rejecting Ho.

t-ratio (t-statistic) – Any statistic that follows the t-distribution.

TYPE I error – When a true null hypothesis is rejected.

TYPE II error – When a false null hypothesis is not rejected.

Chapter 4   Problems

1. A professor has polled 25 students and asked them about their seat belt use (Do you wear your seat belt regularly?) and smoking (Do you smoke cigarettes?).

A) The correlation coefficient (r) between seat belt use and cigarette smoking is -.034. Are you surprised that the correlation is negative? Explain.

B) Do a test to determine if r is different from zero. Show the 5-step procedure.

C) Do a test to determine if r is less than zero. Show the 5-step procedure.

D) Explain why seat belt use and smoking may be correlated despite the tests above.

2. A professor has polled 30 students and asked them about their job situation (Do you have a full-time or part-time job this semester?) and their overall GPA (What is your overall GPA?).

A) The correlation coefficient (r) between having a job and GPA is 0.21. Are you surprised that the correlation is positive? Explain.

B) Do a test to determine if r is different from zero. Show the 5-step procedure.

C) Do a test to determine if r is greater than zero. Show the 5-step procedure.

D) What is the probability that a TYPE I error is being made in the test above?

3. Given the following regression results:

$$CORUPT_i = 5.47 - 0.05\ MIL_i + e_i$$
$$(0.49)\ (0.05) \leftarrow \text{standard errors}$$
$$(0.00)\ (0.34) \leftarrow \text{P-values}$$

$$SER = 2.35 \quad \overline{CORUPT} = 5.14 \quad r^2 = 0.02 \quad n = 48$$

$CORUPT_i$ is the corruption level of the country
(1 is low; 10 is high)
MIL_i is military presence in the country
(military personnel per 1,000 citizens)

A) Do a test of significance on the coefficient on MIL. Show the 5-step procedure.

B) Would the results of your test turn out differently if the critical level of the test was 40% instead of 5%? Explain.

C) Is the constant term significant at the 1% critical level? Answer this question without doing a test of significance. Just explain.

D) Form a 90% confidence interval around the coefficient on MIL.

E) Determine if $r^2 = 0$ for this regression. (The F-statistic $= 0.95$.) Show the 5-step procedure.

F) Would your results for E) be different if the critical level of the test was 33%? Explain. (P-value for this test is 0.34.)

G) Do a test to determine if the coefficient on MIL equals zero or if it is greater than zero. Show the 5-step procedure.

H) Do a test to determine if the coefficient on MIL equals - 0.1 or not. Show the 5-step procedure.

4. Given the following regression results:

$$CORUPT_i = 7.54 - 0.25\ OVER65_i + e_i$$
$$\quad (0.62)\ (0.06)\quad \leftarrow \text{standard errors}$$
$$\quad (0.00)\ (0.00)\quad \leftarrow \text{P-values}$$

$$SER = 1.99 \quad \overline{CORUPT} = 5.14 \quad r^2 = 0.29 \quad n = 32$$

$CORUPT_i$ is the corruption level of the country
(1 is low; 10 is high)
$OVER65_i$ is percentage of the population 65 or older

A) Do a test of significance on the coefficient on OVER65. Show the 5-step procedure.

B) Would the results of your test turn out differently if the critical level of the test was 1% instead of 5%? Explain.

C) Is the constant term significant at the 1% critical level? Answer this question without doing a test of significance. Just explain.

D) Form a 90% confidence interval around the coefficient on OVER65.

E) Determine if $r^2 = 0$ for this regression. (The F-statistic = 12.25.) Show the 5-step procedure.

F) Would your results for E) be different if the critical level of the test was 3%? Explain. (P-value for this test is 0.01.)

G) Do a test to determine if the coefficient on OVER65 equals zero or if it is greater than zero. Show the 5-step procedure.

H) Do a test to determine if the coefficient on OVER65 equals -1.00 or not. Show the 5-step procedure.

Chapter 5

Multiple Regression

5.1 Parameter Estimation in Multiple Regression

In a multiple regression there are two or more explanatory variables. Consider the case of two explanatory variables: $Y_i = \hat{\beta}_0 + \hat{\beta}_1 X1_i + \hat{\beta}_2 X2_i + e_i$.

We still want to min Σe_i^2 or min $\Sigma(Y_i - \hat{\beta}_0 - \hat{\beta}_1 X1_i - \hat{\beta}_2 X2_i)^2$. That requires taking three partial derivatives and setting the resulting equations equal to zero. The three normal equations can then be solved for $\hat{\beta}_0, \hat{\beta}_1$, and $\hat{\beta}_2$:

Take the partial derivative with respect to $\hat{\beta}_0$:

$$\frac{\partial \Sigma(Y_i - \hat{\beta}_0 - \hat{\beta}_1 X1_i - \hat{\beta}_2 X2_i)^2}{\partial \hat{\beta}_0} = 2\Sigma(Y_i - \hat{\beta}_0 - \hat{\beta}_1 X1_i - \hat{\beta}_2 X2_i)(-1) = 0$$

Divide both sides of the above by -2 and distribute the sum sign:

$$\Sigma Y_i - n\hat{\beta}_0 - \hat{\beta}_1 \Sigma X1_i - \hat{\beta}_2 \Sigma X2_i = 0$$

Solve for $\hat{\beta}_0$:

$$\Sigma Y_i = n\hat{\beta}_0 + \hat{\beta}_1 \Sigma X1_i + \hat{\beta}_2 \Sigma X2_i \quad \text{(normal equation)}$$

$$\hat{\beta}_0 = \frac{\Sigma Y_i - \hat{\beta}_1 \Sigma X1_i - \hat{\beta}_2 \Sigma X2_i}{n} = \overline{Y} - \hat{\beta}_1 \overline{X}1_i - \hat{\beta}_2 \overline{X}2_i$$

Take the partial derivative with respect to $\hat{\beta}_1$:

$$\frac{\partial \Sigma(Y_i - \hat{\beta}_0 - \hat{\beta}_1 X1_i - \hat{\beta}_2 X2_i)^2}{\partial \hat{\beta}_1} = 2\Sigma(Y_i - \hat{\beta}_0 - \hat{\beta}_1 X1_i - \hat{\beta}_2 X2_i)(-X1_i) = 0$$

Divide both sides of the above by -2 and distribute the sum sign:

$$\Sigma Y_i X1_i - \hat{\beta}_0 \Sigma X1_i - \hat{\beta}_1 \Sigma X1_i X1_i - \hat{\beta}_2 \Sigma X2_i X1_i = 0$$

Solve for $\hat{\beta}_1$:

$$\Sigma Y_i X1_i = \hat{\beta}_0 \Sigma X1_i + \hat{\beta}_1 \Sigma X1_i X1_i + \hat{\beta}_2 \Sigma X2_i X1_i \quad \text{(normal equation)}$$

$$\vdots$$

$$\hat{\beta}_1 = \frac{(\Sigma y_i x_{1i})(\Sigma x_{2i}{}^2) - (\Sigma y_i x_{2i})(\Sigma x_{1i} x_{2i})}{(\Sigma x_{1i}{}^2)(\Sigma x_{2i}{}^2) - (\Sigma x_{1i} x_{2i})^2} \; ; \text{ where } y_i = Y_i - \overline{Y} \; ; x_{1i} = X1_i - \overline{X}1 \; ; x_{2i} = X2_i - \overline{X}2$$

Take the partial derivative with respect to $\hat{\beta}_2$:

$$\frac{\partial \Sigma (Y_i - \hat{\beta}_0 - \hat{\beta}_1 X1_i - \hat{\beta}_2 X2_i)^2}{\partial \hat{\beta}2} = 2\Sigma(Y_i - \hat{\beta}_0 - \hat{\beta}_1 X1_i - \hat{\beta}_2 X2_i)(-X2_i) = 0$$

Divide both sides of the above by -2 and distribute the sum sign:

$$\Sigma Y_i X2_i - \hat{\beta}_0 \Sigma X2_i - \hat{\beta}_1 \Sigma X1_i X2_i - \hat{\beta}_2 \Sigma X2_i X2_i = 0$$

Solve for $\hat{\beta}_2$:

$$\Sigma Y_i X2_i = \hat{\beta}_0 \Sigma X2_i + \hat{\beta}_1 \Sigma X1_i X2_i + \hat{\beta}_2 \Sigma X2_i X2_i \quad \text{(normal equation)}$$

$$\cdot$$
$$\cdot$$
$$\cdot$$

$$\hat{\beta}_2 = \frac{(\Sigma y_i x_{2i})(\Sigma x_{2i}{}^2) - (\Sigma y_i x_{1i})(\Sigma x_{1i} x_{2i})}{(\Sigma x_{1i}{}^2)(\Sigma x_{2i}{}^2) - (\Sigma x_{1i} x_{2i})^2} \; ; \text{ where } y_i = Y_i - \overline{Y} \; ; x_{1i} = X1_i - \overline{X}1 \; ; x_{2i} = X2_i - \overline{X}2$$

The formulas for $\hat{\beta}_1$ and $\hat{\beta}_2$ are too cumbersome to calculate by hand. We are grateful to have computers to do this sort of thing for us. Here is the formula for $\hat{\beta}_1$ written out in all its glory:

$$\hat{\beta}_1 = \frac{(\Sigma(Y_i - \overline{Y})(X1_i - \overline{X}1))(\Sigma X2_i - \overline{X}2)^2 - (\Sigma(Y_i - \overline{Y})(X2_i - \overline{X}2))(\Sigma(X1_i - \overline{X}1)(X2_i - \overline{X}2))}{(\Sigma X1_i - \overline{X}1)^2(\Sigma X2_i - \overline{X}2)^2 - (\Sigma(X1_i - \overline{X}1)(X2_i - \overline{X}2))^2}$$

The problems at the end of this chapter and beyond require you to use a statistical software package to perform cumbersome calculations such as the one above. Eviews by IHS was used to solve the problems in this book, but any package will do. Excel by Microsoft can be used to run regressions, but it does not calculate all the residual statistics you will need in later chapters. Free shareware is available (such as gretl) that can do all the problems in this text. All of the input data required for any problems in this textbook are available at www.mesharpe-student.com . The data files are in Excel format, which allows them to be imported into a variety of statistical packages including Eviews and gretl.

5.2 The Variance and Standard Errors of the Estimators

As we move to multiple regression from simple regression, our formulas for the standard errors of the structural parameters are changed.

$$\text{var}(\hat{\beta}_0) = \left[\frac{1}{n} + \frac{\overline{X1}^2 \Sigma x_{2i}^2 + \overline{X2}^2 \Sigma x_{1i}^2 - 2\overline{X1}\,\overline{X2}\,\Sigma x_{1i}x_{2i}}{(\Sigma x_{1i}^2)(\Sigma x_{2i}^2) - (\Sigma x_{1i}x_{2i})^2} \right] \bullet \hat{\sigma}^2$$

$$se(\hat{\beta}_0) = \sqrt{\text{var}(\hat{\beta}_0)}$$

$$\text{var}(\hat{\beta}_1) = \frac{\Sigma x_{2i}^2}{(\Sigma x_{1i}^2)(\Sigma x_{2i}^2) - (\Sigma x_{1i}x_{2i})^2} \bullet \hat{\sigma}^2$$

$$se(\hat{\beta}_1) = \sqrt{\text{var}(\hat{\beta}_1)}$$

$$\text{var}(\hat{\beta}_2) = \frac{\Sigma x_{1i}^2}{(\Sigma x_{1i}^2)(\Sigma x_{2i}^2) - (\Sigma x_{1i}x_{2i})^2} \bullet \hat{\sigma}^2$$

$$se(\hat{\beta}_2) = \sqrt{\text{var}(\hat{\beta}_2)}$$

The interpretation of these standard errors is still the same. If we calculate $se(\hat{\beta}_2) = 1.23$ it means that $\hat{\beta}_2$ is expected to vary by 1.23 on average in repeated sampling.

5.3 Goodness-of-Fit in Multiple Regression

The measures of goodness-of-fit that we developed for simple regressions are slightly altered when we move to multiple regressions.

The SER is still interpreted and (almost) calculated the same way: $\hat{\sigma} = \sqrt{\dfrac{\Sigma e_i^2}{n-2}}$

For multiple regression $\hat{\sigma} = \sqrt{\dfrac{\Sigma e_i^2}{n-k}}$; where k is the number of structural parameters.

Interpretation: 0.487   The typical distance of an observation from the regression line is 0.487.

The coefficient of determination is now denoted by R^2 (as opposed to r^2), but it is still calculated with the same formula:

$$R^2 = 1 - \frac{\Sigma e_i^{\ 2}}{\Sigma (Y_i - \overline{Y})^2}$$

Interpretation: .001 - 0.1 percent of the variation in Y is explained by the X variables.

R^2 is monotonically increasing with respect to k. Hence, it is inappropriate to compare R^2 from regressions with a different number of explanatory variables. Instead, use adjusted R^2 ($\overline{R}^2$):

$$\overline{R}^2 = 1 - \frac{\Sigma e_i^{\ 2} / (n - k)}{\Sigma (Y_i - \overline{Y})^2 / (n - 1)}$$

$\overline{R}^2$ will decrease if the additional explanatory variable has little or no impact on the dependent variable. Indeed, it can be shown that $\overline{R}^2$ will decrease if the added explanatory variable has a t-ratio < 1 in absolute value.

5.4 An Illustrative Example with Hypothesis Testing

Let's consider a classic econometric study as an example of multiple regression (Andersen and Jordan 1969). In this study, Andersen and Jordan hypothesized that changes in nominal GDP would depend on changes in monetary and fiscal policy. They measured monetary and fiscal policy in a variety of ways using quarterly data from the first quarter of 1952 through the second quarter of 1968. Here we replicate the study using annual data from 1964 through 2005.

$$NGDP_t = 127.35 + 1.06\ M2_{t-1} - 0.29\ FP_{t-1} + e_t$$
$$\quad\quad (3.75)\quad (5.55)\quad\quad (-0.71)\quad \leftarrow \text{t-ratios}$$

$$SER = 132.65 \quad \overline{NGDP} = 282.42 \quad R^2 = 0.47 \quad n = 42$$

NGDP is the change in nominal GDP
M2 is the change in the M2 money supply
FP is the change in standardized federal budget deficit

Notice that M2 and FP are lagged one period (t-1). This is because monetary and fiscal policy actions last year impact this year's nominal GDP. Our replication confirms Andersen and Jordan's original results -- monetary policy has an impact on nominal GDP but fiscal policy is statistically insignificant.

Before doing any hypothesis testing, let's interpret the regression results noticing how the interpretations differ from those in a simple regression.

Interpretations:

$\hat{\beta}_0 = 127.35$: If $M2_{t-1}$ and $FP_{t-1} = 0$, then $NGDP_t = 127.35$

$\hat{\beta}_1 = 1.06$: If $M2_{t-1}$ increases one unit, then NGDP increases 1.06 units, holding FP_{t-1} constant

$\hat{\beta}_2 = -0.29$: FP_{t-1} increases one unit, then NGDP decreases 0.29 units, holding $M2_{t-1}$ constant

$R^2 = 0.47$: 47 percent of the variation in NGDP is explained by $M2_{t-1}$ and FP_{t-1}

SER = 132.65: The typical regression error is 132.65

Hypothesis Testing

Notice that the coefficient on FP_{t-1} has the correct sign: an increase in the standardized federal budget deficit is expected to contract the economy and decrease nominal GDP. However, the coefficient is not statistically different from zero.

Test of significance on $\hat{\beta}_2$

1) Ho: $\beta_2 = 0$ Ha: $\beta_2 \neq 0$
2) 5%
3) If |t-ratio| > t^c, then reject Ho
4) 0.71 < 2.023 (d.f. = n- k = 42 – 3 = 39)
5) Do Not Reject Ho; $\hat{\beta}_2$ is not statistically significant

Changes in the money supply, however, have a positive impact on nominal GDP according to a positive sign test:

Positive Sign Test on $\hat{\beta}_1$

1) Ho: $\beta_1 = 0$ Ha: $\beta_1 > 0$
2) 5%
3) If t-ratio > t^c, then reject Ho
4) 5.55 > 1.685 (d.f. = n- k = 42 – 3 = 39)
5) Reject Ho; $\hat{\beta}_1$ is significantly positive

These results suggest that monetary policy is an effective macroeconomic policy while fiscal policy is not.

5.5 The Intuition of Multiple Regression

Geometrically, simple regression can be represented by fitting a line between observations in two-dimensional space.

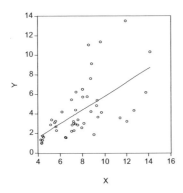

A regression with two explanatory variables is akin to fitting a plane in three-dimensional space.

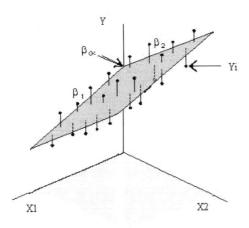

A regression with three explanatory variables would be fitting a three-dimensional object into observations in four-dimensional space. We leave it to the reader to visualize this case.

5.6 Model Specification

Whether or not to include a particular variable in a given regression is not something that can be taught. However, there are some general rules to help researchers decide about model specification. Before we consider those rules, it should be understood that the process of model selection is crucial.

It is completely inappropriate, and unethical, to run regression after regression, slightly altering the set of explanatory variables each time, and then stop when the results conform to your premonitions. Hypothesis testing in this situation is invalid since the researcher has actively worked to ensure that the results would support preconceived notions.

The proper approach to model specification is to thoroughly research which explanatory variables belong in a particular regression. Theory is the best guide. It is important to include every explanatory variable that has a substantial impact on the dependent variable. Re-running the regression with more variables is not a crime, but it begins to look like fishing for preconceived results.

Often, theory does not indicate whether a particular variable should be included or not. In this case there are some statistical indicators that can help.

- Significance – Explanatory variables with anemic t-ratios (< 2 in absolute value) or high p-values ($> .05$) are candidates for exclusion from the model. Such variables will not pass a test of significance.
- Adjusted R^2 – If adjusted R^2 falls upon the addition of an explanatory variable, it is an indication that the variable does not belong. It can be shown that adjusted R^2 will fall when the added variable has a |t-ratio| < 1.
- Akaike information criterion and Schwarz criterion – Like adjusted R^2, these statistics consider how fit is improved by adding an explanatory variable to a regression. Unlike adjusted R-squared, a fall in either of these statistics is an indication that the added variable belongs.

Akaike Information Criterion:
$$AIC = -2[(-n/2)(1 + \log(2\pi) + \log(\hat{\sigma}^2/n))]/n + 2k/n$$

Schwarz Criterion:
$$SC = -2[(-n/2)(1 + \log(2\pi) + \log(\hat{\sigma}^2/n))]/n + (k \log n)/n$$

- Altered coefficients – When a particular variable is removed from the regression and the coefficients on the remaining variables change markedly, it is an indication that the removed variable belongs.
- Ramsey's Reset test – Ramsey (1969) has devised an F- test to determine if explanatory variables might be excluded from a regression:

1) Ho: $\beta_2 = \beta_3 = 0$ Ha: β_2 and/or $\beta_3 \neq 0$
    (No variables excluded)   (Variables excluded)
2) 5%
3) If $F > F^c$, then reject Ho
4) Get F and F^c
5) Reject or Do Not Reject Ho

The F-statistic is calculated with the following formula:

$$F = \frac{(SSR_U - SSR_R)/2}{(1 - SSR_U)/(n-k)}$$

An auxiliary regression must be run that includes the predicted values from the initial regression squared and cubed. Then the sum of the squared residuals from the initial regression (SSR_R) and the sum of the squared residuals from the auxiliary regression (SSR_U) are used to calculate an F-statistic that is compared to an F^c.

$$SSR_R: \ \Sigma e_i^2 \text{ from } Y_i = \hat{\beta}_0 + \hat{\beta}_1 X1_i + e_i$$
$$SSR_U: \ \Sigma e_i^2 \text{ from } Y_i = \hat{\beta}_0 + \hat{\beta}_1 X1_i + \hat{\beta}_2 \hat{Y}_i^2 + \hat{\beta}_3 \hat{Y}_i^3 + e_i$$

The critical F (F^c) is found in the F-table. The degrees of freedom in the numerator are equal to 2 (the two addition variables added to SSR_U) and the degrees of freedom in the denominator are equal to n-k.

If $F > F^c$ then we reject Ho, which indicates that important explanatory variables may be omitted from the specification.

All of these rules are trumped by theory. When theory unequivocally indicates that a variable should be included, then these statistical indicators take a back seat.

Let's continue with our Andersen-Jordan example. They argued that monetary and fiscal policy were the only theoretically justified explanatory variables for their model. However, they were unsure about how to measure these variables. They tried a variety of measures for monetary policy (including changes in M1 and changes in the monetary base) and several fiscal policy variables. They understood that running a bank of regressions could cause skepticism about their results so they reported all their regression results and all the results pointed in the same direction: monetary policy affects nominal GDP but fiscal policy does not.

5.7 Underspecification

Underspecification is when an important explanatory variable is excluded from a regression. Let's omit monetary policy from the model and see what happens:

Correctly Specified Andersen-Jordan Equation

$$\text{NGDP}_t = 127.35 + 1.06 \, \text{M2}_{t-1} - 0.29 \, \text{FP}_{t-1} + e_t$$
$$\quad\quad (3.75) \quad (5.55) \quad\quad (-0.71) \quad \leftarrow \text{t-ratios}$$

$$\text{SER} = 132.65 \quad \overline{\text{NGDP}} = 282.42 \quad R^2 = 0.47 \quad n = 42$$

$$\text{Adjusted } R^2 = 0.45 \quad \text{Akaike} = 12.68 \quad \text{Schwarz} = 12.81$$

Underspecificed Specified Andersen-Jordan Equation

$$NGDP_t = 276.91 - 0.81\ FP_{t-1} + e_t$$
$$(10.15)\ (-1.56)\ \leftarrow \text{t-ratios}$$

$$SER = 175.26 \quad \overline{NGDP} = 282.42 \quad r^2 = 0.06 \quad n = 42$$

$$\text{Adjusted } R^2 = 0.03 \quad \text{Akaike} = 13.22 \quad \text{Schwarz} = 13.30$$

Notice that adjusted R^2 has plummeted indicating that the fit of the underspecified regression is much worse. The Akaike and the Schwarz statistics are higher, which also suggest a worse fit. Also notice how different the estimators are in both regressions. The constant term went from 127.35 to 276.91 and the coefficient on FP_{t-1} went from -0.29 to -0.81. Such dramatic differences imply that the omitted variable belongs in the regression.

Finally, the underspecified regression does not pass Ramsey's Reset test.

1) Ho: $\beta_2 = \beta_3 = 0$ Ha: β_2 and/or $\beta_3 \neq 0$
        (No variables excluded)   (Variables excluded)
2) 5%
3) If $F > F^c$, then reject Ho
4) 3.66 > 3.245; where F^c has d.f. NUM = 2 ; d.f. DEN = n-k = 42-4=38
                       (using NUM=2 and DEN=30 because of our F-table)
5) Reject Ho; Variables are excluded from this regression.

All indications are that the regression without the monetary policy variable is underspecified. The consequence of leaving a relevant explanatory variable out of a regression is severe -- parameter estimates, and therefore all residual statistics, are biased. This means that in repeated sampling the average of the estimates will not equal the true value: $E[\hat{\beta_1}] \neq \beta_1$.

5.8 Overspecification

We can intentionally overspecify the original Andersen-Jordan model by adding a variable we know does not belong -- $RAND_t$ is a series of random numbers generated by a computer.

Overspecified Andersen-Jordan Equation

$$NGDP_t = 152.46 + 1.05\ M2_{t-1} - 0.23\ FP_{t-1} - 8.42\ RAND_t + e_t$$
$$(3.75)\ \ \ (5.55)\ \ \ \ \ \ (-0.71)\ \ \ \ \ \ (-0.93)\ \leftarrow \text{t-ratios}$$

$$SER = 132.87 \quad \overline{NGDP} = 282.42 \quad R^2 = 0.49 \quad n = 42$$

$$\text{Adjusted } R^2 = 0.44 \quad \text{Akaike} = 12.71 \quad \text{Schwarz} = 12.87$$

Adjusted R^2 has fallen very slightly, while the Akaike and Schwarz statistics have both risen a tad. All three statistics thereby suggest that RAND does not belong in the regression. Notice that the estimators have hardly changed with the addition of RAND. The coefficient on FP_{t-1} went from 1.06 to 1.05. This also implies that RAND is extraneous.

Ramsey's Reset test cannot help to discern if a regression is overspecified, so we will not employ it here. It is fairly evident that RAND is an irrelevant explanatory variable given its anemic t-ratio and the indications noted above.

The consequence for including an irrelevant explanatory variable in a regression is inefficient (not best) estimators. An inefficient estimator will vary more in repeated sampling than the efficient estimator. Hypothesis tests should be conducted with caution under these circumstances since the t-ratios used in those tests will be derived from bloated standard errors. Type II errors will become more likely.

Terms

Adjusted R^2 ($\overline{R}^2$) - A statistic that tends to decrease when an irrelevant explanatory variable is added to a regression.

Akaike information criterion – A statistic that tends to increase when an irrelevant explanatory variable is added to a regression.

Biased estimator – In repeated sampling, the average of the estimates will not equal the true value.

Inefficient estimator – An estimator that varies more in repeated sampling than the efficient estimator.

Multiple regression – A regression that includes more than one explanatory variable.

Overspecification – When a regression includes one or more irrelevant explanatory variables.

Ramsey's Reset test – A statistical test to help determine if a regression is underspecified.

Schwarz criterion – A statistic that tends to increase when an irrelevant explanatory variable is added to a regression.

Underspecification – When an important explanatory variable is excluded from a regression.

Chapter 5   Problems

1. Use the data in SDATA.XLS and statistical software to run the following regression:

$$GPA_i = \hat{\beta}_0 + \hat{\beta}_1\ ST_i + e_i$$

where GPA = grade point average
and ST = study time per day

A) Interpret the value you obtained for $\hat{\beta}_0$.

B) Interpret the value you obtained for $\hat{\beta}_1$.

C) How much does $\hat{\beta}_1$ typically vary in repeated sampling?

D) Perform a test of significance on $\hat{\beta}_1$. Show the 5-step procedure.

E) What percent of the variation in GPA is explained by study time?

F) Perform a test to determine if $r^2 = 0$. Show the 5-step procedure.

G) According to these results, how many hours per day would your study time have to increase in order to raise your GPA by 0.1?

H) Plot the scattergram between GPA and ST with the estimated regression line drawn in.

I) What is the average distance of an observation from the regression line?

J) Will you cut back on your study time now that you have seen these results? Explain why.

2. Use the data in SDATA.XLS and statistical software to run the following regression:

$$GPA_i = \hat{\beta}_0 + \hat{\beta}_1\ ST_i + \hat{\beta}_2\ SAT_i + e_i$$

where GPA = grade point average
ST = study time per day
SAT = SAT score

A) Interpret the value you obtained for $\hat{\beta}_0$.

B) Interpret the value you obtained for $\hat{\beta}_1$.

C) Perform a positive sign test on $\hat{\beta}_1$. Show the 5-step procedure.

D) Interpret the value you obtained for $\hat{\beta}_2$.

E) Perform a test to determine if b $\hat{\beta}_0 < 1$. Show the 5-step procedure.

F) Interpret the value you obtained for R^2.

G) Which regression fits the data better, this one or the one in question 1? On what do you base your response?

H) The typical student in the survey studies about 3.0 hours per day and had an SAT score of 1125. What would you expect the average student's GPA to be given your research into this matter?

3. Use the data in CONSUMP.XLS and statistical software to run the following regression:

$$RCONPC_t = \hat{\beta}_0 + \hat{\beta}_1 REALYDPC_t + \hat{\beta}_2 REALR_t + e_t$$

where RCONPC = real consumer spending in the USA per capita
REALYDPC = real disposable income per capita
REALR = real interest rate on one-year Treasury Bonds

A) Do all the explanatory variables attain their expected signs?
B) Aside from CC, what explanatory variables might be missing from this regression?
C) Perform Ramsey's Reset test. Show the 5-step procedure. Are variables missing from the model according to this test?

4. Use the data in MBAPAY.XLS and statistical software to run the following regression:

$$MBAPAY_i = \hat{\beta}_0 + \hat{\beta}_1 AVGMAT_i + \hat{\beta}_2 ACRATE_i + e_i$$

where MBAPAY$_i$ = average starting salary of MBA students from school i
AVGMAT$_i$ = average GMAT score at school i
ACRATE$_i$ = acceptance rate at school i
CC = University of Michigan Index of Consumer Confidence

A) Do all the explanatory variables attain their expected signs?
B) Aside from AVGPA, what explanatory variables might be missing from this regression?
C) Perform Ramsey's Reset test. Show the 5-step procedure. Are variables missing from the model according to this test?

5. Use the data in CONSUMP.XLS and statistical software to run the following regression:

$$RCONPC_t = \hat{\beta}_0 + \hat{\beta}_1 REALYDPC_t + \hat{\beta}_2 REALR_t + \hat{\beta}_3 CC_t + e_t$$

where RCONPC = real consumer spending in the USA per capita
REALYDPC = real disposable income per capita
REALR = real interest rate on one-year Treasury Bonds
CC = University of Michigan Index of Consumer Confidence

A) Does CC attain its expected sign? Explain.
B) Does a test of significance on CC justify its presence in the regression?
C) Does CC belong in the regression according to Adjusted R^2? Explain.
D) Does CC belong in the regression according to the Akaike information criterion? Explain.
E) Does CC belong in the regression according to the Schwarz criterion? Explain.

F) Does this regression fit better than the regression from question 3 above? Explain.

G) Perform Ramsey's Reset test. Show the 5-step procedure. Are variables missing from the model according to this test?

H) Do you think the estimators in $RCONPC_t = \hat{\beta}_0 + \hat{\beta}_1 REALYDPC_t + \hat{\beta}_2 REALR_t + e_t$ are biased? Inefficient? Neither? Explain.

I) Do you think the estimators in $RCONPC_t = \hat{\beta}_0 + \hat{\beta}_1 REALYDPC_t + \hat{\beta}_2 REALR_t + \hat{\beta}_3 CC_t + e_t$ are biased? Inefficient? Neither? Explain.

6. Use the data in MBAPAY.XLS and statistical software to run the following regression:

$$MBAPAY_i = \hat{\beta}_0 + \hat{\beta}_1 AVGMAT_i + \hat{\beta}_2 ACRATE_i + \hat{\beta}_3 AVGPA_i + e_i$$

where $MBAPAY_i$ = average starting salary of MBA students from school i
$AVGMAT_i$ = average GMAT score at school i
$ACRATE_i$ = acceptance rate at school i
$AVGPA_i$ = average GPA of incoming MBA students at school i

A) Does AVGPA attain its expected sign? Explain.

B) Does a test of significance on AVGPA justify its presence in the regression?

C) Does AVGPA belong in the regression according to Adjusted R^2? Explain.

D) Does AVGPA belong in the regression according to the Akaike information criterion? Explain.

E) Does AVGPA belong in the regression according to the Schwarz criterion? Explain.

F) Does this regression fit better than the regression from question 4 above? Explain.

G) Perform Ramsey's Reset test. Show the 5-step procedure. Are variables missing from the model according to this test?

H) Do you think the estimators in $MBAPAY_i = \hat{\beta}_0 + \hat{\beta}_1 AVGMAT_i + \hat{\beta}_2 ACRATE_i + e_i$ are biased? Inefficient? Neither? Explain.

I) Do you think the estimators in $MBAPAY_i = \hat{\beta}_0 + \hat{\beta}_1 AVGMAT_i + \hat{\beta}_2 ACRATE_i + \hat{\beta}_3 AVGPA_i + e_i$ are biased? Inefficient? Neither? Explain.

Test Yourself on Chapters 4 and 5

Dependent Variable: WHY
Method: Least Squares
Sample: 1978 2006
Included observations: 29

Variable	Coefficient	Std. Error	t-Statistic	Prob.
C	1.997710	51.03278	0.039146	0.9691
EX1	15.81597	3.734046	4.235611	0.0003
EX2	3.046501	2.188336	1.392154	0.1761
EX3	-0.000145	0.005735	-0.025229	0.9801
R-squared	0.765250	Mean dependent var		152.0576
Adjusted R-squared	0.737080	S.D. dependent var		51.28692

S.E. of regression	26.29775	Akaike info criterion	9.504286
Sum squared resid	17289.29	Schwarz criterion	9.692879
Log likelihood	-133.8121	F-statistic	27.16539
Durbin-Watson stat	0.723982	Prob(F-statistic)	0.000000

1. Use the Eviews output above and below to help with A) through G).

    A) Interpret the coefficient on EX1.

    B) Interpret the coefficient on the constant term (C).

    C) Is EX2 significant at the 17 percent critical level? Explain.

    D) Perform a positive sign test on the coefficient attached to EX2. Show the 5-step procedure.

    E) Perform a test to determine if the coefficient on EX3 is greater than -1.11. Show the 5-step procedure.

    F) Perform a test to determine if R-squared is greater than zero. Show the 5-step procedure.

    G) Based on the information in the table above (and ignoring Ramsey's Reset test, which we will perform in a moment) do you think the regression above is underspecified or overspecified? Explain.

    H) Perform Ramsey's Reset test on the regression above using the Eviews printout below. Show the 5-step procedure.

Ramsey RESET Test:

| F-statistic | 15.32735 | Probability | 0.000059 |
| Log likelihood ratio | 24.56517 | Probability | 0.000005 |

Test Equation:
Dependent Variable: WHY
Method: Least Squares
Sample: 1978 2006
Included observations: 29

Variable	Coefficient	Std. Error	t-Statistic	Prob.
C	1190.553	228.1171	5.219043	0.0000
EX1	-314.2471	60.00884	-5.236679	0.0000
EX2	-62.55620	12.06659	-5.184249	0.0000
EX3	-0.013078	0.006110	-2.140328	0.0432
FITTED^2	0.119787	0.021647	5.533578	0.0000
FITTED^3	-0.000222	4.06E-05	-5.474315	0.0000

R-squared	0.899370	Mean dependent var	152.0576
Adjusted R-squared	0.877494	S.D. dependent var	51.28692
S.E. of regression	17.95084	Akaike info criterion	8.795142
Sum squared resid	7411.349	Schwarz criterion	9.078031
Log likelihood	-121.5296	F-statistic	41.11217
Durbin-Watson stat	1.018779	Prob(F-statistic)	0.000000

I) What do the terms "FITTED^2" and "FITTED^3" refer to in the Eviews printout above?

2. Define the following terms: (4 pts. each)

    A) Unbiased estimator
    B) Best estimator
    C) Correlation coefficient (r)
    D) Probability value

3. Mark each statement TRUE or FALSE.

    A) If a regression is overspecified, then it would be surprising to see the t-ratios become more robust once the extraneous variables were removed.
    B) If a regression is underspecified, then it would be surprising to see the estimators change markedly once the missing variables were included.
    C) If a regression is overspecified, then it would be surprising to see the estimators change markedly once the extraneous variables were removed.
    D) A 95% confidence interval for a coefficient will be smaller than a 90% confidence interval.
    E) The Andersen-Jordan equation indicates that monetary policy is more effective than fiscal policy.
    F) Deriving the estimators for $Y_i = \hat{\beta}_0 + \hat{\beta}_1 X1_i + \hat{\beta}_2 X2_i + e_i$ will yield three normal equations.
    G) The Akaike information criterion is monotonically decreasing with respect to the number of explanatory variables.
    H) The higher the critical level of the hypothesis test, the less chance there is that the test will result in a TYPE II error.
    I) A coefficient that is significant at the 1% critical level may not be significant at the 2% critical level.
    J) A test of significance is more likely to result in a TYPE I error in an overspecified model.

Chapter 6

Alternate Functional Forms

6.1 Regression through the Origin

By suppressing the intercept term, the regression line is forced through the origin:

$$Y_i = \hat{\beta}_1 X_i + e_i$$

In this situation we still want to minimize Σe_i^2. Since $e_i = Y_i - \hat{\beta}_1 X_i$ in this case, we will minimize $\Sigma (Y_i - \hat{\beta}_1 X_i)^2$. Setting the derivative of this expression with respect to $\hat{\beta}_1$ equal to zero and solving gives:

$$\hat{\beta}_1 = \frac{\Sigma X_i Y_i}{\Sigma X_i^2}$$ (The details of this derivation are left to the reader as an exercise.)

There should be strong theoretical reasons for excluding the constant term. Just as when any important explanatory variable is excluded, the regression results will be biased if the intercept is inappropriately suppressed. In addition, R^2 and adjusted R^2 are invalid in regressions through the origin.

As an example of regression through the origin consider Okun's Law (Okun 1962). In the early 1960s Okun posited a linear relationship between unemployment and economic growth. Specifically, Okun estimated that the gap between potential and real GDP growth would widen 2 to 3 percentage points for each percentage point increase in the unemployment rate.

To test Okun's Law in the postwar United States economy we regressed the gap between potential and real GDP growth on the change in the unemployment rate.

$GDPGAP_t = -0.08 - 1.87\ CHGUN_t + e_t$
         (-0.05) (-10.31)   ← t-ratios

$SER = 1.11$ $\overline{|GDPGAP|} = 1.55$ $R^2 = 0.70$ $n = 47$

where GDPGAP is the real GDP growth minus potential GDP growth
     CHGUN is the change in the unemployment rate

The coefficient on CHGUN implies that a 1 percent increase in the unemployment rate will widen the GDPGAP by 1.87 percent; not quite the 2 to 3 percent Okun stipulated, but that was a different economy back then.

The constant term is not statistically different from zero in this regression and theoretically it should be equal to zero: if the change in the unemployment rate from one year to the next is zero, then the change in the GDPGAP should be zero as well. Therefore, we might test Okun's Law with a regression through the origin.

$$GDPGAP_t = -1.87\ CHGUN_t + e_t$$
$$(-10.39) \qquad \leftarrow \text{t-ratio}$$

$$SER = 1.10 \quad \overline{|GDPGAP|} = 1.55 \quad n = 47$$

The coefficient on CHGUN hardly changes when the constant term is omitted--just what we would expect when an extraneous variable is excluded. R^2 and adjusted R^2 are not reported since they are invalid in this case, as are Akaike and Schwarz. The SER indicates an inadequate fit.

6.2 Units of Measurement and Estimates

Regression estimates will be affected by changes in the units of measurement, but the substance of the regression results will be unaffected. Consider the case where nominal personal consumption expenditures (PCON) are regressed on nominal disposable personal income (DPI). Here are the raw data and the regression results:

Year	PCON	DPI
1959	317.7	350.1
1960	331.8	365.2
1961	342.2	381.6
.	.	.
.	.	.
.	.	.
2011	10,729.00	11,549.30

$$PCON_t = -68.55 + 0.93\ DPI_t + e_t$$
$$(-4.42)\ (322.25) \quad \leftarrow \text{t-ratios}$$

$$SER = 73.64 \quad \overline{PCON} = 3715.54$$

$$r^2 = 0.99 \qquad n = 53$$

The interpretation here is that a 1 unit increase in DPI causes a .93 unit increase in PCON. In other words, the marginal propensity to consume is estimated to be 0.93. Our data are measured in billions of dollars. Wouldn't it be strange if our results changed simply because we measured PCON and DPI in millions of dollars? Here are the regression results when the data are in millions of dollars:

Year	PCON	DPI
1959	317,700	350,100
1960	331,800	365,200
1961	342,200	381,600
.	.	.
.	.	.
.	.	.
2011	10,729,000	11,549,300

$$PCON_t = -68,550 + 0.93\ DPI_t + e_t$$
$$(-4.42)\ (322.25) \quad \leftarrow \text{t-ratios}$$

$$SER = 73,640 \qquad \overline{PCON} = 3,715,540$$

$$r^2 = 0.99 \qquad n = 53$$

The new results still peg the marginal propensity to consume at 0.93. However, the constant term, the SER, and the mean of the dependent variable have been multiplied by 1,000. But nothing has changed in essence. The constant term is interpreted to mean that if DPI = 0, then PCON = -68,550 million dollars; whereas before the constant term was interpreted to mean when DPI = 0, then PCON = -68.55 billion dollars.

We can get the coefficient on DPI to change decimal places as well. Watch what happens if we measure PCON in millions and DPI in billions of dollars.

Year	PCON	DPI
1959	317,700	350.1
1960	331,800	365.2
1961	342,200	381.6
.	.	.
.	.	.
.	.	.
2011	10,729,000	11,549.30

$$PCON_t = -68,550.00 + 930\ DPI_t + e_t$$
$$\quad\quad\quad (-4.42)\quad\ (322.25)\quad \leftarrow \text{t-ratios}$$

$$SER = 73,640 \qquad \overline{PCON} = 3,715,540$$

$$r^2 = 0.99 \qquad n = 53$$

Even now our estimate of the marginal propensity to consume is unaffected because the coefficient on DPI is interpreted to mean if DPI increases by 1 unit (or 1 billion dollars), then PCON is expected to increase 930 units (or 930 million dollars.) In other words, PCON is expected to increase 93 cents when DPI increases by 1 dollar.

There is an important lesson to take away from this exercise: The magnitude of a coefficient says nothing about its significance. We can make coefficients larger or smaller simply by changing the units by which we measure the variables attached to them. However, the t-ratio is invariant with respect to changes in the units of measurement.

6.3 The Double-Log Model

Ordinary-least squares fits straight lines between observations on a scattergram. However, it is possible to fit curvilinear lines by rescaling the data. Alternate functional forms rely on this rescaling.

Consider the demand for milk in the United States from 1959 to 2001.

The Demand for Milk

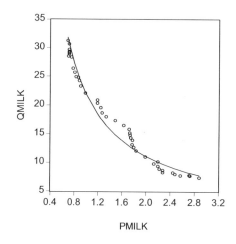

QMILK – milk consumption (gallons per person per year)

PMILK – price of milk (dollars per gallon)

Astute readers may notice that unlike most demand curves, this one has the price on the horizontal axis. Placing the independent variable, PMILK, on the X-axis is mathematically correct. Therefore, the demand curves drawn in economics textbooks and classrooms are incorrect in the mathematical sense. It has been suggested that the tradition of placing the price on the Y-axis is in homage to Alfred Marshall, who thusly drew demand curves in his 1890 text *Principles of Economics*.

It appears as if a bowed line, convex to the origin, would fit the data better than a straight line. This can be accomplished by rescaling -- in this case taking the natural logarithms of the data.

The Demand for Milk (Natural Logarithms)

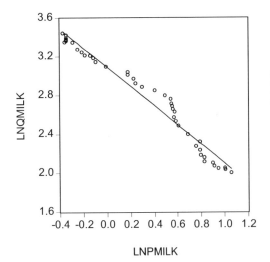

LNQMILK – the natural log of QMILK
LNPMILK – the natural log of PMILK

We can fit a straight line to the logged observations. When the axes of this diagram are put back into the original (non-logged) scale the straight line bends to give the curved line in the original diagram.

It is quite simple to apply this technique. We have data on PMILK and QMILK. Take the natural logarithms of those data (LNPMILK, LNQMILK).

obs	PMILK	QMILK	LNPMILK	LNQMILK
1959	0.690000	31.29000	-0.371064	3.443299
1960	0.710000	30.69000	-0.342490	3.423937
1961	0.710000	29.72000	-0.342490	3.391820
1962	0.710000	29.35000	-0.342490	3.379293
1963	0.710000	29.20000	-0.342490	3.374169
.	.	.	.	.
.	.	.	.	.
.	.	.	.	.
2001	2.880000	7.410000	1.057790	2.002830

Now regress LNQMILK on LNPMILK:

$$LNQMILK_t = 3.09 - 0.99\ LNPMILK_t + e_t$$

This is akin to fitting the straight line to the scattergram of LNQMILK and LNPMILK. Let's interpret these results carefully:

$\hat{\beta}_0 = 3.09 \rightarrow$ If PMILK = 1, then LNQMILK = 3.09 (QMILK = 21.98)

$\hat{\beta}_1 = -0.99 \rightarrow$ If PMILK $\uparrow$ 1%, then QMILK $\downarrow$ 0.99%

The interpretation of $\hat{\beta}_0$ begins "If PMILK = 1" because if PMILK = 1, then LNPMILK = 0. If we plug LNPMILK = 0 into the regression, we are left with LNQMILK = 3.09. Taking the anti-log of 3.09 gives QMILK = 21.98.

Because we have taken the natural logarithms of both variables, a 1-unit increase in LNPMILK can be interpreted as a 1 percent increase in PMILK. Thus, a 1 percent increase in PMILK causes 0.99 percent reduction in QMILK.

These results suggest the elasticity of the demand for milk is nearly unitary. If the price goes up 1 percent, demand falls by 0.99 percent. The interpretation of $\hat{\beta}_1$ as an elasticity is why this particular alternate functional form is sometimes called the "constant elasticity model." It also goes by the names "log-log model" or "double-log model."

The results and interpretations of the double-log model are compared with the linear model in the boxes below:

Linear:	Double-Log:
$QMILK_t = 35.17 - 11.27\ PMILK_t + e_t$ $R^2 = .94$	$LNQMILK_t = 3.09 - 0.99\ LNPMILK_t + e_t$ $R^2 = .96$
If PMILK = 0, then QMILK = 35.17	If PMILK = 1, then LNQMILK = 3.09 (QMILK = 21.98)
If PMILK $\uparrow$ 1 unit, then QMILK $\downarrow$ 11.27 units	If PMILK $\uparrow$ 1%, then QMILK $\downarrow$ 0.99%

The R^2's for both models indicate good fits. However, it is incorrect to say that the double-log model has a better fit than the linear model. The R^2's are not comparable since the dependent variables are not the same for both models. The adjusted R^2's are not comparable as well.

6.4 The Log-Lin Model

Another alternate functional form is the semi-log, or log-lin, model. In this model the natural log of the dependent variable is taken, but not that of the independent variable. This model gives percentage changes in the dependent variable for absolute changes in the independent variable. The box below shows the results of applying the log-lin model to the milk data.

Log-Lin:
$LNQMILK_t = 3.84 - 0.70\ PMILK_t + e_t$ $R^2 = .98$
If PMILK = 0, then LNQMILK = 3.84 (QMILK = 46.53)
If PMILK $\uparrow$ 1 unit, then QMILK $\downarrow$ 70%

The log-lin model has an interesting interpretation in regressions with a trend variable. A trend variable increases one unit each time period. The table below shows real GDP in the Unites States and a trend variable.

obs	RGDP	TREND
1948	1,8520	1
1949	1,843.1	2
1950	2,004.2	3
1951	2,159.3	4
.	.	.
.	.	.
.	.	.
2012	13,588.8	65

Now run the log-lin model: $LNRGDP_t = 7.58 + 0.032\ TREND_t + e_t$

Interpret the coefficient on TREND: If TREND ↑ 1 unit, then RGDP ↑ 3.2%. Each year we expect real GDP to increase 3 percent. In other words, the average annual growth rate of real GDP from 1948 through 2012 was 3.2 percent. The log-lin model gives average annual growth rates when the x-variable is a trend.

6.5 The Lin-Log Model

The lin-log model is appropriate when the dependent variable changes an absolute amount for a given percentage change in the independent variable. Here it is applied to the milk data.

Lin-Log:
$QMILK_t = 23.18 - 16.52\ LNPMILK_t + e_t$ $R^2 = .99$

If PMILK = 1, then QMILK = 23.18

If PMILK ↑ 1%, then QMILK ↓ 0.1652 units

Again, a curvilinear line will be fit to the scattergram. The fit of this regression can be compared to that of the linear regression since both have QMILK as the dependent variable. We can compare R^2's since both regressions have the same number of explanatory variables. The lin-log model fits better with an R^2 of .99 compared to .94 in the linear model.

6.6 The Reciprocal Model

The reciprocal model uses the reciprocal of the independent variable. Often this model is used to estimate asymptotic relationships because of the unique interpretation of the intercept term.

Reciprocal:
$$QMILK_t = 1.34 + 20.37 \, (1/PMILK)_t + e_t \qquad R^2 = .97$$

As $PMILK \to \infty$, $QMILK \to 1.34$

If $PMILK \uparrow$, then $QMILK \downarrow$

As PMILK approaches infinity, the reciprocal term approaches zero. Therefore, QMILK approaches 1.34.

There is no intuitive interpretation of the magnitude of the coefficient attached to the reciprocal (20.37). Since it is positive an increase in PMILK will cause a decrease in QMILK. But the magnitude of that effect depends on the initial level of PMILK.

6.7 The Polynomial Model

The polynomial form is used to draw parabolas between the observations on a scattergram. A parabolic relationship does not make sense for a demand curve because it implies that there could be two prices associated with a given quantity demanded. However, if the demand curve sloped downward at an increasing or decreasing rate, the polynomial form would capture that.

Polynomial:
$$QMILK_t = 44.07 - 24.54 \, PMILK_t + 4.07 \, PMILK^2_t + e_t$$

If $PMILK = 0$, then $QMILK = 44.07$

Since $\hat{\beta}_1 < 0$ and $\hat{\beta}_2 > 0$, then as $PMILK \uparrow$, $QMILK \downarrow$ up to a point and then $QMILK \uparrow$
(the relationship is U-shaped)

The magnitude of the coefficients on PMILK and $PMILK^2$ have no straightforward interpretation. However, when the coefficient on PMILK is negative and the coefficient on $PMILK^2$ is positive, it suggests a U-shaped relationship. If the coefficient on PMILK is positive and the coefficient on $PMILK^2$ is negative, then the parabola is an inverted U.

Another way to interpret the pattern of $\hat{\beta}_1$ and $\hat{\beta}_2$ in a polynomial regression is as follows:

$$Y_t = \hat{\beta}_0 + \hat{\beta}_1 X_t + \hat{\beta}_2 X_t^2 + e_t$$

If $\hat{\beta}_1 > 0$ and $\hat{\beta}_2 > 0$, then as X increases, Y increases at an increasing rate.

If $\hat{\beta}_1 < 0$ and $\hat{\beta}_2 < 0$, then as X increases, Y decreases at an increasing rate.

If $\hat{\beta}_1 > 0$ and $\hat{\beta}_2 < 0$, then as X increases, Y increases at a decreasing rate.

If $\hat{\beta}_1 < 0$ and $\hat{\beta}_2 > 0$, then as X increases, Y decreases at a decreasing rate.

In the milk example we have $\hat{\beta}_1 < 0$ and $\hat{\beta}_2 > 0$, so we expect that as PMILK increases, QMILK will decrease at a decreasing rate:

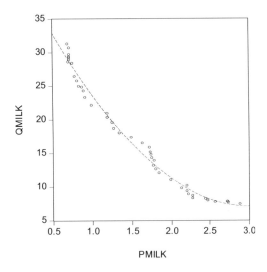

The price of milk does not go above 3.0 in our sample. If it did, the polynomial regression line would eventually turn upward.

6.8 Mixing and Matching Alternate Forms

It is perfectly legitimate to mix and match alternate functional forms as in the multiple regression below. Each coefficient is interpreted individually, holding the others constant.

Mix and Match:
$$QMILK_t = 22.59 - 15.82 \ LNPMILK_t + 3.58 \ (1/PCOOKIE)_t + e_t$$

(where PCOOKIE is the price of cookies)

If PMILK = 1 and as PCOOKIE $\to \infty$, QMILK $\to$ 22.59

If PMILK $\uparrow$ 1%, then QMILK $\downarrow$ .1582 units, holding PCOOKIE constant

If PCOOKIE $\uparrow$, then QMILK $\downarrow$, holding PMILK constant

Hopefully there are good theoretical reasons for choosing such a peculiar alternate functional form.

6.9 Finding the Correct Functional Form

It is critical that regressions are run in the appropriate functional form. If the relationship between X and Y is curvilinear and the regression is run in the linear form, the results will be biased. Therefore, it is just as important to specify the correct functional form as it is to include all the important independent variables.

Theory is the best guide for determining the appropriate functional form. If a particular relationship is likely to be asymptotic, then the reciprocal form should be used. It is often instructive to see which functional form other researchers used on a given topic.

Unfortunately, theory and previous work are not always specific about the functional form of a statistical relationship. The second best solution is to let the data suggest the appropriate functional form. For instance, one functional form may fit much better than the others. Not all of the various functional forms can be directly compared for fit. Still, one can often discern whether a linear specification is appropriate or not.

Just looking at a scattergram of the relationship can be useful. We saw that the milk data suggested an alternate functional form.

Finally, Ramsey's Reset test is also a test for appropriate functional form. This is important to understand. Even if a regression includes all the relevant explanatory variables, it may not pass Ramsey's Reset test if it is in the wrong functional form.

Terms

Alternate functional form – A regression where at least one of the variables is transformed into different units such as natural logarithms or raised to some exponential power.

Regression through the origin – A regression where the constant term is suppressed.

Trend variable – An explanatory variable that takes on integer values that increase by one each period.

Chapter 6   Problems

1. Derive the formula for $\hat{\beta}_1$ in $Y_i = \hat{\beta}_1 X_i + e_i$ that minimizes Σe_i^2.

2. Use the data in OKUNUK.XLS and statistical software to run the following regression:

$$GDPGAP_t = \hat{\beta}_0 + \hat{\beta}_1 \; CHGUN_t + e_t$$

where GDPGAP = real GDP growth minus potential GDP growth in the UK
CHGUN = change in the unemployment rate in the UK

   A) According to a test of significance, does $\hat{\beta}_0$ belong in the regression?

   B) According to economic reasoning, does $\hat{\beta}_0$ belong in the regression?

   C) Re-run the regression excluding $\hat{\beta}_0$. Does $\hat{\beta}_1$ change much from the prior regression?

   D) Which regression of the two fits best? On what do you base your response?

3. In the regression below, what would be the new values of $\hat{\beta}_0$, $\hat{\beta}_1$, their t-ratios, SER, r^2, and the mean of WEIGHT if WEIGHT was measured in ounces instead of pounds?

$$WEIGHT_i = 51.12 + 1.85 \; HEIGHT_i + e_i$$
$$\quad\quad (4.72) \quad (9.85) \quad \leftarrow \text{t-ratios}$$

$$SER = 20.38 \quad \overline{WEIGHT} = 156.78$$

$$r^2 = 0.49 \quad n = 4800$$

4. In the regression below, what would be the new values of $\hat{\beta}_0$, $\hat{\beta}_1$, their t-ratios, SER, r^2, and the mean of HEIGHT if AGE was measured in months instead of years and height was measured in inches instead of feet?

$$HEIGHT_i = 1.68 + 0.35 \; AGE_i + e_i$$
$$\quad\quad (7.723) \quad (2.11) \quad \leftarrow \text{t-ratios}$$

$$SER = 12.45 \quad \overline{HEIGHT} = 5.54$$

$$r^2 = 0.38 \quad n = 120$$

5. Use the data in EGG.XLS and statistical software to do the following problems:

Run the following regression: $QEGG_t = \hat{\beta}_0 + \hat{\beta}_1 PEGG_t + e_t$

where QEGG is per capita egg consumption each year 1973–1997
PEGG is the average price of a dozen eggs in the USA

A) i) Interpret the value you obtained for $\hat{\beta}_0$.

ii) Interpret the value you obtained for $\hat{\beta}_1$.

iii) If the price of eggs goes up $1 per dozen, what is the expected change in egg consumption according to this regression?

B) Run the regression in the double-log form.

i) Interpret the value you obtained for $\hat{\beta}_0$.

ii) Interpret the value you obtained for $\hat{\beta}_1$.

iii) If the price of eggs goes up 1 percent, what is the expected percentage change in egg consumption according to this regression?

C) Run the regression in the semi-log form (where the natural log of PEGG is taken).

i) Interpret the value you obtained for $\hat{\beta}_0$.

ii) Interpret the value you obtained for $\hat{\beta}_1$.

iii) If the price of eggs goes up 1 percent, what is the expected change in egg consumption according to this regression?

D) Run the regression in the semi-log form (where the natural log of QEGG is taken).

i) Interpret the value you obtained for $\hat{\beta}_0$.

ii) Interpret the value you obtained for $\hat{\beta}_1$.

iii) If the price of eggs goes up $1 per dozen, what is the expected percentage change in egg consumption according to this regression?

E) Run the regression in the reciprocal form.

i) Interpret the value you obtained for $\hat{\beta}_0$.

ii) Interpret the value you obtained for $\hat{\beta}_1$.

iii) If the price of eggs goes up $1 per dozen, will egg consumption increase or decrease according to this regression?

F) Run the regression in the polynomial form.

i) Interpret the value you obtained for $\hat{\beta}_0$.

ii) Interpret the values you obtained for $\hat{\beta}_1$ and $\hat{\beta}_2$.

G) i) Do you think the data in this study require an alternate functional form or is the linear form satisfactory? Explain.

ii) Which of the six regressions fits the data best?

6. Use the data in MATISSE.XLS and statistical software to do the following problems:

Does the size of a master's painting have an effect on its price? To shed light on this issue run the following regression:

$$PRICE_i = \hat{\beta}_0 + \hat{\beta}_1 \; SIZE_i + e_i$$

where PRICE is the price of paintings by Matisse sold at auction in dollars
SIZE is the size of the paintings in square inches

A) i) Interpret the value you obtained for $\hat{\beta}_0$.

ii) Interpret the value you obtained for $\hat{\beta}_1$.

iii) If one Matisse canvas is 60 square inches larger than another, will it cost more? Exactly how much more (or less)?

iv) According to this regression, what would a 1,500-square-inch Matisse sell for at auction?

B) Run the regression in the double-log form.

i) Interpret the value you obtained for $\hat{\beta}_0$.

ii) Interpret the value you obtained for $\hat{\beta}_1$.

iii) If one Matisse canvas is 5% larger than another, will it cost more? Exactly how much more (or less) in percentage terms?

iv) According to this regression, what would a 1,500-square-inch Matisse sell for at auction?

C) Run the regression in the semi-log form (where the natural log of price is taken).

i) Interpret the value you obtained for $\hat{\beta}_0$.

ii) Interpret the value you obtained for $\hat{\beta}_1$.

iii) If one Matisse canvas is 60 square inches larger than another, will it cost more? Exactly how much more (or less) in percentage terms?

iv) According to this regression, what would a 1,500-square-inch Matisse sell for at auction?

D) Run the regression in the semi-log form (where the natural log of size is taken).

i) Interpret the value you obtained for $\hat{\beta}_0$.

ii) Interpret the value you obtained for $\hat{\beta}_1$.

iii) If one Matisse canvas is 5% larger than another, will it cost more? Exactly how much more (or less)?

iv) According to this regression, what would a 1,500-square-inch Matisse sell for at auction?

E) Run the regression in the reciprocal form.

   i) Interpret the value you obtained for $\hat{\beta}_0$.

   ii) Interpret the value you obtained for $\hat{\beta}_1$.

   iii) If one Matisse canvas is 60 square inches larger than another, will it cost more? Exactly how much more (or less)?

   iv) According to this regression, what would a 1,500-square-inch Matisse sell for at auction?

F) Run the regression in the polynomial form.

   i) Interpret the value you obtained for $\hat{\beta}_0$.

   ii) Interpret the values you obtained for $\hat{\beta}_1$ and $\hat{\beta}_2$.

   iii) If one Matisse canvas is 60 square inches larger than another, will it cost more? Exactly how much more (or less)?

   iv) According to this regression, what would a 1,500-square-inch Matisse sell for at auction?

G) i) Do you think the data in this study require an alternate functional form or is the linear form satisfactory? Explain.

   ii) Which of the six regressions fits the data best?

7. Use the data in SDATA.XLS and statistical software to do the following problem:

Which functional form do you think is appropriate for the regression below:

$$GPA_i = \hat{\beta}_0 + \hat{\beta}_1 ST_i + e_i$$

Explain your response.

8. Use the data in EKC.XLS and statistical software to test the environmental Kuznets's theory. This theory posits an inverted–U shaped relationship between pollution and economic development (Dasgupta et al. 2002).

A) Run the following polynomial regression and discuss its implications for the Kuznets's curve:

$$CO2CAP_i = \hat{\beta}_0 + \hat{\beta}_1 GDPCAP_i + \hat{\beta}_2 GDPCAP_i^2 + e_i$$

where CO2CAP is per capita carbon dioxide emissions in 48 nations
     GDPCAP is per capita GDP in these nations

B) Run the following regression and discuss its implications for the Kuznets's curve:

$$SO2CAP_i = \hat{\beta}_0 + \hat{\beta}_1 \, GDPCAP_i + \hat{\beta}_2 \, GDPCAP_i^2 + e_i$$

where SO2CAP is per capita sulfur dioxide emissions in 48 nations

C) Run the following regression and discuss its implications for the Kuznets's curve:

$$PART = \hat{\beta}_0 + \hat{\beta}_1 \, GDPCAP_i + \hat{\beta}_2 \, GDPCAP_i^2 + e_i$$

where PART is suspended particulates in the largest city of the nation.

9. Interpret every structural parameter in each of the following regressions considering:

      WAGES = pay per hour of work
      LNWAGES = natural log of WAGES
      EXP = years of experience
      EXPSQ = EXP squared

A) $LNWAGES_i = 2.1 + 1.3 \, EXP_i + e_i$

B) $WAGES_i = 2.1 + 1.3 \, EXP_i - 2.3 \, EXPSQ_i + e_i$

C) $WAGES_i = 2.5 - 0.1 \, (1/EXP)_i + e_i$

10. In the spaces below draw the following regression results:

A) $LNWAGES = 2.1 + 1.3 \, EXP$ B) $WAGES = 2.1 + 1.3 \, EXP - 2.3 \, EXPSQ$

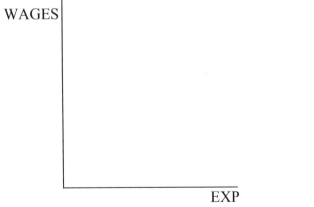

C) WAGES = 2.5 - 0.1 (1/EXP)

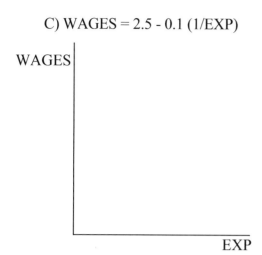

Chapter 7

Dichotomous Variables

7.1 Dichotomous Variables

Dichotomous variables take on values of zero or one only. Dichotomous variables are more commonly called "dummy" variables and sometimes are referred to as "limited" variables.

In the regression below, MALE is a dummy variable.

$$DRINKS_i = 18.31 - 3.75 \; GPA_i + 4.74 \; MALE_i + e_i$$
$$\quad\quad (8.56) \; (-6.23) \quad\quad (7.55) \quad \leftarrow \text{t-ratios}$$

$$SER = 8.62 \quad \overline{DRINKS} = 7.59 \quad R^2 = 0.13 \quad n = 695$$

where   DRINKS – an undergraduate's number of alcoholic drinks per week
GPA – the student's GPA
MALE – 1 if male; 0 otherwise

Here are the first few observations in the data set:

Obs	DRINKS	GPA	MALE
1	3	3.7	0
2	30	3.3	0
3	4	3	1
4	0	3	0
5	0	4	1
6	15	3	1

The formulas for estimating the structural parameters and the residual statistics are unaffected by the presence of a dummy variable. However, the interpretations are somewhat different.

$\hat{\beta}_0 = 18.31 \rightarrow$ A female with 0 GPA is expected to have 18.31 alcoholic drinks per week.

$\hat{\beta}_1 = -3.75 \rightarrow$ If GPA increases 1 unit, DRINKS (males and females) decreases 3.75 units.

$\hat{\beta}_2 = 4.74 \rightarrow$ A male has 4.74 more drinks than a female with the same GPA.

Graphing the interpretations indicates that the dummy variable allows for different intercepts for males and females. However, the slopes of the two regression lines are parallel.

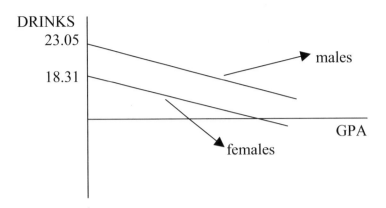

If the dummy variable was defined in the opposite manner (i.e. MALE = 1 if female; 0 otherwise), then our regression results will be slightly altered. However, after interpretation, our diagram would remain unchanged. The new regression results would be:

$$DRINKS_i = 23.05 - 3.75\ GPA_i - 4.74\ MALE_i + e_i$$

$\hat{\beta}_0 = 23.05 \rightarrow$ A male with 0 GPA is expected to have 25.05 alcoholic drinks per week.

$\hat{\beta}_1 = -3.75 \rightarrow$ If GPA increases 1 unit, DRINKS (males and females) decreases 3.75 units.

$\hat{\beta}_2 = 4.74 \rightarrow$ A female has 4.74 fewer drinks than a male with the same GPA.

Graphing the interpretations gives exactly the same diagram as previously.

7.2 Dummies for Seasonal Analysis

Dummy variables can be used to make more than two categories. In the example below, retail sales are divided into the four quarters of the year.

$$RSALES_t = 517462.20 + 63804.40\ D2_t + 66323.00\ D3_t + 115777.80\ D4_t + e_t$$

where RSALES is quarterly retail sales in the USA (millions of $)
D2 is 1 in the second quarter; 0 otherwise
D3 is 1 in the third quarter; 0 otherwise
D4 is 1 in the fourth quarter; 0 otherwise

$\hat{\beta}_0 \rightarrow$ In the 1st qrt RSALES average 51746.20.

$\hat{\beta}_1 \rightarrow$ In the 2nd quarter RSALES are expected to be 63804.40 units higher than the 1st qtr.

$\hat{\beta}_2 \rightarrow$ In the 3rd quarter RSALES are expected to be 66323.00 units higher than the 1st qtr.

$\hat{\beta}_3 \rightarrow$ In the 4th quarter RSALES are expected to be 115777.80 units higher than the 1st qtr.

The coefficients on the dummy variables tell us how much we can expect retail sales to differ from the first quarter due to seasonal factors. We can discern that retail sales are seasonally lowest in the first quarter, higher in the second quarter, still higher in the third, and highest in the fourth quarter.

Also notice that we need only three dummies to divide retail sales into four categories. That is because when D2 = D3 = D4 = 0, then by default we must be in the first quarter.

Finally, we can obtain seasonally adjusted retail sales figures by adding the residuals from the regression above to the mean of retail sales. The graph below shows RSALES and the seasonally adjusted series.

Retail Sales and Seasonally Adjusted Retail Sales

It should be pointed out that almost all economic data in the United States are adjusted with a procedure that is much more sophisticated than the one outlined here. The top seasonal adjustment procedures take into account such things as where particular holidays fall and leap years.

7.3 Interactive Terms

Interactive terms interact with dummy variables to allow for different slopes for different categories. Going back to our earnings example, we have added an interactive term: MALE*GPA.

$$DRINKS_i = 11.66 - 1.86 \, GPA_i + 17.67 \, MALE_i - 3.75 \, MALE*GPA_i + e_i$$

MALE = 1 if male; 0 otherwise
MALE*GPA = MALE x GPA

$\hat{\beta}_0 = 11.66 \rightarrow$ A female with 0 GPA is expected to have 11.66 alcoholic drinks per week.

$\hat{\beta}_1 = -1.86 \rightarrow$ If GPA increases 1 unit, DRINKS for females decreases 1.86 units.

$\hat{\beta}_2 = 17.67 \rightarrow$ A male with zero GPA drinks 17.67 units more than a female with zero GPA.

$\hat{\beta}_3 = -3.75 \rightarrow$ If GPA increases 1 unit then DRINKS for a male will decrease 3.75 units over and above the 1.86 units for a female.

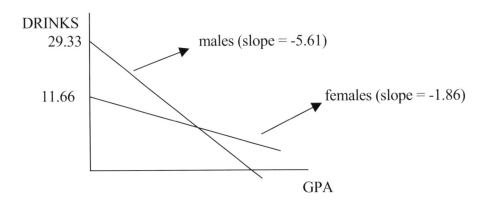

How would the regression results change if the dummy was flip-flopped? Again, the regression results would be altered, but so would the interpretations. The diagram above would be unchanged.

$$DRINKS_i = 29.33 - 5.61\ GPA_i - 17.67\ MALE_i + 3.75\ MALE*GPA_i + e_i$$

MALE = 1 if female; 0 otherwise
MALE*GPA = MALE x GPA

$\hat{\beta}_0 = 29.33 \rightarrow$ A male with zero GPA is expected to have 29.33 alcoholic drinks per week.

$\hat{\beta}_1 = -5.61 \rightarrow$ If GPA increases 1 unit, DRINKS for males decreases 5.61 units.

$\hat{\beta}_2 = -17.67 \rightarrow$ A female with zero GPA drinks 17.67 units less than a male with zero GPA.

$\hat{\beta}_3 = 3.75 \rightarrow$ If GPA increases 1 unit then DRINKS for a female will decrease 3.75 units less than the -5.61 units for a male.

7.4 Linear Probability Models

Up to this point, we have considered using dummy variables only as independent variables. Dichotomous variables can be used as dependent variables as well. If ordinary least-squares is used to estimate a regression with a dummy dependent variable then it is known as a linear probability model.

Let's consider a classic econometric study that uses a dichotomous dependent variable. Spector and Mazzeo (1980) investigated the factors affecting whether or not a student got a final letter grade of A in intermediate macroeconomics. Here are the results when ordinary least-squares is applied to their data:

$$AMACRO_i = -1.4980 + .4639\ GPA_i + .0111\ TUCE_i + .3786\ PSI_i + e_i$$
$$\qquad\qquad\quad (2.86)\qquad\quad (0.54)\qquad\quad (2.72)\quad \leftarrow \text{t-ratios}$$

AMACRO = 1 if final grade in Macro Analysis is an A ; 0 otherwise
GPA = GPA of student at the beginning of Macro Analysis
TUCE = score on the TUCE exam prior to Macro Analysis (the TUCE is a 33 multiple-choice exam that Tests Understanding of College Economics)
PSI = 1 if student received personalized instruction (tutoring); 0 otherwise

AMACRO is the dichotomous dependent variable. The regression also includes a dummy independent variable: PSI.

Interpretations:

If GPA, TUCE, and PSI = 0, then the probability of obtaining an A in Macro Analysis = -149.80%.

If GPA increases 1 unit then the probability of obtaining an A in Macro Analysis increases 46.39%, holding TUCE constant, regardless of PSI.

If TUCE increases 1 unit then the probability of obtaining an A in Macro Analysis Increases 1.11%, holding GPA constant, regardless of PSI.

A student who receives personalized instruction increases his or her odds of obtaining an A in Macro Analysis by 37.86%, holding GPA and TUCE constant.

These results are informative, but all linear probability models suffer from some drawbacks.

Problems with the linear probability model:

- The error terms are binomially, not normally, distributed, thereby invalidating hypothesis testing in small samples.
- R-squared is not a good measure of fit.
- Predicted probabilities can be out of bounds (i.e., >1 or < 0).

The fact that predicted probabilities can be out of bounds is especially disconcerting. Let's plug some numbers into our linear probability model. First, consider a student with a 3.5 GPA, a score of 28 on the TUCE exam, and who received personalized instruction:

$$A\hat{M}ACRO_i = -1.4980 + .4639\ GPA_i + .0111\ TUCE_i + .3786\ PSI_i$$

$$.815 \quad = -1.4980 + .4639\ (3.5)\ + .0111\ (28)\ + .3786\ (1)$$

This student has an 81.5 percent chance of receiving an A in intermediate macroeconomics. However, a student with a GPA of 3.9, a 33 on the TUCE exam and who received personalized instruction has a 106 percent chance of obtaining an A:

$$A\hat{M}ACRO_i = -1.4980 + .4639\ GPA_i + .0111\ TUCE_i + .3786\ PSI_i$$

$$1.06 \quad = -1.4980 + .4639\ (3.9)\ + .0111\ (33)\ + .3786\ (1)$$

This is what is meant by a prediction that is out-of-bounds. Only the gods know for certain whether this student will receive an A in the course. And even they are only 100 percent sure.

Another out-of-bounds prediction occurs with this next student as well:

$$A\hat{M}ACRO_i = -1.4980 + .4639\ GPA_i + .0111\ TUCE_i + .3786\ PSI_i$$

$$-.26 \quad = -1.4980 + .4639\ (2.2)\ + .0111\ (20)\ + .3786\ (0)$$

According to the results above, a student with a GPA of 2.2, a TUCE score of 20, and who did not receive personalized instruction will definitely not get an A. Indeed, it makes no sense to have a negative probability. The diagram below depicts what is happening.

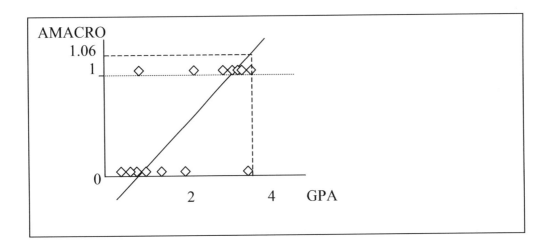

AMACRO can only be 1 or 0. Therefore, the observations on the scattergram will lie on these values. Here, AMACRO is plotted against GPA. High GPAs will be associated with AMACRO = 1, while low GPA students are less likely to obtain an A. A linear probability model fits a straight line through the observations using the ordinary least-squares formulas. A student with a 3.9 GPA has a 106 percent chance of obtaining an A when the ordinary least-squares line is used to make the prediction.

7.5 Logistic Models

Logistic models are based on the logistic equation. These models fit an S-shaped curve to scattergrams with dichotomous dependent variables. Logistic models give predictions that are less than one and greater than zero in all instances and thus avoid one of the drawbacks of linear probability models.

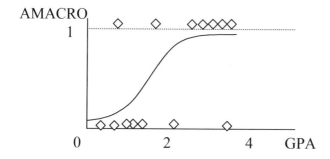

The logistic specification of Spector and Mazzeo's model for A's in macroanalysis is:

$$AMACRO_i = \frac{1}{1 + e^{-(\hat{\beta}_0 + \hat{\beta}_1 GPA_i + \hat{\beta}_2 TUCE_i + \hat{\beta}_3 PSI_i + e_i)}}$$

With a little algebra, this specification can be re-written as:

$$\ln(\frac{AMACRO_i}{1 - AMACRO_i}) = \hat{\beta}_0 + \hat{\beta}_1 GPA_i + \hat{\beta}_2 TUCE_i + \hat{\beta}_3 PSI_i + e_i$$

There is an estimation problem with the logistic model. If $AMACRO_i = 0$ or 1, then $\ln(\frac{AMACRO_i}{1 - AMACRO_i})$ is undefined. The maximum likelihood procedure overcomes this problem and is typically applied to the original logistic specification to obtain estimates of the structural parameters.

The maximum likelihood procedure is an algorithm that begins with initial values for the estimators and adjusts them based on the residuals (e_i's). The adjusted values of the estimators result in new e_i's and the algorithm decides how to adjust the estimates again given these new e_i's. This iterative process continues until sequential estimates of the estimators do not vary much.

Applying the maximum likelihood procedure to Spector and Mazzeo's data gives:

$$\ln(\frac{AMACRO_i}{1-AMACRO_i}) = \text{-}13.0 + 2.8 \text{ GPAi} + 0.1 \text{ TUCEi} + 2.4 \text{ PSIi} + \text{ei}$$

$$(2.24) \qquad (0.72) \qquad (2.23) \qquad \text{Maddala } R^2 = .3821$$

Interpretations:

The estimators in logistic models do not have intuitive interpretations so we will only interpret two of them as examples.

If GPA, TUCE, and PSI = 0, then the natural log of the odds ratio = -13.0.

If GPA increases 1 unit, then the natural log of the odds ratio increases 2.8 units, holding TUCE constant, regardless of PSI status.

Predicting with logistic models:

The predictions generated by the logistic model are between zero and one. Even the students with out-of-bounds predictions in the linear probability model are within bounds here.

It takes some effort to obtain these predictions. The students' GPA, TUCE, and PSI are plugged into:

$$\ln(\frac{AMACRO_i}{1-AMACRO_i}) = \text{-}13.0 + 2.8 \text{ GPA}_i + 0.1 \text{ TUCE}_i + 2.4 \text{ PSI}_i + \text{e}_i$$

Then we can calculate $\ln(\frac{AMACRO_i}{1-AMACRO_i})$ for each of our three students:

1.909	$= \text{-}13.0 + 2.8 \, (3.5) + 0.1 \, (28) + 2.4 \, (1)$
3.620	$= \text{-}13.0 + 2.8 \, (3.9) + 0.1 \, (33) + 2.4 \, (1)$
-4.904	$= \text{-}13.0 + 2.8 \, (2.2) + 0.1 \, (20) + 2.4 \, (0)$

Finally, these can be converted into probabilities:

$$\ln(\frac{AMACRO_i}{1-AMACRO_i}) = 1.909 \, ; \, \frac{AMACRO_i}{1-AMACRO_i} = 6.746 \, ; \, AMACRO = .87$$

$$\ln(\frac{AMACRO_i}{1-AMACRO_i}) = 3.620 \, ; \, \frac{AMACRO_i}{1-AMACRO_i} = 37.34 \, ; \, AMACRO = .97$$

$$\ln(\frac{AMACRO_i}{1 - AMACRO_i}) = \text{-}4.904 \; ; \; \frac{AMACRO_i}{1 - AMACRO_i} = 0.007 \; ; AMACRO = .007$$

The student with an 81.5 percent chance of obtaining an A according to the linear probability model has an 87 percent chance according to the logistic model. The student with a 106 percent chance of obtaining an A according to the linear probability model has a 97 percent chance here. Finally, the student who had a negative 26 percent chance of obtaining an A has a 0.7 percent chance according to the logistic model.

Terms

Dummy variable (Dichotomous variable) – Independent or dependent variables that take on the values of zero or one only.

Interactive term – A dummy variable combined with another independent variable.

Linear probability model – A regression with a dichotomous dependent variable that is estimated with ordinary least-squares.

Logistic model – An alternate function form that fits an S-shape to regressions with dichotomous dependent variables.

Maximum likelihood procedure – A technique for estimating the structural parameters of a non-linear econometric model, such as a logistic model.

Chapter 7 Problems

1. A) Interpret every structural parameter in the following regression:

$$PROFSAL_i = 17.969 + 1.3707 \; EXP_i + 3.3336 \; DUM_i + e_i$$

where PROFSAL is the professor's salary
EXP is the professor's experience in years
DUM = 1 if the professor is male; 0 otherwise

  B) Draw a diagram reflecting the regression results with PROFSAL on the vertical axis and EXP on the horizontal axis.
  C) A male professor with 10 years' experience is expected to make how much in salary?
  D) A female professor with 10 years' experience is expected to make how much in salary?
  E) What would be the new values of the structural parameters if the dummy was flip-flopped?
  F) Using the flip-flopped results, how much would a male professor with 10 years' experience make in salary?

2. Use the data in SDATA.XLS and statistical software to run the following regression:

$$GPA_i = \hat{\beta}_0 + \hat{\beta}_1\, ST_i + \hat{\beta}_2\, SAT_i + \hat{\beta}_3\, MALE_i + e_i$$

where GPA = grade point average
ST = study time per day
SAT = SAT score
MALE = 1 if the student is male; 0 otherwise

A) Interpret the coefficient on SAT.
B) Interpret the coefficient on the dummy variable.
C) Would a male or a female student with the same SAT scores and study time be expected to have a higher GPA? By exactly how much?
D) What would be the values of the four structural coefficients if the dummy variable had been defined as 1 = female ; 0 otherwise?

3. A) Interpret every structural parameter in the following regression:

$$PROFSAL_i = 16.1718 + 1.2016\, EXP_i + 3.2245\, DUM_i - 1.0001\, DUM*EXP_i + e_i$$

where PROFSAL is the professor's salary
EXP is the professors' experience in years
DUM = 1 if the professor is male; 0 otherwise

B) Draw a diagram reflecting the regression results with PROFSAL on the vertical axis and EXP on the horizontal axis.
C) What would be the new values of the structural parameters if the dummy was flip-flopped?

4. Use the data in SDATA.XLS and statistical software to run the following regression:

$$GPA_i = \hat{\beta}_0 + \hat{\beta}_1\, ST_i + \hat{\beta}_2\, MALE_i + \hat{\beta}_3\, INTER_i + e_i$$

where INTER is MALE x ST

A) Interpret all four structural parameters.
B) Who benefits more from an extra unit of ST, men or women? Exactly how much more?
C) What would be the new values for the structural parameters if the dummy for gender was defined: 1 = female ; 0 otherwise?
D) Graph your regression results labeling all intercepts and slopes.

5. A) Interpret every structural parameter in the following regression:
$$GPA_i = 0.37 + 0.81\, HSGPA_i + 0.00001\, SAT_i - 0.38\, GREEK_i + e_i$$

where GPA is grade point average in college
HSGPS is high school GPA
SAT is SAT score
GREEK = 1 if student is a member of a sorority or fraternity;
0 otherwise

B) Draw a diagram reflecting the regression results with GPA on the vertical axis and SAT on the horizontal axis.

6. A) Interpret every structural parameter in the following regression:

$$PERSAV_t = 41.8081 + 0.0321 \, INC_t - 19.7655 \, DUM_t - 0.0021 \, DUM*INC_t + e_t$$

where PERSAV is personal savings in the USA
INC is disposable personal income in the USA
DUM = 1 if 1982 or later;
0 otherwise

B) Draw a diagram reflecting the regression results with PERSAV on the vertical axis and INC on the horizontal axis.

C) What would be the new values of the structural parameters if the dummy was flip-flopped?

7. Use the data in WAGES.XLS and statistical software run to run a regression where wages are explained by a constant term, education, experience, and a dummy variable for gender.

NAME	VARIABLE
WAGES	wages
LNWAGES	the natural logarithm of wages
ED	education in years
NONWH	1 if nonwhite; 0 otherwise
FEM	1 if female; 0 otherwise
MARRIED	1 if married; 0 otherwise
EXPER	experience in years
EXPSQ	experience squared
UNION	1 if union member; 0 otherwise
PRO	1 if employed in a profession; 0 otherwise

A) Interpret the coefficient on education.
B) Interpret the coefficient on the dummy variable.

8. Use the data in WAGES.XLS and statistical software to run a regression where wages are explained by a constant term, education, a dummy variable for gender, and an interactive term.

A) Interpret all four structural parameters.
B) Draw the regression results labeling the values of all intercepts and slopes.
C) What would be the values of the structural parameters if the gender dummy was defined to be 1 if male; 0 otherwise?

9. Use the data in WAGES.XLS and statistical software to run a regression where the natural logarithm of wages is explained by a constant term, education, experience, and dummy variables for marital status, gender, race, union membership, and professional status.

A) Interpret the coefficient on education.
B) Interpret the coefficient on marital status.
C) Interpret the coefficient on union membership.
D) Does this regression provide evidence of racial and gender discrimination? Explain.

10. Use the data in WAGES.XLS and statistical software to run a regression where MARRIED is explained by a constant term, WAGES, ED, and PRO.

A) Interpret all four structural parameters.
B) What is the probability that a college grad (ED=16) in a profession with WAGES = 9.0 is married?

11. Use the data in EXTRAMARITAL.XLS and statistical software to estimate a linear probability model where EXTRA is explained by a constant term, AGE, HPPYM, RELIG, and YRSMAR.

EXTRA = 1 if person participated in an extramarital affair in the past year; 0 otherwise
AGE = the age of the person
HPPYM = person's perception of their marital happiness (1 = very unhappy; 5 = very happy)
RELIG = person's perception of their religiousness (1 = very unreligious; 5 = very religious)
YRSMAR = years married

A) Interpret all 5 structural parameters.
B) What is the probability that a 52-year-old person married for 27 years had an extramarital affair last year? Assume the person's RELIG = 2 and HAPPYM = 3.

12. Use the data in EXTRAMARITAL.XLS and statistical software to estimate a logistic model where EXTRA is explained by a constant term, AGE, HPPYM, RELIG, and YRSMAR. What is the probability that a 52-year-old person married for 27 years had an extramarital affair last year? Assume the person's RELIG = 2 and HAPPYM = 3.

Test Yourself on Chapters 6 and 7

1. Interpret every structural parameter in each of the following regressions considering:

   WAGES = pay per hour of work
   EXP = years of experience
   EXPSQ = EXP squared
   ED = years of education
   DGEN = 1 if male; 0 otherwise
   INTACT = DGEN X EXP
   LN --- = the natural log of a variable

A) $LNWAGES_i = 2.1 + 1.3\ EXP_i + e_i$ Adjusted $R^2 = .77$

B) $LNWAGES_i = 2.1 + 1.3\ LNEXP_i + 2.3\ LNED_i + e_i$ Adjusted $R^2 = .79$

C) $WAGES = 2.1 + 1.3\ EXP_i + 3.5\ DGEN_i + 4.2\ INTACT_i + e_i$ Adjusted $R^2 = .80$

2. Which regression of the three above fits best? On what do you base your response?

3. What would be the values for the structural parameters for the regression above, 1 C), if DGEN was defined as 0 if male; 1 otherwise?

4. Draw diagrams that reflect the following regressions. Put WAGES on the Y-axis and EXP on the X-axis in each case.

A) $WAGES = 2.5 - .01\ (1/EXP)$
   (Also, show where 2.5 is on the Y-axis.)

B) $WAGES = 2.5 + 1.1\ EXP + 3.5\ DGEN - 3.0\ INTACT$
   (Label all intercepts and slopes with their values.)

C) $WAGES = 2.5 + 1.1\ EXP - 0.22\ EXPSQ$

5. Given:

Dependent Variable: BINGE
Method: Least Squares
Sample(adjusted): 1 695
Included observations: 695 after adjusting endpoints

Variable	Coefficient	Std. Error	t-Statistic	Prob.
C	0.818558	0.125126	6.541884	0.0000
GPA	-0.125652	0.033407	-3.761217	0.0002
MALE	0.135596	0.036207	3.745041	0.0002

R-squared	0.056816	Mean dependent var	0.628777
Adjusted R-squared	0.052721	S.D. dependent var	0.483480
S.E. of regression	0.470563	Akaike info criterion	1.335963

Sum squared resid	153.0075	Schwarz criterion	1.362115
Log likelihood	-460.2471	F-statistic	13.87497
Durbin-Watson stat	2.015544	Prob(F-statistic)	0.000000

where   BINGE = 1 if student is a binge drinker; 0 otherwise
               GPA = grade point average
         MALE = 1 if male; 0 otherwise

A) Interpret the constant term.
B) Interpret the coefficient on GPA.

6. Given the following logistic regression results:

Dependent Variable: BINGE
Method: ML - Binary Logit (Quadratic hill climbing)
Sample(adjusted): 1 695
Included observations: 695 after adjusting endpoints
Convergence achieved after 4 iterations
Covariance matrix computed using second derivatives

Variable	Coefficient	Std. Error	z-Statistic	Prob.
C	2.174010	0.565780	3.842498	0.0001
GPA	-0.552753	0.159758	-3.459934	0.0005
MALE	0.581107	0.163816	3.547312	0.0004

What is the probability that a male with a GPA = 3.2 is a binge drinker? Show your calculations.

7. Label each statement below TRUE or FALSE.

A) In a regression through the origin, $\hat{\beta}_1 = \dfrac{\Sigma X_i Y_i}{\Sigma X_i^2}$.

B) Altering the units that the variables in a regression are measured in may alter the values of the structural parameters, but never their t-ratios.

C) If two models have the exact same dependent variable, then the one with the better fit is the better model.

D) R-squared is not a good measure of fit for a linear probability model.

E) The magnitude of a coefficient by itself says nothing about its significance.

F) A logistic model can yield a predicted value for the dependent variable that is equal to one, but never greater than one.

G) A linear probability model can yield a predicted value for the dependent variable that is equal to one, but never greater than one.

H) R-squared is invalid in regressions including dummy independent variables.

I) Regressions in the wrong functional form are biased.

J) Ramsey's Reset test can help to determine if a regression is in the correct functional form.

Chapter 8

Properties of Ordinary Least-Squares Estimators

The Ordinary Least-Squares Estimators are BLUE

Linear

Unbiased

Best

The Classical Linear Regression Model

Terms

Chapter 8 Problems

8.1 The Ordinary Least-Squares Estimators are BLUE

Although several choices are available when faced with calculating the structural parameters of $Y_i = \hat{\beta}_0 + \hat{\beta}_1 X_i + e_i$, the most popular technique is ordinary least-squares. That is because when we calculate $\hat{\beta}_0$ and $\hat{\beta}_1$ so that Σe_i^2 is minimized, our estimates have some very desirable statistical qualities. These qualities are captured in the acronym BLUE -- best, linear, unbiased estimators.

8.2 Linear

The ordinary least-squares estimators are linear under certain conditions. Linear in this case means that the formulas for $\hat{\beta}_0$ and $\hat{\beta}_1$ are linear-- that is, they do not contain any non-linearities such as exponents, reciprocals, or logarithms. This is certainly true of our formula for $\hat{\beta}_0 = \bar{Y} - \hat{\beta}_1 \bar{X}$. However, the formula for $\hat{\beta}_1 = \dfrac{\Sigma(X_i - \bar{X})Y_i}{\Sigma(X_i - \bar{X})^2}$ has a quotient and an exponent. We can get rid of these non-linearities by writing the formula as $\hat{\beta}_1 = \Sigma w_i Y_i$ where $w_i = \dfrac{(X_i - \bar{X})}{\Sigma(X_i - \bar{X})^2}$. You may rightly claim that this does not get rid of the non-linearities. It only masks them in the term w_i.

However, we may consider the w_i's to be constants if the X_i's, which form the w_i's, are predetermined. This is rarely the case. Consider the following regression:

$$GPA_i = \hat{\beta}_0 + \hat{\beta}_1 \, ST_i + e_i$$

where GPA_i is grade point average of the ith student

ST_i is average daily study time of the ith student

ST is our X-variable. It is predetermined if prior to collecting any data from students, we decided that ST should equal 0.5 hours, 1.0 hour, 1.5 hours, 2.0 hours, 2.5 hours, and 3.0 hours. Then we randomly selected a group of students who studied 0.5 hours and asked them their GPAs. Next we randomly select a group of students that studied 1.0 hour and asked them their GPAs. We continue in this manner through ST = 3.0 hours.

Typically data are not collected this way. Instead, we randomly select a student and ask them their ST and GPA. If a student reports ST = 0.75, we do not exclude that student from our study. In other words, our data on ST is stochastic, not predetermined. In this situation, our formula for $\hat{\beta}_1$ will not be linear.

A non-linear $\hat{\beta}_1$ is not an immediate problem and in no way makes $\hat{\beta}_1$ less desirable. However, some upcoming proofs will be more conveniently accomplished with a linear $\hat{\beta}_1$. In addition, it can be shown that $\hat{\beta}_1$ is linear even if the X_i's are not predetermined if the X_i's are not correlated with the error terms (u_i's) from the regression.

Concisely stated, $\hat{\beta}_0$ and $\hat{\beta}_1$ are linear if the X_i's are predetermined or if the X_i's are not correlated with the error terms from the regression. Linearity is not a highly desirable statistical attribute, but it will make some upcoming proofs easier.

8.3 Unbiased

Unbiased results are desirable in any scientific study. This is true of regression analysis as well. However, the term "unbiased" has a particular meaning in regard to statistical estimators. An estimator is unbiased if its expected value is equal to the true value of the parameter. More succinctly, $\hat{\beta}_1$ is unbiased if $E[\hat{\beta}_1] = \beta_1$.

It is highly unlikely that any particular sample regression will exactly yield the true values of β_1. However, if our estimate of β_1 is unbiased and we run the regression 10,000 times (using fresh data each time) and average together all 10,000 estimates of $\hat{\beta}_1$, the average will equal the true β_1.

How can we know this? We will do the proof in a moment. But the proof that the ordinary least-squares estimators are unbiased has been verified with Monte Carlo studies. A Monte Carlo study draws repeated samples from a known population and then analyzes the characteristics of the sample regressions.

In a sense we can play God by getting 5,000 observations on X and Y and assume that this is the entire population of observations. The structural parameters of a regression line through these 5,000 observations are the true β_0 and β_1. Now we can take a random sample of 40 observations from the 5,000 and run a sample regression. Indeed, we could program a computer to run 10,000 of these sample regressions drawing a fresh sample of 40 observations each time. For an unbiased estimator, the average $\hat{\beta}_0$ and $\hat{\beta}_1$ from the 10,000 regressions with 40 observations each will be equal to the true β_0 and β_1 from the population regression with 5,000 observations.

With this intuition in hand, we can now prove that $\hat{\beta}_1$ is an unbiased estimate of β_1:

Assume $\hat{\beta}_1$ is a linear estimator of β_1.

$$\hat{\beta}_1 = \frac{\Sigma(X_i - \overline{X})Y_i}{\Sigma(X_i - \overline{X})^2} = \Sigma w_i Y_i; \quad \text{where } w_i = \frac{(X_i - \overline{X})}{\Sigma(X_i - \overline{X})^2}$$

$$\hat{\beta}_1 = \Sigma w_i Y_i = \Sigma w_i(\beta_0 + \beta_1 X_i + u_i) = \beta_0 \Sigma w_i + \beta_1 \Sigma w_i X_i + \Sigma w_i u_i$$

$$\hat{\beta}_1 = \beta_1 + \Sigma w_i u_i \text{ since } \Sigma w_i = 0 \text{ and } \Sigma w_i X_i = 1$$

Then $E[\hat{\beta}_1] = E[\beta_1 + \Sigma w_i u_i] = \beta_1$ only if $E[\Sigma w_i u_i] = 0$

It is fairly easy to show that $\Sigma w_i = 0$ and $\Sigma w_i X_i = 1$. These proofs are left to the reader as an exercise. For $\hat{\beta}_1$ to be unbiased we need $E[\Sigma w_i u_i] = 0$. This will hold if $E[u_i | X_i] = 0$. Thus we must assume that the expected value of the error terms is zero for each value of X_i in order to prove that $\hat{\beta}_1$ is an unbiased estimator of β_1.

It is straightforward to show that $\hat{\beta}_0 (= \bar{Y} - \hat{\beta}_1 \bar{X})$ is an unbiased estimator of β_0. Since $\bar{Y}$, $\bar{X}$, and $\hat{\beta}_1$ are unbiased estimators of the true $\bar{Y}$, $\bar{X}$, and β_1, then $\hat{\beta}_0$ will be an unbiased estimator of β_0. This is because $\hat{\beta}_0$ is a linear combination of these three unbiased estimators.

We are now in a position to see that a regression in the incorrect functional form will yield biased estimates of the structural parameters. In such a regression, $E[u_i | X_i] \neq 0$, which is a direct violation of the assumption needed to prove unbiased parameter estimates. To see this, consider the example of the demand for milk from chapter 6:

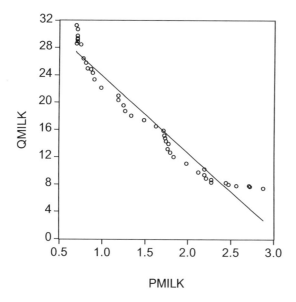

Here we have applied a straight line when an alternate functional form is appropriate. Notice $E[u_i | X_i] \neq 0$. When the value of X (PMILK) is low, u_i is likely to be positive, not 0. Similarly, when the value of X (PMILK) > 2.5, u_i is likely to be positive. When 1.0 < PMILK < 2.5, u_i is likely to be negative. Thus, $E[u_i]$ depends on Xi and is not always equal to zero.

If we are in the correct functional form but exclude an important explanatory variable from a regression, the structural parameters will biased. Again, this is because $E[u_i | X_i] \neq 0$. Consider this example where you have left X_2, an important explanatory variable, out of a regression.

TRUTH: $Y_i = \beta_0 + \beta_1 X_{1i} + \beta_2 X_{2i} + u_i$

YOU: $Y_i = \hat{\beta}_0 + \hat{\beta}_1 X_{1i} + e_i$

In this case, $e_i = \beta_2 X_{2i} + u_i$. Your error term, e_i, is composed of the u_i's plus the variable you omitted, X_2, times its coefficient, $\hat{\beta}_2$. It can be shown that

$$E[\hat{\beta}_1] = E[\beta_1 + \Sigma w_i u_i] = \beta_1 + \beta_2 (\alpha_1), \text{ where } \alpha_1 \text{ is from } X_{2i} = \alpha_0 + \alpha_1 X_{1i} + u_i.$$

Thus, we may conclude that the bias to $\hat{\beta}_0$ and $\hat{\beta}_1$ from omitting X_2 from the regression will be larger the more X_1 and X_2 are correlated. On the other hand, the structural parameters of the underfit regression will not be biased at all if $\alpha_1 = 0$-- that is, if X_1 and X_2 are completely uncorrelated. Nevertheless, all measures of goodness-of-fit are biased regardless of the value of α_1 since the e_i's are biased estimates of the u_i's. And the SE($\hat{\beta}_0$) and SE($\hat{\beta}_1$) are biased regardless of the zero correlation. Therefore, t-ratios are biased and hypothesis testing is invalid.

8.4 Best

We will now show that the ordinary least-squares estimators are best. It sounds as if our estimates are unbeatable, but the term "best" has a very particular meaning in this context. An estimator is said to be best if it varies the least out of all possible estimators in repeated sampling.

Consider once again our Monte Carlo experiment in which we have 5,000 observations on Y and X that are assumed to be the entire population of observations. If we run 10,000 regressions of Y on X with randomly drawn samples of 40 from this population, then we will have 10,000 separate estimates of β_0 and β_1. If the 10,000 estimates of β_1 average to the true β_1, then the ordinary least-squares estimator is unbiased. If the 10,000 estimates of β_1 have a smaller standard error than any other linear and unbiased estimator, then the ordinary least-squares estimator is best.

More concisely, the best estimator has minimum variance in its class. The best estimator is often referred to as an efficient estimator: it varies the least in repeated sampling. Monte Carlo experiments can be used to show one estimator is more efficient than another. But we can prove that the ordinary least-squares estimators are best. This is the proof of the famous Gauss-Markov theorem: The ordinary least-squares estimators are best in the class of all linear, unbiased estimators. Here is the proof that $\hat{\beta}_1$ is best:

Assume $\hat{\beta}_1$ is a linear and unbiased estimator of β_1.

$$\hat{\beta}_1 = \frac{\Sigma(X_i - \bar{X})Y_i}{\Sigma(X_i - \bar{X})^2} = \Sigma w_i Y_i; \quad \text{where } w_i = \frac{(X_i - \bar{X})}{\Sigma(X_i - \bar{X})^2}$$

$$VAR(\hat{\beta}_1) = E[(\hat{\beta}_1 - \beta_1)^2] = E[(\beta_1 + \Sigma w_i u_i - \beta_1)^2] = \sigma^2 \Sigma w_i^2$$

Now consider another arbitrary estimator:

$$\tilde{\beta}_1 = \Sigma c_i Y_i; \text{ where } c_i = w_i + d_i$$

$$\tilde{\beta}_1 = \Sigma c_i (B_0 + B_1 X_i + u_i) = B_0 \Sigma c_i + B_1 \Sigma c_i X_i + \Sigma c_i u_i$$

$\tilde{\beta}_1$ is unbiased if and only if $\Sigma c_i = 0$ and $\Sigma c_i X_i = 1$, the c_i are fixed and $\Sigma u_i = 0$.

We can deduce that $\Sigma d_i = 0$ since $\Sigma c_i = \Sigma w_i + \Sigma d_i$ and $\Sigma c_i = 0$ and $\Sigma w_i = 0$.

Also, $\Sigma d_i X_i = 0$ since $\Sigma c_i X_i = \Sigma w_i X_i + \Sigma d_i X_i$ and $\Sigma c_i X_i = 1$ and $\Sigma w_i X_i = 1$.

$$VAR(\tilde{\beta}_1) = E[(\tilde{\beta}_1 - \beta_1)^2] = E[(\beta_1 + \Sigma c_i u_i - \beta_1)^2] = \sigma^2 \Sigma c_i^2$$

$\Sigma c_i^2 = \Sigma w_i^2 + \Sigma d_i^2 + 2\Sigma w_i d_i = \Sigma w_i^2 + \Sigma d_i^2$ since $\Sigma w_i d_i = 0$ (using $\Sigma d_i = 0$ and $\Sigma d_i X_i = 0$)

So that:

$$VAR(\tilde{\beta}_1) = \sigma^2 (\Sigma w_i^2 + \Sigma d_i^2) = \sigma^2 \Sigma w_i^2 + \sigma^2 \Sigma d_i^2 =$$

$$VAR(\hat{\beta}_1) + \sigma^2 \Sigma d_i^2$$

If $\Sigma d_i^2 \neq 0$, then $VAR(\tilde{\beta}_1) > VAR(\hat{\beta}_1)$; If $\Sigma d_i^2 = 0$, then $VAR(\tilde{\beta}_1) = VAR(\hat{\beta}_1)$
Q.E.D.

The most difficult step of this proof is in the third line:

$VAR(\hat{\beta}_1) = E[(\hat{\beta}_1 - \beta_1)^2] = E[(\beta_1 + \Sigma w_i u_i - \beta_1)^2] = \sigma^2 \Sigma w_i^2$ It is not easy to see that

$E[(\beta_1 + \Sigma w_i u_i - \beta_1)^2] = \sigma^2 \Sigma w_i^2$. The positive β_1 cancels with the negative β_1 and we are left with:

$E[(\Sigma w_i u_i)^2] = \sigma^2 \Sigma w_i^2$ Expanding the left side:

$$E[(\Sigma w_i u_i)^2] = E[(w_1 u_1 + w_2 u_2 + \ldots + w_n u_n)(w_1 u_1 + w_2 u_2 + \ldots + w_n u_n)] =$$

$$E[w_1^2 u_1^2 + w_2^2 u_2^2 + \ldots + w_n^2 u_n^2 + 2w_1 u_1 w_2 u_2 + 2w_1 u_1 w_3 u_3 + \ldots + 2w_2 u_2 w_3 u_3 + 2w_2 u_2 w_4 u_4 + \ldots + 2w_{n-1} u_{n-1} w_n u_n]$$

However, if we assume that $E[u_i u_j] = 0$ for all $i \neq j$, then this last expression becomes:

$$E[w_1^2 u_1^2 + w_2^2 u_2^2 + ... + w_n^2 u_n^2]$$

Finally, assuming $E[u_i^2] = E[u_j^2] = \sigma^2$ we have:

$$E[w_1^2 u_1^2 + w_2^2 u_2^2 + ... + w_n^2 u_n^2] = \sigma^2 E[w_1^2 + w_2^2 + ... + w_n^2] = \sigma^2 \Sigma w_i^2$$

Thus we are required to make two more assumptions in order to prove that $\hat{\beta}_1$ is best: 1) $E[u_i u_j] = 0$ for all $i \neq j$, which means the error terms are not related to each other. Autocorrelation, or serial correlation, is when the error terms are related to one another. Therefore, we are assuming that the error terms are not serially correlated. 2) $E[u_i^2] = E[u_j^2] = \sigma^2$, which means that all the error terms have the same variance. When the error terms do not all have the same variance it is called heteroskedasticity. So we are assuming that the error terms are homoskedastic.

8.5 The Classical Linear Regression Model

Ordinary least-squares fits a straight line between observations on X and Y such that Σe_i^2 is minimized. We have just shown that this line will be best, linear, and unbiased if four assumptions are met.

The Assumptions of the Classical Linear Regression Model

1. The independent variable(s) is (are) predetermined or at least not correlated with the error term: $E[u_i X_i] = 0$

2. The expected value of the error terms is zero: $E[u_i | X_i] = 0$

3. The error terms are not related to one another: $E[u_i u_j] = 0$ for all $i \neq j$

4. The error terms all have the same variance: $E[u_i^2] = E[u_j^2] = \sigma^2$ for all $i \neq j$

Underspecified econometric models violate assumption 2. If assumption 2 does not hold, then we cannot get through the proof of unbiasedness. Indeed, underspecified regressions yield biased parameter estimates.

Similarly, regressions run using the incorrect functional form will yield biased results. This is because such regressions violate assumption 2.

If assumption 3 does not hold, then the error terms are said to be autocorrelated. We saw that assumption 3 was necessary to complete the Gauss-Markov proof. Hence, regressions that violate assumption 3 will yield inefficient (not best) estimators.

If assumption 4 is violated, then the error terms are said to be heteroskedastic. We saw that assumption 4 was necessary to complete the Gauss-Markov proof. Therefore, regressions that violate assumption 3 will yield inefficient (not best) estimators.

In Chapter 4 we did all sorts of hypothesis testing. In order to conduct hypothesis tests it is necessary to make an additional assumption about the regression model: the error terms are normally distributed. If the error terms are normally distributed, then $\hat{\beta}_0$ and $\hat{\beta}_1$ will be normally distributed since they are linear functions of the error terms. In the section on bias above, we saw that $\hat{\beta}_1$ is indeed a linear function of the u_i's:
$\hat{\beta}_1 = \Sigma w_i Y_i = \Sigma w_i (\beta_0 + \beta_1 X_i + u_i)$. And $\hat{\beta}_0$ is a linear function of $\hat{\beta}_1$: $\hat{\beta}_0 = \bar{Y} - \hat{\beta}_1 \bar{X}$.

Once we know $\hat{\beta}_0$ and $\hat{\beta}_1$ are normally distributed we are able to carry out hypothesis tests based on the normal distribution. The t-table and F-table we use to look up critical values are only applicable if the error terms, and thus $\hat{\beta}_0$ and $\hat{\beta}_1$, are normally distributed.

There is a mathematical notation that succinctly sums up almost everything we have assumed about the error terms:

$$u_i \sim N(0, \sigma^2) \text{ for all i}$$

This states that the error terms are normally distributed with a mean of 0 and a variance of σ^2. Since $\hat{\beta}_0$ and $\hat{\beta}_1$ are linear functions of the u_i's, we know that:

$$\hat{\beta}_0 \sim N(\beta_0, \text{VAR}(\hat{\beta}_0))$$
$$\hat{\beta}_1 \sim N(\beta_1, \text{VAR}(\hat{\beta}_1))$$

Terms

Autocorrelation – When the error terms of a regression are related to one another: $E[u_i u_j] \neq 0$ for all $i \neq j$.

Best estimator (efficient estimator) – The estimator that varies the least out of all possible estimators in repeated sampling.

BLUE – An acronym for best, linear, unbiased estimator.

Gauss-Markov proof – The proof that $\hat{\beta}_0$ and $\hat{\beta}_1$ are best.

Heteroskedasticity – The error terms of a regression do not all have the same variance: $E[u_j^2] = \sigma^2$.

Linear estimator – An estimator whose formula is linear.

Monte Carlo study – An econometric study that draws repeated samples from a known population and then analyzes the characteristics of the sample regressions.

Unbiased estimator – An estimator whose expected value is equal to the true value of the parameter: $E[\hat{\beta}_1] = \beta_1$.

Chapter 8   Problems

1. Prove $\Sigma w_i = 0$ and $\Sigma w_i X_i = 1$.

2. Suppose $u_i \sim N(7, \sigma^2)$ for all i. Will $\hat{\beta}_1$ be biased? Explain.

3. Suppose $u_i \sim N(0, \sigma^2)$ for all i. Why can't we guarantee $\hat{\beta}_1$ will be efficient?

4. Given: Stalk Height$_i$ = 2.0 + 3.0 Rainfall$_i$ + 4.0 Fertilizer$_i$ + e$_i$

    A) Interpret the value of the intercept.
    B) Interpret the value of the coefficient on Rainfall.
    C) Suppose you were told that the true value of the coefficient on Rainfall is 3.1. Does this mean the estimate above is biased? Explain.
    D) Suppose you were told that the equation does not meet assumption 2 of the Classical Linear Regression Model (The error term has a zero population mean.) Does this mean that the coefficient on Rainfall is definitely not 3.0? Explain.
    E) When the data for this regression were gathered, Fertilizer was carefully applied to the various plots of corn so that each plot received exactly 2 lbs/acre of fertilizer more than the previous plot. Rainfall was measured using "dip canisters" in the standard meteorological way. Which of these explanatory variables is stochastic? Explain.
    F) Why can't we conclude that the estimates above are biased since one of the explanatory variables is stochastic?

5. From the article "Econometrics in Theory and Practice" by Steven Caudill (1990), http://college.holycross.edu/eej/Volume16/V16N3P249_256.pdf

    A) What is the "Axiom of Specification"?
    B) Is the Axiom of Specification an assumption of the Classical Linear Regression Model? If not, then should it be? If so, then which assumption corresponds to it?
    C) What is the difference between "applied econometricians" and "econometric theorists"?
    D) What is "data mining"?

6. From the article "Let's Take the Con Out of Econometrics" by Edward E. Leamer (1983)
    http://www.mtholyoke.edu/~mirobins/leamer.pdf

A) Distinguish between "experimental" and "nonexperimental" data. What is the drawback of using nonexperimental data?
B) What is data mining? What is the drawback of data mining?
C) What is sensitivity analysis?

Chapter 9

Multicollinearity

The Nature of Multicollinearity

Perfect Multicollinearity

Multicollinearity Defined

Consequences of Multicollinearity

Detecting Multicollinearity

Remedies for Multicollinearity

Terms

Chapter 9 Problems

Test Yourself on Chapters 8 and 9

9.1 The Nature of Multicollinearity

In a multiple regression there are two or more explanatory variables. At times, some of these variables will be highly linearly related -- a condition known as multicollinearity. When this occurs, ordinary least-squares has trouble discerning how much of the impact on the dependent variable can be attributed to each explanatory variable since changes in one explanatory variable are mirrored in the others.

Multicollinearity means that some or all of the explanatory variables move in lockstep or near lockstep. In this situation, regression analysis struggles to disentangle the effect each explanatory variable has on the Y-variable.

The material in this chapter is organized as follows:

- The difference between ordinary and perfect multicollinearity is explained.
- The consequences of multicollinearity are spelled out.
- Detection techniques are presented.
- Remedies are considered.

9.2 Perfect Multicollinearity

Perfect multicollinearity is when the explanatory variables in a regression are perfectly linearly related. Consider X1 and X2 below:

X1	X2
10.0	6.0
17.0	2.5
12.0	5.0
21.0	0.5

You might stare at these numbers for a long time before realizing that X2 = 11 - .5 X1. In other words, X2 is a perfect linear re-write of X1. The two variables are perfectly collinear. Notice that if the first observation on X1 was 10.1 instead of 10.0, then the two variables would be highly linearly related, but no longer perfectly collinear.

When the explanatory variables in a regression are perfectly collinear, the structural parameters are undefined. From Chapter 5 we know that the formulas for $\hat{\beta}_1$ and $\hat{\beta}_2$ in $Y_i = \hat{\beta}_0 + \hat{\beta}_1 X1_i + \hat{\beta}_2 X2_i + e_i$ are:

$$\hat{\beta}_1 = \frac{(\Sigma y_i x_{1i})(\Sigma x_{2i}^2) - (\Sigma y_i x_{2i})(\Sigma x_{1i} x_{2i})}{(\Sigma x_{1i}^2)(\Sigma x_{2i}^2) - (\Sigma x_{1i} x_{2i})^2} \; ; \text{ where } y_i = Y_i - \bar{Y} \; ; x_{1i} = X_{1i} - \bar{X}1 \; ; x_{2i} = X_{2i} - \bar{X}2$$

and

$$\hat{\beta}_2 = \frac{(\Sigma y_i x_{2i})(\Sigma x_{2i}^2) - (\Sigma y_i x_{1i})(\Sigma x_{1i} x_{2i})}{(\Sigma x_{1i}^2)(\Sigma x_{2i}^2) - (\Sigma x_{1i} x_{2i})^2} \quad ; \text{ where } y_i = Y_i - \bar{Y} \; ; x_{1i} = X_{1i} - \bar{X}1 \; ; x_{2i} = X_{2i} - \bar{X}2$$

It can be shown that the denominators of both of these equations are equal to zero when X1 and X2 are perfectly collinear. With the denominators equal to zero, both $\hat{\beta}_1$ and $\hat{\beta}_2$ are undefined. Therefore, $\hat{\beta}_0 = \bar{Y} - \hat{\beta}_1 \bar{X}1_i - \hat{\beta}_2 \bar{X}2_i$ is undefined as well.

You may wonder why a researcher would include perfectly collinear variables in a regression. Usually it happens by mistake. For instance, in a regression explaining GPA a researcher might include study time per day (ST/DAY) and study time per week (ST/WK) before realizing that ST/WK = 0 + 7 ST/DAY.

In another example, a regression explaining wages may include the number of unemployed people, the unemployment rate, and the number of people in the labor force.

$$\text{WAGES}_i = \hat{\beta}_0 + \hat{\beta}_1 \text{ \#UNEM}_i + \hat{\beta}_2 \text{ UNEMRATE}_i + \hat{\beta}_3 \text{ LFORCE}_i + \text{e}_i$$

In this case, the UNEMRATE = #UNEM / LFORCE. A linear combination of two of the explanatory variables equals the third explanatory variable. This is perfect multicollinearity and the structural parameters are undefined.

There is only one thing to do in the face of perfect multicollinearity -- drop one or more of the collinear variables.

9.3 Multicollinearity Defined

Multicollinearity is when the explanatory variables in a regression are highly, but not perfectly, linearly related. In this case, the structural parameters and all the residual statistics can be calculated with the usual formulas.

Indeed, the ordinary least-squares estimators are BLUE in the presence of multicollinearity. There is no other linear estimator that will yield estimates that vary less in repeated sampling. However, the standard errors of the estimators will be larger than if there were no multicollinearity.

To understand this more clearly, consider the following regression:

$$Y_i = \hat{\beta}_0 + \hat{\beta}_1 X1_i + \hat{\beta}_2 X2_i + \text{e}_i$$

The standard error of $\hat{\beta}_1$ in the following regression can be written as:

$$SE(\hat{\beta}_1) = \sqrt{\frac{\Sigma e_i^2 / (n-k)}{\Sigma (X_{i1} - \bar{X}_1)^2 (1 - r_{12}^2)}} \quad ; \text{ where } r_{12}^2 \text{ is the square of the correlation coefficient}$$

between X1 and X2. Thus the more collinear X1 and X2, the larger the standard error of $\hat{\beta}_1$. In other words, the more severe the multicollinearity, the larger the standard errors of the estimators.

9.4 Consequences of Multicollinearity

Notice that multicollinearity does not violate any of the assumptions of the Classical Linear Regression Model. Therefore, OLS estimators are unbiased and best in the presence of multicollinearity. "Best" means minimum variance and no other technique for estimating the structural parameters of a regression yield lower standard errors than OLS, even when the regression suffers from multicollinearity. However, if we could somehow remedy the multicollinearity, the OLS standard errors would be even lower.

The main consequence of multicollinearity is bloated (but still minimum) standard errors of the structural parameters. This will lead to further problems. Since the t-ratios are calculated from the standard errors they will be smaller in absolute value than if there were no multicollinearity. This makes hypothesis testing precarious. Artificially anemic t-ratios can lead to more TYPE II errors.

In addition, the bloated standard errors can cause parameter estimates to be sensitive to model specification. Dropping an irrelevant variable, let alone a relevant one, can cause large swings in parameter estimates under multicollinearity. Model selection becomes tricky when multicollinearity is severe.

9.5 Detecting Multicollinearity

There are a few techniques available to detect multicollinearity. The simplest and most common technique is to check the correlation coefficient between the explanatory variables:

$$r = \frac{\Sigma(X_{1i} - \overline{X}_1)(X_{2i} - \overline{X}_2)}{(S.D.X_1)(S.D.X_2)}$$

Remember, r ranges between plus and minus unity. $|r| > 0.7$ means severe multicollinearity.

A more formal procedure for detecting multicollinearity requires the calculation of a set of variance inflation factors (VIFs). To find the VIFs, 1) regress each explanatory variable on all the others in a bank of auxiliary regressions and 2) calculate VIF for each regression:

$$VIF = \frac{1}{1 - R_i^2}$$

If any VIF > 5, then multicollinearity is severe.

As an example, consider the regression:

$$Y_t = \hat{\beta}_0 + \hat{\beta}_1 X1_t + \hat{\beta}_2 X2_t + \hat{\beta}_3 X3_t + e_t$$

The required bank of auxiliary regressions is:

$$X1_t = \hat{\beta}_0 + \hat{\beta}_1 X2_t + \hat{\beta}_2 X3_t + e_t$$
$$X2_t = \hat{\beta}_0 + \hat{\beta}_1 X1_t + \hat{\beta}_2 X3_t + e_t$$
$$X3_t = \hat{\beta}_0 + \hat{\beta}_1 X1_t + \hat{\beta}_2 X2_t + e_t$$

The three R^2's from these regressions are plugged into

$$VIF = \frac{1}{1 - R_i^2}$$

in order to obtain the three VIFs. If any one VIF > 5, then the original regression suffers from severe multicollinearity.

9.6 Remedies for Multicollinearity

Once they have been detected, there are one or two things to consider when working with multicollinear explanatory variables. Often, doing nothing is the best response. The consequences are not totally debilitating and can be taken into account. For instance, hypothesis testing should be conducted with a mind toward the fact that TYPE II errors are more likely to occur.

Dealing with multicollinearity is much like dealing with a common cold. There are some things you can do to alleviate the symptoms, but most of the time you simply have to put up with them. And like the common cold, the consequences of having multicollinearity usually are not life threatening.

Another thing to consider is dropping one of the collinear explanatory variables. This would be done only if it was determined that the variable could be expended without causing an underspecified model.

A better option would be to somehow combine the collinear variables. Sometimes it is possible to form ratios or differences of variables and thereby avoid dropping the information that belongs in the regression. With time-series data, taking first differences often remedies multicollinearity.

Finally, sometimes moving to an alternate functional form can alleviate the multicollinearity. Notice that it does not pay to change into an inappropriate functional form to relieve multicollinearity since the consequences of being in the wrong form are much worse than the consequences of multicollinearity.

Terms

Correlation coefficient – A statistic that estimates the degree of linear relationship between two variables.

Multicollinearity – When the explanatory variables in a regression are highly linearly related.

Perfect multicollinearity – When the explanatory variables in a regression are perfectly linearly related.

Variance inflation factor – A statistic used to detect multicollinearity.

Chapter 9   Problems

1. Use the data in CONSUMP.XLS and statistical software to run the following regression:

$$RCONPC_t = \hat{\beta}_0 + \hat{\beta}_1 REALYDPC_t + \hat{\beta}_2 REALR_t + \hat{\beta}_3 CC_t + e_t$$

where RCONPC = real consumer spending in the USA per capita
       REALYDPC = real disposable income per capita
       REALR = real interest rate on 1-year Treasury Bonds
       CC = University of Michigan Index of Consumer Confidence

A) Which explanatory variables do not obtain their expected signs?

B) According to the correlation coefficients between the explanatory variables, would you classify the multicollinearity in this regression as severe, moderate, mild, or non-existent? Explain.

C) According to the correlation coefficients between the explanatory variables, which two variables are most collinear?

D) Calculate the three VIFs for this regression. Would you classify the multicollinearity in this regression as severe, moderate, mild, or non-existent? Explain.

E) Run the regression in first difference form. Which explanatory variables do not obtain their expected signs?

F) According to the correlation coefficients between the explanatory variables, would you classify the multicollinearity in this regression as severe, moderate, mild, or non-existent? Explain.

G) Calculate the three VIFs for this regression. Would you classify the multicollinearity in this regression as severe, moderate, mild, or non-existent? Explain.

H) Based on your look into this matter, what do you recommend doing about the multicollinearity in the original regression? Explain.

2. Use the data in ANMACRO.XLS and statistical software to run a regression where the demand for money (m2) is explained by a constant term, income (ngdp), interest rates (aaa), and prices (cpi).

VARIABLE	DESCRIPTION
m2	demand for m2
ngdp	nominal GDP
aaa	aaa corporate bond rate
cpi	consumer price index

A) Which explanatory variables do not obtain their expected signs?

B) According to the correlation coefficients between the explanatory variables, would you classify the multicollinearity in this regression as severe, moderate, mild, or non-existent? Explain.

C) According to the correlation coefficients between the explanatory variables, which two variables are most collinear?

D) Calculate the three VIFs for this regression. Would you classify the multicollinearity in this regression as severe, moderate, mild, or non-existent? Explain.

E) Run the regression in first difference form. Which explanatory variables do not obtain their expected signs?

F) According to the correlation coefficients between the explanatory variables, would you classify the multicollinearity in this regression as severe, moderate, mild, or non-existent? Explain.

G) Calculate the three VIFs for this regression. Would you classify the multicollinearity in this regression as severe, moderate, mild, or non-existent? Explain.

H) Based on your look into this matter, what do you recommend doing about the multicollinearity in the original regression? Explain.

Test Yourself on Chapters 8 and 9

1. Is a study that uses "experimental" data superior to a similar study that uses "nonexperimental" data? Explain.

2. Prove that $E[\hat{\beta}_1] = \beta_1$.

3. Assume $\hat{\beta}_1$ is linear and unbiased. Use that information to argue that $\hat{\beta}_0 (= \bar{Y} - \hat{\beta}_1\bar{X})$ is unbiased as well.

4. Defend the process known as "data mining." Does this process not violate the theories of inference?

5. Discuss the pros and cons of the following remedies for multicollinearity:
   A) Drop a variable
   B) Try first differences
   C) Try an alternate functional form such as the reciprocal form
   D) Do nothing

6. Use the following equation to argue that the SE($\hat{\beta}_1$) is undefined under perfect

   multicollinearity: $SE(\hat{\beta}_1) = \sqrt{\dfrac{\Sigma e_i^2 /(n-k)}{\Sigma(X_{i1} - \bar{X}_1)^2 (1 - r^2_{12})}}$; where r^2_{12} is the square of

   the correlation coefficient between X1 and X2.

Mark each of the following statements TRUE or FALSE.

A) $\hat{\beta}_1$ is BLUE in the presence of serial correlation.

B) In order to show that $\hat{\beta}_1$ is best, it must be assumed that the e_i's are not correlated with each other.

C) In order to show that $\hat{\beta}_1$ is unbiased, it must be assumed that the true error terms are not correlated with each other.

D) One of the conditions necessary for hypothesis testing is that the u_i's are normally distributed.

E) One of the conditions necessary to prove that the OLS estimators are BLUE is that the u_i's are normally distributed.

F) A regression in the incorrect functional form violates assumption 4 of the Classical Linear Regression Model (CLRM).

G) In the presence of multicollinearity, the estimate of R-squared will be biased.

H) $VAR(\hat{\beta}_1) = E[(\hat{\beta}_1 - \beta_1)^2] = E[(\beta_1 + \Sigma w_i u_i - \beta_1)^2] = \sigma^2 \Sigma w_i^2$

I) It is possible, although unlikely, that the structural parameters in an underspecified regression are unbiased.

J) With perfect multicollinearity, the OLS estimators are undefined.

K) Consider $Y_i = \hat{\beta}_0 + \hat{\beta}_1 X1_i + \hat{\beta}_2 X2_i + \hat{\beta}_3 X3_i + \hat{\beta}_4 X4_i + e_i$, t. If X1 and X2 are highly collinear, then the standard errors of $\hat{\beta}_1$ and $\hat{\beta}_2$ will be bloated, but not those of $\hat{\beta}_3$ and $\hat{\beta}_4$.

L) $\Sigma w_i X_i = 0$; where $w_i = \dfrac{(X_i - \bar{X})}{\Sigma (X_i - \bar{X})^2}$

M) A predetermined explanatory variable is stochastic.

N) A VIF (variance inflation factor) less than 5 means multicollinearity is non-existent.

O) $u_i \sim N(0, \sigma^2)$ indicates that the true error terms are normally distributed with an expected value of 0 and that each true error term has a variance equal to some constant, σ^2.

P) Assumptions 1 and 2 of the CLRM are necessary to prove that the OLS estimators are linear.

Q) Assumptions 1 and 2 of the CLRM are necessary to prove that the OLS estimators are unbiased.

R) Assumptions 3 and 4 of the CLRM are necessary to prove that the OLS estimators are linear.

S) Assumptions 3 and 4 of the CLRM are necessary to prove that the OLS estimators are unbiased.

T) Assumptions 3 and 4 of the CLRM are necessary to prove that the OLS estimators are best.

Assumptions of the Classical Linear Regression Model

1. The independent variable(s) is (are) predetermined or at least not correlated with the error term: $E[u_i X_i] = 0$

2. The expected value of the error terms is zero: $E[u_i | X_i] = 0$

3. The error terms are not related to one another: $E[u_i u_j] = 0$ for all $i \neq j$

4. The error terms all have the same variance: $E[u_i^2] = E[u_j^2] = \sigma^2$ for all $i \neq j$

Chapter 10

Heteroskedasticity

What is Heteroskedasticity?

Consequences of Heteroskedasticity

Detection

Remedies

Terms

Chapter 10 Problems

10.1 What Is Heteroskedasticity?

Heteroskedasticity literally means different (hetero) spread (skedasticity). It occurs when the error terms from a regression do not all have the same variance. This is a direct violation of assumption 4 of the Classical Linear Regression Model, which states that the error terms all have the same variance: $E[u_i^2] = E[u_j^2] = \sigma^2$.

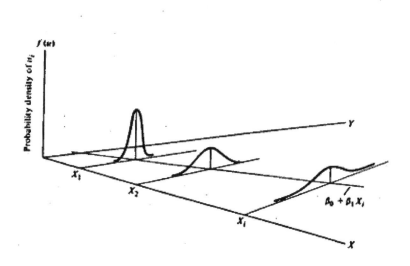

Heteroskedasticity

Cross-sectional data are most likely to be heteroskedastic. The example below considers the relationship between the savings and income of 50 families.

Example: $SAVING_i = -2.28 + 0.43\ INCOME_i + e_i$

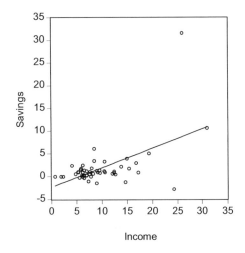

When family income is low, the regression errors tend to be small. As income increases, so does the magnitude of the residuals. Intuitively, this makes sense. When a family has low income, it is easy to predict their savings. However, there is more room for error when predicting the savings of a family with high income.

Heteroskedasticity is not the larger errors associated with higher levels of income. It is the wider frequency distributions of the error terms associated with higher levels of income. The difference is subtle, but important.

In practice, we detect heteroskedasticity by checking to see if the magnitude of the errors varies with one of the explanatory variables. The idea is that larger errors are evidence of wider frequency distributions. But let us consider the consequences of heteroskedasticity before turning to detection techniques.

10.2 Consequences of Heteroskedasticity

The structural parameters of a regression suffering from heteroskedasticity are not best. Since assumption 4 (the error terms all have the same variance: $E[u_i^2] = E[u_j^2] = \sigma^2$) of the Classical Linear Regression Model is violated, it is impossible to get through the Gauss-Markov proof. It is, however, possible to prove that the structural parameters are linear and unbiased.

The estimated SER, the estimated standard errors of the structural parameters, and therefore the t-ratios, the R^2, and F-statistics are all biased. So hypothesis testing of any sort is invalid in the presence of heteroskedasticity.

10.3 Detection

There are a variety of tests available to detect heteroskedasticity. Here we introduce three of them.

The graphical method involves plotting the squared residuals from the regression against the "culprit" variable. The culprit variable is the explanatory variable that is giving rise to the heteroskedasticity. In our example, there is no question that INCOME is the culprit variable -- it is the only explanatory variable.

Here are the squared residuals from our example (EISSQ) graphed against income:

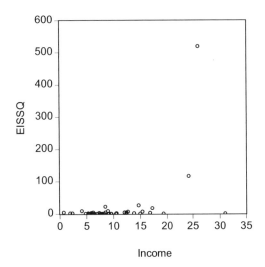

It is not obvious, but a case could be made that the squared residuals are getting larger as income increases. In general, any pattern to the squared residuals indicates heteroskedasticity. The chart on the left below shows no pattern, while the one on the right is indicative of heteroskedasticity.

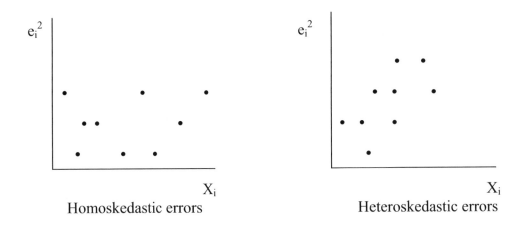

The Park test (Park 1966) is a more formal way to look for patterns in the squared residuals. To test if $Y_i = \hat{\beta}_0 + \hat{\beta}_1 X_i + e_i$ suffers from heteroskedasticity, square the residuals and regress them on the explanatory variable giving rise to the heteroskedasticity. Use the double-log form if possible; if that is not possible, the semi-log form will do:

$$\ln(e_i^2) = \alpha_0 + \alpha_1 \ln(X_i) + \varepsilon_i$$

If α_1 is statistically significant, then heteroskedasticity is present.

To test if $SAVING_i = -2.28 + 0.43\ INCOME_i + e_i$ suffers from heteroskedasticity, square the residuals and regress them on the explanatory variable giving rise to heteroskedasticity:

$$\ln(e_i^2) = -1.49 + 0.70\ \ln(INCOME_i) + \varepsilon_i$$
$$(1.29) \quad \leftarrow \quad \text{t-ratio} \quad n = 50$$

1) Ho: $\alpha_1 = 0$ (no hetero)   Ha: $\alpha_1 \neq 0$ (hetero exists)
2) 5%
3) If |t-ratio| > tc, reject Ho
4) 1.29 < 2.011 (d.f.= n-k)
5) Do Not Reject Ho; heteroskedasticity is not present in the original regression

The Park test contradicts what we suspected from the graphical analysis and finds no evidence of heteroskedasticity.

One of the most popular tests for heteroskedasticity is the White test (White 1980).

To test if $Y_i = \hat{\beta}_0 + \hat{\beta}_1 X1_i + \hat{\beta}_2 X2_i + e_i$ suffers from heteroskedasticity, run an auxiliary regression:

$$e_i^2 = \alpha_0 + \alpha_1 X1_i + \alpha_2 X1_i^2 + \alpha_3 X2_i + \alpha_4 X2_i^2 + \alpha_5(X1_i)(X2_i) + \varepsilon_i$$

If at least one of the coefficients α_1 through α_5 is significant, then heteroskedasticity is evident.

Let's add another explanatory variable to the example so that we may put the White test to full use. SIZE is the number of people in the family.

$$SAVING_i = -2.62 + 0.42\ INCOME_i + 0.08\ SIZE_i + e_i$$

To test if this regression suffers from heteroskedasticity, run the auxiliary regression:

$$e_i^2 = \alpha_0 + \alpha_1 INCOME_i + \alpha_2 INCOME_i^2 + \alpha_3 SIZE_i + \alpha_4 SIZE_i^2 + \alpha_5(INCOME_i)(SIZE_i) + \varepsilon_i$$

$$n = 50\ ;\ R^2 = .42$$
1) Ho: no hetero   Ha: hetero exists
2) 5%
3) If $nR^2 > \chi c$, then reject Ho
4) 50(.42) = 21.0 ; χc = 11.07 (d.f. = k-1 from the auxiliary regression = 5)
5) Reject Ho; heteroskedasticity is present in the original regression

The White test finds evidence of heteroskedasticity in the multiple regression of INCOME and SIZE on SAVINGS.

10.4 Remedies

As with multicollinearity and serial correlation, it is perfectly legitimate to do nothing in the face of heteroskedasticity. You will want to use the residual statistics with caution, or not at all, since they are biased. And hypothesis testing should be taken with a grain of salt. But the estimates of the structural parameters are unbiased and forecasts based on the regression are valid.

Sometimes running a regression in an alternate functional form can alleviate heteroskedasticity. It is left as an exercise for the reader to show that the heteroskedasticity in the example above is remedied by running the regression in the semi-log form. However, if you move to an incorrect functional form in order to remedy the heteroskedasticity, then you will be creating a more severe problem. Remember, regressions run in the wrong functional form yield biased results.

Another sly way to deal with heteroskedasticity is to form ratios as opposed to levels of the variables when possible. For instance, we might run a regression such as:

$$\frac{SAVING_i}{SIZE_i} = \hat{\beta}_0 + \hat{\beta}_1 \frac{INCOME_i}{SIZE_i} + e_i$$

Again, it is left to the reader to show that in this particular case heteroskedasticity is reduced by forming these ratios. This regression explains savings per family member with income per family member.

Newey and West (1987) have developed superior estimates of the standard errors of the coefficients when the regression suffers from heteroskedasticity. The Newey-West standard errors are still biased, but less so than the usual estimates of the standard errors.

The Newey-West technique leaves the ordinary least-squares parameter estimates untouched. Remember that the ordinary least-squares parameter estimates are unbiased in the presence of autocorrelation. The standard errors of the parameter estimates, however, are biased. The Newey-West technique corrects for this bias. This technique has become so popular that many econometric software packages ask if you want to see "robust" standard errors for every regression, whether it suffers from heteroskedasticity or not.

Weighted least-squares is yet another possible way to cope with heteroskedasticity. It can be shown that weighted least-squares is the best, linear, unbiased estimation technique in the presence of heteroskedasticity. The trick is finding the appropriate weights to correct for the non-constant variance of the error terms.

Suppose the error terms from $SAVING_i = \beta_0 + \beta_1 INCOME_i + u_i$ are heteroskedastic in that the variance of the error terms varies with INCOME. Multiply through the original regression by 1/INCOME.

$$\frac{SAVING_i}{INCOME_i} = \beta_0 \frac{1}{INCOME_i} + \beta_1 \frac{INCOME_i}{INCOME_i} + \frac{u_i}{INCOME_i}$$

Note that $INCOME_i/INCOME_i = 1$, so we can write:

$$\frac{SAVING_i}{INCOME_i} = \beta_0 \frac{1}{INCOME_i} + \beta_1 + \frac{u_i}{INCOME_i}$$

$\left(\dfrac{u_i}{INCOME_i}\right)$ are the new error terms. They will be homoskedastic if the variance of the u_i's is proportional to the square of INCOME.

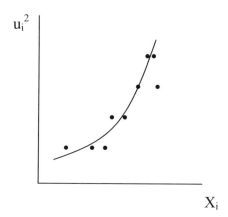

Error Terms Proportional to Income Squared

If we applying ordinary least-squares to the regression above, it is known as weighted least-squares. Notice that in practice this amounts to regressing $\dfrac{SAVING_i}{INCOME_i}$ on $\dfrac{1}{INCOME_i}$.

If the variance of the error terms is proportional to INCOME, rather than the square of INCOME, then multiplying through by $1/\sqrt{INCOME_i}$ will result in homoskedastic errors:

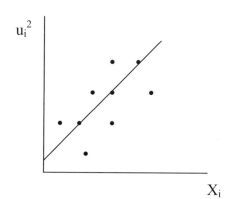

Error Terms Proportional to Income

$$\frac{SAVING_i}{\sqrt{INCOME_i}} = \beta_0 \left[\frac{1}{\sqrt{INCOME_i}} \right] + \beta_1 \left[\frac{INCOME_i}{\sqrt{INCOME_i}} \right] + \frac{u_i}{\sqrt{INCOME_i}}$$

Again, applying ordinary least-squares to the weighted data above is known as weighted least-squares. The error terms in the weighted least-squares regression $\left(\frac{u_i}{\sqrt{INCOME_i}} \right)$ are homoskedastic only if the variance of the u_i's is proportional to INCOME.

Most econometric software packages apply weighted least-squares on command. The researcher only needs to specify the weight. Typically, this is the reciprocal of the explanatory variable giving rise to the heteroskedasticity or the reciprocal of the square root of the culprit variable.

Possible Remedies for Heteroskedasticity

- Apply weighted least-squares
- Apply the Newey-West technique
- Take ratios if possible
- Try alternate functional forms (but don't switch into the wrong form)

Terms

Culprit variable – The independent variable causing the heteroskedasticity.

Heteroskedasticity – The error terms of a regression do not all have the same variance: $E[u_j^2] = \sigma^2$.

Newey-West technique – Formulas for the standard errors of the estimators that are less biased in the presence of heteroskedasticity.

Weighted least-squares – A technique that remedies heteroskedasticity by dividing the data by some version of the culprit variable.

Chapter 10   Problems

1. Given $Y_i = \hat{\beta}_0 + \hat{\beta}_1 X1_i + \hat{\beta}_2 X2_i + e_i$

   A) Write the auxiliary regression required for the Park test assuming X2 is the "culprit" variable.

   B) Suppose n = 23 and the t-ratio on X2 in the auxiliary regression is –2.222. Is heteroskedasticity present? Show the 5-step procedure for the Park test.

   C) Write the auxiliary regression required for the White test.

   D) Suppose n = 23 and the R-squared on the auxiliary regression is 0.55. Is heteroskedasticity present? Show the 5-step procedure for the White test.

   E) Write the weighted least-squares regression that would remedy the heteroskedasticity if it were proportional to X2.

2. A) Use the data in XFILE.XLS and statistical software to test the following regression for heteroskedasticity by applying White's test. Show the 5-step procedure.

$$SAVING_i = \hat{\beta}_0 + \hat{\beta}_1 INCOME_i + \hat{\beta}_2 SIZE_i + e_i$$

   B) Run the original regression using weighted least-squares. Assume 1/INCOME is the correct weight. Then apply White's test for heteroskedasticity to the errors from this weighted regression. Show the 5-step procedure.

   C) Run the original regression using weighted least-squares. Assume $1/\sqrt{INCOME}$ is the correct weight. Then apply White's test for heteroskedasticity to the errors from this weighted regression. Show the 5-step procedure.

   D) Now apply White's test to the following regression. Show the 5-step procedure.

$$SAVING_i = \hat{\beta}_0 + \hat{\beta}_1 \ln INCOME_i + \hat{\beta}_2 \ln SIZE_i + e_i$$

   E) Now apply White's test to the following regression. Show the 5-step procedure.

$$\frac{SAVINGS_i}{SIZE_i} = \hat{\beta}_0 + \hat{\beta}_1 \frac{INCOME_i}{SIZE_i} + e_i$$

   F) Now apply the Newey-West technique to the regression in 2.A). Based on the results do you think the standard errors of the structural parameters are biased upward or downward in the regression in 2.A)?

---

3. Use the data in ALCO5.XLS and statistical software to run a regression where drinks is explained by a constant term, gpa, male, ofage, cig, pot, intra, and white.

Variable	Description
drinks	number of alcoholic drinks consumed per week
gpa	grade point average 0–4 scale
male	1 if the student is male; 0 otherwise
ofage	1 if the student is 21 or older; 0 otherwise
cig	1 if the student uses tobacco; 0 otherwise
pot	1 if the student uses marijuana; 0 otherwise
intra	1 if the student participates in intramural athletics; 0 otherwise
white	1 if the student is white; 0 otherwise

A) Which variables do not attain their expected signs?

B) Which variables are not significant at the 5% critical level?

C) Plot the squared residuals from the regression against gpa. Does the plot show evidence of heteroskedasticity? Explain.

D) Do a Park test for heteroskedasticity assuming gpa is the "culprit" variable. Show the 5-step procedure.

E) Perform White's test for heteroskedasticity. Show the 5-step procedure.

F) Run the original regression using weighted least-squares. Assume 1/gpa is the correct weight. Then apply White's test for heteroskedasticity to the errors from this weighted regression. Show the 5-step procedure.

G) Run the original regression using weighted least-squares. Assume $1/\sqrt{gpa}$ is the correct weight. Then apply White's test for heteroskedasticity to the errors from this weighted regression. Show the 5-step procedure.

H) Use the Newey-West technique to obtain heteroskedasticity-corrected standard errors with the original regression. Did heteroskedasticity appear to be biasing the standard errors of the structural parameters very much? Explain.

4. Linear probability models are prone to being heteroskedastic. Use the data in BINGE.XLS and statistical software to run a regression where BINGE is explained by a constant term, cig, class, intra, male, pot, and white.

Variable	Description
binge	1 if the student binged in the last two weeks; 0 otherwise
cig	1 if the student uses tobacco; 0 otherwise
class	1 if frshman; 2 if soph; 3 if jr; 4 if senior

intra	1 if the student participates in intramural athletics; 0 otherwise
male	1 if the student is male; 0 otherwise
pot	1 if the student uses marijuana; 0 otherwise
white	1 if the student is white; 0 otherwise

A) Which variables do not attain their expected signs?

B) Which variables are not significant at the 5% critical level?

C) Perform White's test for heteroskedasticity. Show the 5-step procedure.

D) Apply the Newey-West technique to obtain heteroskedasticity-corrected standard errors with the original regression. Did heteroskedasticity appear to be biasing the standard errors of the structural parameters very much? Explain.

Chapter 11

Serial Correlation

11.1 What Is Serial Correlation?

Serial correlation, also known as autocorrelation, is when the error terms from a regression are related to one another.

A common way in which the error terms can be related is a first-order Markov scheme: $e_t = \rho e_{t-1} + \varepsilon_t$ where $-1 < \rho < +1$ and ε_t is white noise (i.e., $\varepsilon_t \sim N(0, \sigma^2)$ for all t).

positive autocorrelation is when $\rho > 0$

negative autocorrelation is when $\rho < 0$

Autocorrelation is a time-series problem that occurs frequently with economic data. Second-order serial correlation is much less frequently encountered. As you might imagine, second-order serial correlation is when the current error term is related to the two prior error terms: $e_t = \rho_1 e_{t-1} + \rho_2 e_{t-2} + \varepsilon_t$

11.2 Consequences of Serial Correlation

Serial correlation is a direct violation of assumption 3 of the Classical Linear Regression Model: The error terms are not related to one another: $E[u_i \, u_j] = 0$ for all $i \neq j$. Recall that assumption 3 was required to prove that the estimators are best, but not unbiased.

Therefore, in the presence of autocorrelation the structural parameters are not best. In addition, the residual statistics from the regression are biased:AE

SER, S.E.(B's), T-ratios, F, R^2
 - -   + + +

The signs under each statistic indicate the direction of the bias. Notice that each statistic is biased in a way that makes it appear better. For instance, the standard error of the regression (SER) indicates a good fit when it is low and it will be biased downward in the presence of autocorrelation.

The consequences of serial correlation are the same as those of heteroskedasticity with one small difference. In the presence of serial correlation, the direction of the bias in the residual statistics is known. With heteroskedasticity, the direction of the bias is unknown.

Since the standard errors and t-ratios are biased, hypothesis tests must be carried out with extreme caution in the presence of serial correlation. TYPE I errors will be more likely because the standard errors are biased downward.

11.3 Detection

Many techniques are available to detect serial correlation. We will consider three of them. Since serial correlation is when one error term is related to its predecessor, we might detect it by looking for patterns in the error terms. One way to see these patterns is to make a graph of the error terms from the regression over time.

Here are the residuals from a regression of consumer spending on disposable income from 1959 through 2005:

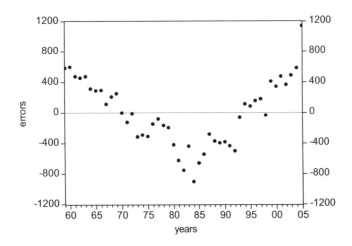

The pattern revealed here is indicative of positive serial correlation:
$e_t = \rho e_{t-1} + \varepsilon_t$ and $\rho > 0$. Since ρ is positive, any error term is likely to have the same sign as the one before it. This holds in the graph above. From 1959 through 1970, every error is positive. Once the error term becomes negative in 1971, there is a run of negative error terms until 1994 when they once again become positive. These long runs of positive and negative error terms are characteristic of positive serial correlation.

Another type of graph can indicate the phenomenon. Here the error terms from the same regression are plotted against their lagged values:

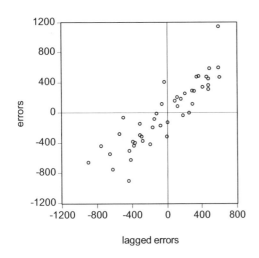

Almost all of the observations lie in the first and third quadrants. This implies that when an error term is positive, the one before it is as well. And when an error term is negative, so is its predecessor. In other words, error terms tend to have the same sign as their predecessors. This implies a positive ρ in the first-order Markov scheme ($e_t = \rho\, e_{t-1} + \varepsilon_t$) and positive serial correlation.

The graphs below reflect negative serial correlation:

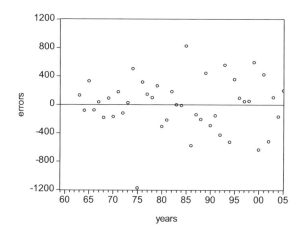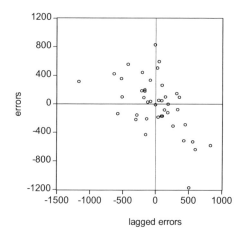

The graph on the left shows that the error terms zig-zag from positive to negative in sequence. If the current error term is positive, the subsequent error term is very likely to be negative. The graph on the right shows most of the observations in the second and fourth quadrants.

How do the graphs look when there is no serial correlation?

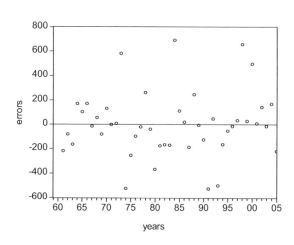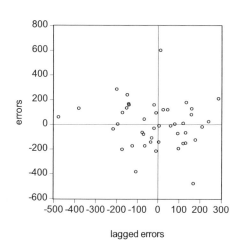

The graph on the left shows no pattern, but a random splay of errors over time. The observations on the graph on the right are almost evenly divided between all four quadrants.

One problem with the graphical method for detecting autocorrelation is that patterns can be difficult to discern. In practice, the graphs usually are not as clear-cut as the ones shown here.

The most popular technique for detecting serial correlation is the Durbin-Watson test (Durbin and Watson 1951). The test involves obtaining the residuals from the regression and calculating d, the test statistic:

$$d = \frac{\Sigma(e_t - e_{t-1})^2}{\Sigma e_t^2}$$

d ranges between 0 and 4 and will tend toward 2 if the error terms are not autocorrelated. If d < 2, suspect positive autocorrelation and apply the following 5-step procedure:

1) Ho: no positive auto   Ha: positive auto
2) 5%
3) If d < d_L, then reject Ho
   If d_L < d < d_U, then inconclusive
4) Calculate d and look up d_L and d_U in a table
5) Reject or Do Not Reject Ho

If d > 2, suspect negative autocorrelation and apply the following 5-step procedure:

1) Ho: no negative auto   Ha: negative auto
2) 5%
3) If 4 - d_L < d, then reject Ho
   If 4 - d_U < d < 4 - d_L, then inconclusive
4) Calculate d and look up d_L and d_U in a table
5) Reject or Do Not Reject Ho

Examples:

(1) Y_t = 9734.2 - 3782.2 $X1_t$ + 2815.3 $X2_t$ + e_t ; n = 16

Since d = 2.21, suspect negative autocorrelation:

   1) Ho: no negative auto   Ha: negative auto
   2) 5%
   3) If 4 - d_L < d < 4, then reject Ho
      If 4 - d_U < d < 4 - d_L, then inconclusive
   4) d = 2.21 d_L = .98 d_U = 1.54   (n = 16; k = 3)
   5) Do Not Reject Ho; no negative auto

---

(2) $Y_t = 0.568 + 0.907 \, X1_t + e_t$; $n = 25$

Since $d = .66$, suspect positive autocorrelation:

    1) Ho: no positive auto   Ha: positive auto
    2) 5%
    3) If $0 < d < d_L$, then reject Ho
      If $d_L < d < d_U$, then inconclusive
    4) $d = .66$ $d_L = 1.29$ $d_U = 1.45$ ($n = 25$; $k = 2$)
    5) Reject Ho; positive auto is present

The Durbin–Watson test is invalid in certain situations:

- The test is not valid in regressions without a constant term.
- The test is not valid for small samples ($n < 15$).
- The test is not valid for autoregressive models.

Autoregressive models are regressions that include the lagged dependent variable as an explanatory variable: $Y_t = \hat{\beta}_0 + \hat{\beta}_1 X1_t + \hat{\beta}_2 Y_{t-1} + e_t$. The Durbin–Watson statistic is biased toward 2 in such models. Use Durbin's h-statistic instead (Durbin 1970):

$$h = (1 - \frac{d}{2})\sqrt{\frac{n}{1 - n(\text{var}(\hat{\beta}))}}$$

    1) Ho: no autocorrelation Ha: auto present
    2) 5%
    3) If $|h| > t^c$, then reject Ho (d.f. $= n-k$)
    4) Calculate h and get t^c
    5) Reject or Do Not Reject Ho

Durbin's h is undefined if $n(\text{var}(\hat{\beta})) > 1$. In this case, the Lagrange multiplier test may be used to test for serial correlation.

Lagrange multiplier tests for serial correlation are increasingly popular since they overcome all the debilities of the Durbin-Watson test: they are fine for small samples, autoregressive models, and models without a constant term. In addition, these tests for serial correlation have no inconclusive zone. The following Lagrange multiplier test is attributed to Breusch (1978) and Godfrey (1978):

If $Y_t = \beta_0 + \beta_1 X_t + \beta_2 Y_{t-1} + u_t$ is suspected of suffering from serial correlation:

Run: $u_t = \alpha_0 + \alpha_1 X_t + \alpha_2 Y_{t-1} + \alpha_3 u_{t-1} + \gamma_t$

1) Ho: no serial correlation   Ha: serial correlation exists
2) 5%
3) If $nR^2 > \chi c$, then reject Ho (d.f. = # of lagged residual terms = 1)
4) Calculate nR^2 and χc
5) Reject or Do Not Reject Ho

Serial correlation has more serious consequences in autoregressive models and it is tricky to remedy. If an autoregressive model suffers from serial correlation then the structural parameters are biased as well as the residual statistics.

Remedies include respecifying the model. Maybe pseudoautocorrelation is the real problem. Instrumental variables and two-stage least squares are other possibilities, but we will not discuss those.

All of the tests outlined above check for first-order serial correlation only. That is, the serial correlation is expected to follow a first-order Markov scheme: $e_t = \rho\, e_{t-1} + \varepsilon_t$. Second-order serial correlation ($e_t = \rho_1\, e_{t-1} + \rho_2\, e_{t-2} + \varepsilon_t$) is rare, but not unheard of, with economic data.

11.4 Remedies

Consider $\qquad\qquad Y_t = \beta_0 + \beta_1 X_t + u_t$; where $u_t = \rho\, u_{t-1} + \varepsilon_t$

lag and mult by ρ: $\quad \rho\, Y_{t-1} = \rho\, \beta_0 + \beta_1\, \rho\, X_{t-1} + \rho\, u_{t-1}$

subtract: $\qquad\qquad Y_t - \rho\, Y_{t-1} = \beta_0 - \rho\, \beta_0 + \beta_1\, X_t - \beta_1\, \rho X_{t-1} + u_t - \rho\, u_{t-1}$

re-arrange: $\qquad\qquad Y_t - \rho\, Y_{t-1} = \beta_0\,(1-\rho) + \beta_1\,(X_t - \rho\, X_{t-1}) + u_t - \rho\, u_{t-1}$

This last equation is the generalized difference equation. The generalized differences of Y_t ($Y_t - \rho\, Y_{t-1}$) are regressed on the generalized differences of X_t ($X_t - \rho\, X_{t-1}$). When a regression is run using the generalized differences of the data, it is known as generalized least-squares (GLS). The error terms ($u_t - \rho\, u_{t-1}$) in the GLS regression are free from serial correlation. This can be seen by substituting $u_t = \rho\, u_{t-1} + \varepsilon_t$ into ($u_t - \rho\, u_{t-1}$). The result is ε_t which is white noise: a normally distributed stochastic variable that has a mean of zero, constant standard error, and is independently distributed (i.e., free from serial correlation).

The GLS estimators are efficient and the residual statistics are unbiased. GLS is the one and only remedy for autocorrelation. The problem, in practice, is that ρ is never known. It must be estimated. We consider four ways to estimate ρ:

1) OLS technique: Suppose the residuals of the following regression are autocorrelated: $Y_t = \hat{\beta}_0 + \hat{\beta}_1 X1_t + e_t$. Now estimate ρ by regressing the residuals on their lagged values: $e_t = \hat{\beta}_1 e_{t-1} + \varepsilon_t$. Notice there is no $\hat{\beta}_0$. $\hat{\beta}_1$ is the estimate of ρ. Run GLS with this estimate of ρ.

2) Hildreth-Lu scanning procedure: Since ρ is expected to lie between plus and minus unity, a computer can easily check to see which value of ρ gives the best results in a GLS regression.

Assume $\rho = -1$; Run GLS; Assume $\rho = -.9$; Run GLS; Assume $\rho = -.8$; Run GLS; ...; Assume $\rho = +.9$; Run GLS; Assume $\rho = +1$; Run GLS. Of all these GLS regressions, use the one that has the best fit according to the R^2 or SER.

3) Cochrane-Orcutt iterative procedure: This procedure estimates ρ with a formula and then runs the GLS regression. However, it does not stop there. The GLS regression will have its own residuals, which can be plugged back into the formula for estimating ρ. Then GLS can be run again. Once again, the GLS residuals can be plugged into the formula for ρ and GLS can be re-applied. This process iterates until sequential estimates of ρ do not vary significantly.

A) Estimate ρ with this formula $\rightarrow \rho = \dfrac{\Sigma e_t e_{t-1}}{\Sigma e_{t-1}^{\,2}}$

B) Run GLS and obtain the new e_t's.

C) Go back to A).

D) Stop when sequential estimates of ρ do not vary by much.

4) Maximum likelihood procedure: Most statistical software packages estimate the parameters of GLS regressions using a maximum likelihood procedure. Basically, this procedure assigns initial values to $\hat{\beta}_0$, $\hat{\beta}_1$, and ρ, then considers the residuals from this GLS model. The pattern of the residuals indicates adjustments to the initial values of $\hat{\beta}_0$, $\hat{\beta}_1$ and ρ. The residuals from the adjusted GLS model are considered and used to make further adjustments to $\hat{\beta}_0$, $\hat{\beta}_1$, and ρ. The process stops when sequential estimates of $\hat{\beta}_0$, $\hat{\beta}_1$, and ρ do not vary significantly.

11.5 Final Thoughts

Regressions that are underspecified or in the wrong functional form often test positive for serial correlation. When this occurs, it is known as pseudoautocorrelation. Graphs and/or the Durbin-Watson test pick up autocorrelation, but this is due to the regression missing an important explanatory variable or being in the wrong functional form. Both of these mistakes have worse consequences than autocorrelation. If autocorrelation is detected and remedial measures are ineffective, it is most likely pseudoautocorrelation.

One of the main consequences of serial correlation is the biased residual statistics. Especially troublesome are the biased standard errors of the coefficients of the regression because hypothesis testing is hazardous under these circumstances.

The Newey-West technique we employed to cope with heteroskedasticity is applicable in cases of autocorrelation as well. The technique corrects the biased standard errors of the structural parameters and leaves the estimates themselves alone. This allows for hypothesis testing in the presence of serial correlation.

Terms

Autoregressive model – A regression that uses the lagged dependent variable as an explanatory variable.

Cochrane-Orcutt iterative procedure – A procedure to estimate ρ for a generalized least-squares regression.

Durbin-Watson test – A test for serial correlation.

First-order Markov scheme ($e_t = \rho e_{t-1} + \varepsilon_t$) – A common way in which the error terms from a regression can be related.

Generalized least-squares (GLS) – A regression using the generalized differences of the data.

Hidreth-Lu scanning procedure – A procedure to estimate ρ for a generalized least-squares regression.

Lagrange multiplier test – A test for serial correlation.

Maximum likelihood procedure – A technique for estimating the structural parameters of an econometric model, such as a GLS model.

Newey-West technique – Formulas for the standard errors of the structural parameters of a regression that correct for the bias caused by serial correlation or heteroskedasticity.

Pseudoautocorrelation – When a regression tests positive for autocorrelation but the symptoms are due to underspecification or using the wrong functional form.

Second-order serial correlation ($e_t = \rho_1 e_{t-1} + \rho_2 e_{t-2} + \varepsilon_t$) – When the current error term is related to the two prior error terms.

Serial correlation (autocorrelation) – When the error terms from a regression are related to one another.

White noise – A normally distributed stochastic variable that has a mean of zero, constant standard error, and is independently distributed (i.e., free from serial correlation).

Chapter 11   Problems

1. Complete the following table:

Sample Size	k	d stat	Autocorrelation present?
20	2	0.83	
32	3	1.24	
45	4	1.98	
100	5	3.72	
150	7	1.71	

2. Complete the following table:

Sample Size	k	d stat	Autocorrelation present?
15	2	1.60	
25	3	1.80	
45	4	2.48	
100	6	2.72	
150	10	2.11	

3. Use the data in CONSUMP.XLS and statistical software to run the following regression:

$$RCONPC_t = \hat{\beta}_0 + \hat{\beta}_1 REALYDPC_t + e_t$$

A) Plot the error terms over time. Do you suspect serial correlation? Explain.
B) Plot the error terms against their lagged values. Do you suspect serial correlation? Explain.
C) Perform a Durbin-Watson test. Show the 5-step procedure.

4. Use the data in ANMACRO.XLS and statistical software to run the following regression:

$$m2/cpi_t = \hat{\beta}_0 + \hat{\beta}_1 ngdp/cpi_t + e_t$$

A) Plot the error terms over time. Do you suspect serial correlation? Explain.
B) Plot the error terms against their lagged values. Do you suspect serial correlation? Explain.
C) Perform a Durbin-Watson test. Show the 5-step procedure.

5. Use the data in CONSUMP.XLS and statistical software to run the following regression:

$$RCONPC_t = \hat{\beta}_0 + \hat{\beta}_1 REALYDPC_t + \hat{\beta}_2 REALR_t + \hat{\beta}_3 CC_t + e_t$$

Where RCONPC = real consumer spending in the USA per capita
REALYDPC = real disposable income per capita
REALR = real interest rate on 1-year Treasury Bonds
CC = University of Michigan Index of Consumer Confidence

A) Plot the residuals from the regression over time. Does this plot suggest serial correlation is present? Positive or negative? Explain.
B) Plot the residuals from the regression against their lagged values. Does this plot suggest serial correlation is present? Positive or negative? Explain.
C) Does the regression suffer from serial correlation? Show the 5-step procedure of the Durbin-Watson test.
D) Estimate ρ by regressing the residuals on their lagged values (no constant term). What is the estimate of ρ?
E) Check for second-order serial correlation. Do you think it is present? Explain.
F) Estimate ρ and correct for first-order serial correlation using GLS with maximum likelihood estimation. What is this estimate of ρ?
G) Did GLS remedy the serial correlation? Show the 5-step procedure.
H) Compare the t-ratios from the original regression and the GLS regression. Are you surprised by which ones turn out to be larger? Explain.
I) Apply the Newey-West technique to the original regression. Are you surprised at the new standard errors of the estimators? Explain.

6. Use the data in ANMACRO.XLS and statistical software to run a regression where the demand for money (m2) is explained by a constant term, income (ngdp), interest rates (aaa), and prices (cpi).

A) Plot the residuals from the regression over time. Does this plot suggest serial correlation is present? Positive or negative? Explain.
B) Plot the residuals from the regression against their lagged values. Does this plot suggest serial correlation is present? Positive or negative? Explain.
C) Does the regression suffer from serial correlation? Show the 5-step procedure of the Durbin-Watson test.
D) Estimate ρ by regressing the residuals on their lagged values (no constant term). What is the estimate of ρ?
E) Check for second-order serial correlation. Do you think it is present? Explain.
F) Estimate ρ and correct for first-order serial correlation using GLS with maximum likelihood estimation. What is this estimate of ρ?
G) Did GLS remedy the serial correlation? Show the 5-step procedure.
H) Compare the t-ratios from the original regression and the GLS regression. Are you surprised by which ones turn out to be larger? Explain.

I) Apply the Newey-West technique to the original regression. Are you surprised at the new standard errors of the estimators? Explain.

Test Yourself on Chapters 10 and 11

1. Describe the following procedures:
   A) Park test
   B) Weighted least-squares
   C) Generalized least-squares
   D) Cochrane-Orcutt iterative procedure
   E) Hildreth-Lu scanning procedure
   F) Maximum likelihood procedure

2. Draw a diagram indicative of heteroskedasticity. Label the horizontal axis "culprit" and be sure to correctly label the vertical axis. Draw a diagram indicative of negative serial correlation. Be sure to label the axes of your diagram.

3. Describe the pros and cons of any three remedies for heteroskedasticity.

4. What is a first-order Markov scheme? What is second-order serial correlation? What is "white noise"?

5. Does the White test below indicate heteroskedasticity? Show the 5-step procedure.

White Heteroskedasticity Test:

F-statistic	0.491592	Probability	0.780723
Obs*R-squared	2.645362	Probability	0.754462

Test Equation:
Dependent Variable: RESID^2
Method: Least Squares
Sample: 1 50
Included observations: 50

Variable	Coefficient	Std. Error	t-Statistic	Prob.
C	-275.2148	329.0460	-0.836402	0.4074
ED	18.22919	33.65147	0.541706	0.5908
ED^2	-0.211078	0.952250	-0.221662	0.8256
ED*EXPER	-0.453429	0.645192	-0.702781	0.4859
EXPER	16.12281	15.23650	1.058170	0.2958
EXPER^2	-0.236866	0.208270	-1.137306	0.2616

R-squared	0.052907	Mean dependent var	19.62276
Adjusted R-squared	-0.054717	S.D. dependent var	66.54024

S.E. of regression	68.33644	Akaike info criterion	11.39893
Sum squared resid	205474.2	Schwarz criterion	11.62837
Log likelihood	-278.9733	F-statistic	0.491592
Durbin-Watson stat	2.086374	Prob(F-statistic)	0.780723

6. Does the regression featured in the Eviews printout below suffer from autocorrelation according to a Durbin-Watson test at the 5% critical level? Show the 5-step procedure.

Dependent Variable: WHY
Method: Least Squares
Sample: 1956 1980
Included observations: 25

Variable	Coefficient	Std. Error	t-Statistic	Prob.
C	-0.325482	8.371100	-0.038882	0.9693
EX1	0.913309	0.032584	28.02956	0.0000
EX2	-0.558162	2.745564	-0.203296	0.8408

R-squared	0.997461	Mean dependent var	640.6560
Adjusted R-squared	0.997230	S.D. dependent var	173.4284
S.E. of regression	9.127571	Akaike info criterion	7.372643
Sum squared resid	1832.876	Schwarz criterion	7.518908
Log likelihood	-89.15804	F-statistic	4321.229
Durbin-Watson stat	1.655326	Prob(F-statistic)	0.000000

---

1) Ho: no positive auto Ha: positive auto
2) 5%
3) If $0 < d < d_L$, then reject Ho
   If $d_L < d < d_U$, then inconclusive
4) Get the numbers
5) Reject or Do Not Reject Ho

1) Ho: no negative auto   Ha: negative auto
2) 5%
3) If $4 - d_L < d < 4$, then reject Ho
   If $4 - d_U < d < 4 - d_L$, then inconclusive
4) Get the numbers
5) Reject or Do Not Reject Ho

Mark each of the following statements TRUE or FALSE.

1. The "culprit variable" is the dependent variable in a heteroskedastic regression.
2. Application of the Newey-West technique will alter the estimate of the SER.
3. The standard error of the regression (SER) is biased downward in a regression suffering from heteroskedasticity.
4. $E[\varepsilon_i^2] = E[\varepsilon_j^2] = \sigma^2$ for all $i \neq j$ is the definition of homoskedasticity.
5. In the presence of heteroskedasticity, tests of significance must be carried out with caution since the T-ratios of the structural parameters are biased.
6. The standard error of $\hat{\beta}_1$ is biased downward in the presence of serial correlation.
7. The R-squared from a GLS regression is not directly comparable to the R-squared from the same regression run using OLS.

8. The standard error of the regression (SER) is biased downward in a regression suffering from serial correlation.
9. After correcting for autocorrelation, one would expect the standard errors of the structural parameters to increase.
10. After correcting for heteroskedasticity, one would expect the standard errors of the structural parameters to increase.

Chapter 12

Time-Series Models

12.1 Distributed Lag Models

A distributed lag model occurs when one or more of the independent variables is lagged one or more periods:

$$Y_t = \beta_0 + \beta_1 X_t + \beta_2 X_{t-1} + \beta_3 X_{t-2} + \beta_4 Z_t + \beta_5 Z_{t-1} + u_t$$

There are several justifications for using lagged explanatory variables. For instance, changes in the explanatory variable may take time to impact the dependent variable. Or it may be that the trend in the explanatory variable over several periods is what affects the dependent variable.

The Permanent Income Hypothesis (PIH) offers an interesting application of a distributed lag model. The PIH asserts that spending depends not on actual income but expected future income. It has been observed that spending (CON) is smoother over time than disposable personal income (DPI). The explanation for this is that windfalls do not change expected future income, so CON remains relatively more stable than DPI.

In econometrics terms, the PIH predicts that CON is better explained by expected DPI (EXDPI) as opposed to actual DPI:

$$CON_t = \hat{\beta}_0 + \hat{\beta}_1 EXDPI_t + e_t$$

The difficulty is that EXDPI is hard to measure especially for aggregate data. One of the first attempts to approximate EXDPI was to use the pattern of past and current incomes:

$$CON_t = \hat{\beta}_0 + \hat{\beta}_1 DPI_t + \hat{\beta}_2 DPI_{t-1} + \hat{\beta}_3 DPI_{t-2} + \hat{\beta}_4 DPI_{t-3} + e_t$$

Here a distributed lag model is used as a proxy for expected future income. If the lagged values of DPI are significant, then the PIH is supported.

Multicollinearity is typically a problem in distributed lag models. The correlation coefficient between DPI and DPI_{t-1} is typically close to unity. And distributed lag models can use up degrees of freedom.

The Koyck model (Koyck 1954) is an ingenious way to employ a distributed lag model while avoiding these drawbacks.

Suppose current consumption is a weighted average of DPI going back many periods. The weights decline geometrically:

$$CON_t = \beta_0 + \beta_1 (DPI_t + \lambda DPI_{t-1} + \lambda^2 DPI_{t-2} + \lambda^3 DPI_{t-3} + \ldots + \lambda^{n-1} DPI_{t-n+1}) + u_t$$

Lag this equation one period and multiply by λ:

$$\lambda CON_{t-1} = \lambda \beta_0 + \beta_1 (\lambda DPI_{t-1} + \lambda^2 DPI_{t-2} + \lambda^3 DPI_{t-3} + \ldots + \lambda^n DPI_{t-n}) + \lambda u_{t-1}$$

Subtract the second equation from the first and you are left with:

$$CON_t - \lambda CON_{t-1} = \beta_0 - \lambda \beta_0 + \beta_1 DPI_t + u_t - \lambda u_{t-1}$$

Which can be re-written:

$$CON_t = (1-\lambda)\beta_0 + \beta_1 DPI_t + \lambda CON_{t-1} + \varepsilon_t; \text{ where } \varepsilon_t = u_t - \lambda u_{t-1}$$

This is a Koyck distributed lag model. It amounts to regressing CON on contemporaneous DPI and CON_{t-1}. A distributed lag of n periods is estimated with the loss of just one observation. Multicollinearity is usually reduced in the Koyck model compared to the regular distributed lag model.

The coefficient on CON_{t-1} is an estimate of the weight (λ). The short run impact of DPI on CON is equal to β_1. The long run impact is equal to $\beta_1/(1-\lambda)$.

Any model that includes some form of the dependent variable as an explanatory variable can be called "autoregressive." The Koyck model is one example of an autoregressive model. The Durbin-Watson statistic is invalid in autoregressive models; use Durbin's h-statistic instead (Durbin 1970).

$$h = (1 - \frac{d}{2}) \sqrt{\frac{n}{1 - n(\text{var}(\hat{\beta}))}}$$

1) Ho: no autocorrelation Ha: auto present
2) 5%
3) If $|h| > t^c$, then reject Ho (d.f. = n-k)
4) Calculate h and get t^c
5) Reject or Do Not Reject Ho

Durbin's h is undefined if $n(\text{var}(\hat{\beta})) > 1$. In this case, the Lagrange multiplier test may be used to test for serial correlation (Breusch 1978 and Godfrey 1978).

If $Y_t = \beta_0 + \beta_1 X_t + \beta_2 Y_{t-1} + u_t$ is suspected of suffering from serial correlation:

Run: $u_t = \alpha_0 + \alpha_1 X_t + \alpha_2 Y_{t-1} + \alpha_3 u_{t-1} + \gamma_t$

1) Ho: no serial correlation   Ha: serial correlation exists
2) 5%
3) If $nR^2 > \chi c$, then reject Ho (d.f. = # of lagged residual terms = 1)

4) Calculate nR^2 and χc

5) Reject or Do Not Reject Ho

Serial correlation has more serious consequences in autoregressive models and it is tricky to remedy. If an autoregressive model suffers from serial correlation, then the structural parameters are biased as well as the residual statistics.

Remedies include respecifying the model. Maybe pseudoautocorrelation is the real problem. Instrumental variables and two-stage least squares are other possibilities, but we will not discuss those.

12.2 Granger Tests

Often in time-series analysis, it pays to know if changes in one variable generally occur before changes in another variable. For instance, it would be hard to argue that inflation causes the Federal Reserve to slow money growth when changes in the inflation rate do not consistently precede changes in the money supply.

Granger (1969) has developed a test to determine precedence in time-series data. In order to determine if changes in inflation rates precede changes in the money supply, run the following regression where M is the money supply and INFL is the inflation rate:

$$M_t = \hat{\beta}_0 + \hat{\beta}_1 M_{t-1} + \hat{\beta}_2 M_{t-2} + \hat{\beta}_3 INFL_{t-1} + \hat{\beta}_4 INFL_{t-2} + e_t$$

$\hat{\beta}_3$ and/or $\hat{\beta}_4$ will be statistically significant if changes in inflation do indeed precede changes in the money supply. The test for this is as follows:

1) Ho: $\hat{\beta}_3$ and $\hat{\beta}_4 = 0$; INFL does not precede M

Ha: $\hat{\beta}_3$ and/or $\hat{\beta}_4 \neq 0$; INFL precedes M

2) 5%

$$\boxed{F = \frac{(SSR_R - SSR)/R}{SSR/(n-k)}}$$

3) If $F > F^C$, reject Ho

4) 0.83 vs 3.32 (d.f. num. = R = 2; d.f. den. = n-k = 40-5=35)

5) Do Not Reject Ho; changes in INFL do not precede changes in M

Thus, we can conclude that changes in the inflation rate do not precede changes in the money supply. Regardless of how this test turned out, it is advisable to conduct the reverse Granger test as well by running the following regression:

$$INFL_t = \hat{\beta}_0 + \hat{\beta}_1 INFL_{t-1} + \hat{\beta}_2 INFL_{t-2} + \hat{\beta}_3 M_{t-1} + \hat{\beta}_4 M_{t-2} + e_t$$

And then perform the following 5-step procedure:

1) Ho: $\hat{\beta}_3$ and $\hat{\beta}_4 = 0$; M does not precede INFL

Ha: $\hat{\beta}_3$ and/or $\hat{\beta}_4 \neq 0$; M precedes INFL

2) 5%

$$\boxed{F = \frac{(SSR_R - SSR)/R}{SSR/(n-k)}}$$

3) If F > F^C , Reject Ho
4) 2.58 vs 3.32 (d.f. num. = R = 2; d.f. den. = n-k = 40-5=35)
5) Do Reject Ho; changes in M do not precede changes in INFL

The results of this reverse test are a shocker since most economists think that inflation is most often the result of growth in the money supply. Perhaps we should only be lagging the dependent variables one period instead of two. The number of lags to use is left to the discretion of the researcher.

Even had we found that changes in the money supply precede changes in the inflation rate, we could not conclude that changes in the money supply CAUSE changes in the inflation. Precedence does not necessarily imply causation. One observes many umbrellas being carried by pedestrians before a rainstorm, but surely those umbrellas do not cause the rain.

From the tests above we conclude that INFL does not "Granger-cause" M and M does not "Granger-cause" INFL.

Granger tests are useful to test for reverse causality. Recall that the structural parameters in the following regression will be biased if Y has an impact on X1:

$$Y_t = \beta_0 + \beta_1 \ X1_t + u_t$$

In regression analysis, it is critical that changes in the explanatory variable (X1) cause changes in the dependent variable (Y). However, if Y impacts X1 we have a case of reverse causality. In such a case, it can be shown that the error terms (u_t) are correlated with X1. This violates assumption 1 of the Classical Linear Regression Model and the structural parameters will be biased.

12.3 Spurious Correlation and Nonstationarity

Spurious correlation is a strong relationship between variables that is the result of a statistical fluke, not an underlying causal relationship. This occurs often with economic data because economic variables have a tendency to grow over time. Thus, variables that are not causally related have high correlation coefficients anyway.

As an example, the correlation coefficient between the money supply (M2) and per capita milk consumption in the United States is -.95. Yet it is highly unlikely that increases in the money supply cause people to consume less milk. The correlation between the two is merely coincidental.

As you can imagine, spurious correlations are common with time-series data since so many variables exhibit long-term growth trends. Special care must be taken when working with trended data because regression results can be biased as a result of spurious correlations.

In the best circumstances, time-series regressions will use only stationary data -- time-series whose basic properties do not change over time. Specifically, a time-series, X, is said to be stationary if:

1) the mean of X is constant over time
2) the variance of X is constant over time

3) the correlation between X_t and X_{t-k} (for all k) is constant.

If one or more of these properties is not met, then X is nonstationary. The use of nonstationary time-series in regressions may result in spurious correlation and that means biased estimates of the structural parameters.

The graph below shows real GDP (rgdp) over the years since 1945. This time-series exhibits a pronounced upward trend and therefore cannot have a constant mean.

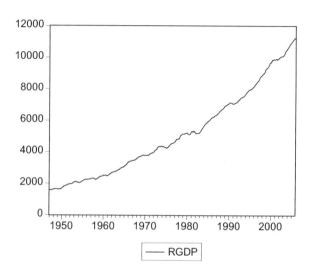

Whether or not the variance of rgdp is constant over time is difficult to tell from visual inspection. We could take the variance of the first half of the time-series and compare it to the variance of the second half.

There is no way to tell from visual inspection whether or not observations a given distance apart have a constant correlation. Checking the correlation between X_t and X_{t-k} requires a correlogram -- a chart that shows the degree to which observations k spaces apart are correlated. Correlograms that do not approach zero quickly indicate nonstationary data.

It is quite tedious to obtain a correlogram by hand and we are glad to have computers do this for us. Given time-series data such as rgdp, take each pair of observations that are adjacent. This means taking the first and second observation, the second and third, the third and fourth, and so on. Now calculate the correlation coefficient (r) between all these pairs.

We are just getting started. Now take observations of rgdp that are a space apart. These are observations one and three, two and four, three, and five, and so on. Now calculate the correlation coefficient (r) between all these pairs. Repeat this for all pairs of observations up to 12 spaces apart (k = 12).

k	r
1	0.99
2	0.97
3	0.96
4	0.94
5	0.93
6	0.91
7	0.9
8	0.89
9	0.87
10	0.86
11	0.85
12	0.83

The table above indicates that adjacent observations in rgdp are highly correlated (r = 0.99). Even observations twelve years ago are highly correlated with this year's level of rgdp (r = 0.83).

If we make a chart from the table above, we have a correlogram:

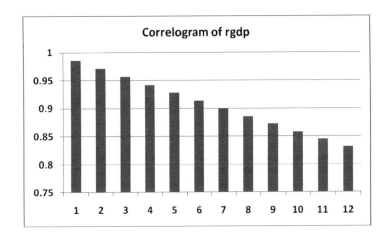

The vertical axis of the correlogram reports the correlation coefficients from the table, while the horizontal axis measures k. Correlgrams that do not quickly decay toward r = 0, such as the one above, are typical of nonstationary time-series. Regressions that use nonstationary data will probably suffer from spurious correlation and yield biased results.

If a time-series is nonstationary, then it may be best to work with the first-differences of the data. First differences are the change from one period to the next in the data series. The graphs below depict the first differences in rgdp (fd1rgdp):

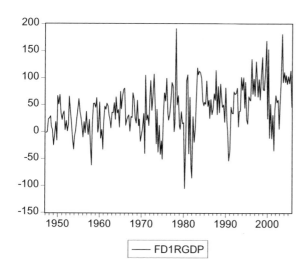

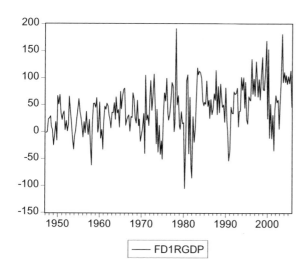
FD1RGDP

Visual inspection suggests a constant mean (perhaps), but it appears as if the latter half of the line has a larger variance than the first half. It is a tough call. The correlogram suggests significant correlations between observations at k = 1 through 4. In other words, the first differences in rgdp may be stationary since the correlations become insignificant after four lags.

k	r
1	0.42
2	0.38
3	0.21
4	0.20
5	0.11
6	0.13
7	0.07
8	0.02
9	0.14
10	0.11
11	0.10
12	-0.04

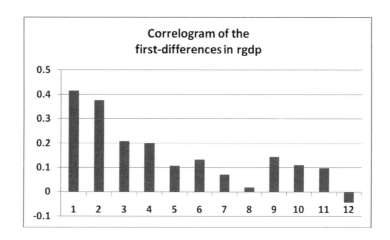

Correlogram of the first-differences in rgdp

The second differences in rgdp (fd2rgdp) are the differences in the first differences, or the change in the change, in rgdp.

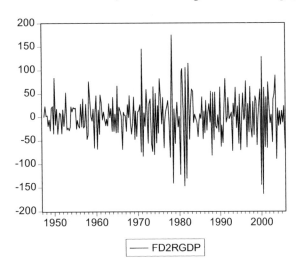

The correlogram suggests that the second differences are stationary since they become insignificant after k =1.

k	r
1	-0.47
2	0.12
3	-0.14
4	0.08
5	-0.11
6	0.07
7	-0.01
8	-0.15
9	0.14
10	-0.02
11	0.12
12	-0.18

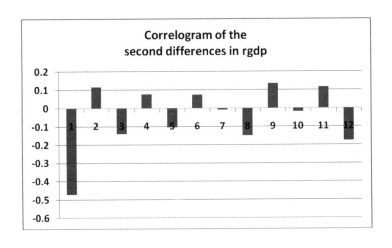

It appears as if any regressions that use rgdp are using a nonstationary variable. This is a serious allegation because the results of any such regressions may be biased. It would be better to use the first differences in rgdp since they appear to be stationary according to a check of the correlogram.

The premier test for stationarity is the Dickey-Fuller, or unit root, test (Dickey and Fuller 1979). To test if a time-series, X_t, is stationary:

A) Run $(X_t - X_{t-1}) = \hat{\beta}_0 + \hat{\beta}_1 X_{t-1} + e_t$

B) Perform a negative sign test on $\hat{\beta}_1$

    1) Ho: $\beta_1 = 0$ (X is nonstationary)   Ha: $\beta_1 < 0$ (X is stationary)
    2) 5%
    3) If t-ratio $< -t^c*$, reject Ho
    4) The t-ratio is the usual one, but t^c* is about 60% higher than tc from the usual t table. As n approaches infinity, t^c* approaches 2.86 from higher levels.
    5) State the results of the test

Using the data on rgdp as an example, we have:

A) $(rgdp_t - rgdp_{t-1}) = 25.92 + 0.03\ rgdp_{t-1} + e_t$
                            (5.72) ←t-ratio

B) Negative sign test on $\hat{\beta}_1$:

    1) Ho: $\beta_1 = 0$ (X is nonstationary)   Ha: $\beta_1 < 0$ (X is stationary)
    2) 5%
    3) If 5.72 < -2.91*, reject Ho
    4) Eviews gives the t^c for the Dickey Fuller test
    5) Do Not Reject Ho; rgdp is nonstationary

Now let's test if the first differences in rgdp are stationary:

A) $(d(rgdp_t) - d(rgdp)_{t-1}) = 90.68 - 0.51\ d(rgdp)_{t-1} + e_t$
                            (-4.31) ←t-ratio

B) Negative sign test on $\hat{\beta}_1$:

    1) Ho: $\beta_1 = 0$ (X is nonstationary)   Ha: $\beta_1 < 0$ (X is stationary)
    2) 5%
    3) If -4.31 < -2.91*, reject Ho
    4) Eviews gives the t^c for the Dickey Fuller test
    5) Reject Ho; the first differences in rgdp are stationary

The augmented Dickey-Fuller test for a unit root (i.e., nonstationarity) adds a lagged dependent variable to the right-hand side:

$$(X_t - X_{t-1}) = \hat{\beta}_0 + \hat{\beta}_1 X_{t-1} + \hat{\beta}_2 (X_{t-1} - X_{t-2}) + e_t$$

It is left to the reader as an exercise to determine if the augmented Dickey-Fuller test gives the same results concerning the stationarity of rgdp and the first differences of rgdp.

If you discover that one or more of the time-series variables you are working with are nonstationary, then you might take first or second differences in order to avoid spurious correlation. However, it is unnecessary to difference nonstationary variables in a regression when they are cointegrated. Cointegrated variables are nonstationary to the same degree.

Suppose you are interested in this regression:

$$Y_t = \hat{\beta}_0 + \hat{\beta}_1 X_t + e_t$$

Suppose X and Y are both nonstationary so that the regression may suffer from spurious correlation. Further suppose that their first differences are stationary. To determine if X and Y are cointegrated, apply a Dickey-Fuller test to e_t:

A) Run the regression: $Y_t = \hat{\beta}_0 + \hat{\beta}_1 X_t + e_t$

B) Run the Dickey-Fuller regression: $(e_t - e_{t-1}) = \hat{\beta}_0 + \hat{\beta}_1 e_{t-1} + z_t$

C) Perform a negative sign test on $\hat{\beta}_1$:

    1) Ho: $\beta_1 = 0$ (e_t is nonstationary)   Ha: $\beta_1 < 0$ (e_t is stationary)
       (X and Y are not cointegrated)   (X and Y are cointegrated)
    2) 5%
    3) If t-ratio < -tc*, reject Ho
    4) The t-ratio is the usual one, but tc* is about 60% higher than tc from the usual t table. As n approaches infinity, tc* approaches 2.86 from higher levels.
    5) State the results of the test

Cointegrated variables can be used "as is" in regressions without concern for spurious correlation.

As an example, let's check a regression where the demand for money (m2) is explained by a constant term, income (ngdp), interest rates (aaa), and prices (cpi):

$$m2_t = \hat{\beta}_0 + \hat{\beta}_1 ngdp_t + \hat{\beta}_2 aaa_t + \hat{\beta}_3 cpi_t + e_t$$

Certainly m2, ngdp, and cpi are nonstationary since they exhibit obvious upward trends. Unit root tests indicate that all four variables are nonstationary in their levels. In addition, all four variables require second differencing in order to pass augmented Dickey-Fuller tests for stationarity. To check if the variables in this regression are cointegrated, we apply an augmented Dickey-Fuller test to e_t by running the following regression:

$$(e_t - e_{t-1}) = \hat{\beta}_0 + \hat{\beta}_1 e_{t-1} + \hat{\beta}_2 (e_{t-1} - e_{t-2}) + z_t$$

And then applying a negative sign test to $\hat{\beta}_1$:

1) Ho: $\hat{\beta}_1 = 0$ (e_t is nonstationary)   Ha: $\hat{\beta}_1 < 0$ (e_t is stationary)
   (X and Y are not cointegrated)   (X and Y are cointegrated)
2) 5%
3) If -2.84 < -2.94, reject Ho
4) Eviews provides the t^c for this test
5) Do Not Reject Ho; the variables are not cointegrated

It is close, but at the 5 percent critical level the variables in the regression are not cointegrated. It would be best to take second differences of all four time-series before running the regression in order to scrupulously avoid spurious correlation.

Terms

Autoregressive model – A regression that uses the lagged dependent variable as an independent variable.

Cointegrated variables – When the time-series in a regression are nonstationary to the same degree.

Correlogram – A chart that shows the degree to which observations k spaces apart are correlated.

Distributed lag model – A regression that lags one or more independent variables one or more times.

First differences – The change from one period to the next in a time-series.

Koyck model – An autoregressive model used to mimic a distributed lag model with declining weights.

Second differences – The change in the change of a time-series.

Spurious correlation – A strong relationship between variables that is the result of a statistical fluke, not an underlying causal relationship.

Stationary variable – A time-series with constant mean, variance, and correlation between observations any given distance apart.

Chapter 12   Problems

1. Consider the following regression:

$$M_t = 2.00 - 0.10 \ R_t + 0.70 \ Y_t + 0.60 \ M_{t-1} + e_t$$
$$\quad\quad (0.10) \quad\ (0.35) \quad\ (0.10) \quad\ \leftarrow \text{standard errors}$$

$$R^2 = .9 \quad\quad\quad DW = 1.80 \quad\quad\quad n = 26$$

>   where M is the demand for M1
>   R is the interest rate on 10-year Treasuries
>   Y is national income

   A) Do the variables attain their expected signs?
   B) Test for serial correlation in this regression. Show the 5-step procedure.
   C) What is the short-run impact of a change in the interest rate on money demand?
   D) What is the long-run impact?

2. Use the data in CONS.XLS and statistical software to run regressions of the following sort:

$$cons_t = \hat{\beta}_0 + \hat{\beta}_1 dpi_t + \hat{\beta}_2 dpi_{t-1} + \hat{\beta}_3 dpi_{t-2} + \hat{\beta}_4 dpi_{t-3} + ... + e_t$$
   cons – the change in real consumer spending
   dpi – the change in real disposable income

   A) What lag length seems appropriate? Explain.
   B) Is multicollinearity a problem in the regression with the appropriate lag length? Explain.
   C) Is serial correlation a problem in the regression with the appropriate lag length? Explain.
   D) Run the Koyck version of this distributed lag model. What is the short-run impact of a change in disposable income on consumer spending?
   E) What is the long-run impact?
   F) Does the Koyck version of the model suffer from multicollinearity? Explain.
   G) Does the Koyck version of the model suffer from autocorrelation? Explain.

3. Use the data in QLEISCOIN and statistical software to do the following problems.

   COIN = percentage change in the composite index of coincident economic indicators
   LEIS = percentage change in the composite index of leading economic indicators

   A) Run a regression to determine if COIN is affected by LEIS and LEIS lagged 1 through 8 quarters. Do you think LEIS 8 quarters ago helps predict COIN this quarter? Explain.

B) How many lags of the LEIS should be used to explain COIN? Explain how you came to this conclusion.

C) Does the regression you settled on in B) above suffer from serial correlation according to the Durbin-Watson test? Show the 5-step procedure.

D) Does the regression you settled on in B) above suffer from serial correlation according to the Lagrange multiplier test? Show the 5-step procedure.

E) Does the regression you settled on in B) above suffer from multicollinearity? On what do you base your response?

F) Employ a Koyck lag structure in the COIN/LEIS regression. Does this regression suffer from serial correlation according to the h test? Show the 5-step procedure.

G) Employ a Koyck lag structure in the COIN/LEIS regression. Does this regression suffer from serial correlation according to the Lagrange multiplier test? Show the 5-step procedure.

H) Employ a Koyck lag structure in the COIN/LEIS regression. Does this regression suffer from multicollinearity? On what do you base your response?

I) According to the Koyck model, a 1-unit increase in LEIS implies COIN will be how much higher or lower in the short run?

J) In the long-run, the 1-unit increase in LEIS implies COIN will eventually change how much?

4. Use the data in MACRO.XLS and statistical software to determine if changes in real disposable personal income (RDPI) precede changes in real consumer spending (RCONS) or vice versa use lag lengths of 8 for both variables.

A) Do you reject the null hypothesis that RDPI does not precede RCONS at the 5% critical level?

B) Would you reject the null hypothesis that RDPI does not precede RCONS at the 10% critical level? Explain.

C) Do you reject the null hypothesis that RCONS does not precede RDPI at the 5% critical level?

D) Would you reject the null hypothesis that RCONS does not precede RDPI at the 10% critical level? Explain.

5. Use the data in QLEISCOIN and statistical software to do Granger tests to determine if changes in the leading economic indicators (LEIS) precede changes in the coincident indicators (COIN).

A) Using lag lengths of 6, show the 5-step procedure for the Granger test that changes in LEIS do not precede changes in COIN.

B) Using lag lengths of 6, show the 5-step procedure for the Granger test that changes in COIN do not precede changes in LEIS.

C) Given your results in A) and B) above, can you unequivocally conclude that changes in LEIS precede changes in COIN?

D) Does your answer to C) above change when lag lengths of 10 are used?

E) Does your answer to C) above change when lag lengths of 12 are used?

6. Use the data in MACRO.XLS and statistical software to run Granger tests to determine if reverse causality is a problem in the following regression:

$$RGDP_t = \hat{\beta}_0 + \hat{\beta}_1 \, RINV_t + e_t$$

where RGDP is real GDP and RINV is real business spending on plant and equipment

Is reverse causality a problem in the regression above? On what do you base your response?

7. Use the data in MACRO.XLS and statistical software to run Granger tests to determine if changes in M2 Granger-cause INFL or vice-versa.

A) What are the appropriate lag lengths? Explain.
B) What do you conclude? Explain.

8. Which of the following sets of variables are most likely to suffer from spurious correlation?

A) The population of America and the Dow Jones Industrial average
B) GDP and the unemployment rate
C) The inflation rate and government expenditures
D) The change in the money supply and the federal funds rate

9. Using the data in MACRO.XLS and statistical software, which of the following variables appear to be nonstationary because of nonconstant means or nonconstant variances? Produce the graph for each variable and say if the problem is a nonconstant mean or variance, both, or neither.

A) Real investment (rinv)
B) The first difference in real investment
C) The second difference in real investment
D) The first difference in the money supply (m2)
E) Interest rate on AAA corporate bonds (aaa)

10. Which variables from the list above appear to be nonstationary based on their autocorrelation functions? Produce the autocorrelation function for each variable and indicate if a variable is stationary, nonstationary, or questionable.

11. Which variables from the list above are nonstationary according to the Dickey-Fuller test? Show the 5-step procedure for each variable.

12. Use the data in RGDP.XLS to apply the augmented Dickey-Fuller test to real GDP (rgdp) and the first differences in rgdp. Show the 5-step procedure for each test.

13. Use the data in AJ.XLS to replicate the famous Andersen-Jordan study by regressing a constant term, lagged money supply (m2), and the lagged standardized federal deficit (fp) on nominal GDP (ngdp): $ngdp_t = \hat{\beta}_0 + \hat{\beta}_1 m2_{t-1} + \hat{\beta}_2 fp_{t-1} + e_t$

    A) Which explanatory variable has the more profound impact on nominal GDP? Explain your response.

    B) Which variables in the regression are nonstationary? Explain.

    C) Check for cointegration among the variables in the regression. Show the 5-step Dickey-Fuller procedure.

Test Yourself on Chapter 12

1. Given:

Dependent Variable: WHY
Method: Least Squares
Sample(adjusted): 1960 2001
Included observations: 42 after adjusting endpoints

Variable	Coefficient	Std. Error	t-Statistic	Prob.
C	-179.2567	163.7257	-1.094860	0.2803
EX	0.259430	0.091487	2.835696	0.0072
WHY(-1)	0.739760	0.198066	3.734916	0.0034

R-squared	0.997038	Mean dependent var	14665.26
Adjusted R-squared	0.996886	S.D. dependent var	4023.018
S.E. of regression	224.5044	Akaike info criterion	13.73442
Sum squared resid	1965686.	Schwarz criterion	13.85854
Log likelihood	-285.4227	F-statistic	6563.263
Durbin-Watson stat	0.866017	Prob(F-statistic)	0.000000

    A) What is the short-run impact of EX on WHY?

    B) What is the long-run impact of EX on WHY?

    C) Does this regression suffer from serial correlation according to Durbin's h-test? Show the 5-step procedure.

$$h = (1 - \frac{d}{2})\sqrt{\frac{n}{1 - n(var(\hat{\beta}))}}$$

D) Does this regression suffer from serial correlation according to the Lagrange multiplier test? Show the 5-step procedure.

Breusch-Godfrey Serial Correlation LM Test:

F-statistic	20.57279	Probability	0.000056
Obs*R-squared	14.75185	Probability	0.000123

Test Equation:
Dependent Variable: RESID
Method: Least Squares
Date: 02/26/03   Time: 15:29
Presample missing value lagged residuals set to zero.

Variable	Coefficient	Std. Error	t-Statistic	Prob.
C	-93.87846	135.1921	-0.694408	0.4917
EX	0.104824	0.078148	1.341348	0.1878
WHY(-1)	-0.113005	0.083810	-1.348355	0.1855
RESID(-1)	0.622442	0.137231	4.535724	0.0001

E) Suppose the regression does suffer from serial correlation. What is the major consequence?

2. A) Using lags of two periods on both independent variables, write the Granger equation to test if the chicken came before the egg.
   B) Given the Eviews printout below, did the chicken come before the egg? Explain how you know.

Pairwise Granger Causality Tests
Sample: 1951 1994
Lags: 2

Null Hypothesis:	Obs	F-Statistic	Probability
CHICK does not Granger Cause EGG	42	0.09849	0.04644
EGG does not Granger Cause CHICK		12.55461	0.17900

3. Are the first differences of M1 (FDM1) stationary? Using the Eviews printout below, show the 5-step procedure.

ADF Test Statistic	-0.615077	1% Critical Value*	-3.7667
		5% Critical Value	-3.0038
		10% Critical Value	-2.6417

Unit root test on FDM1.

4. A) List the three conditions for a variable to be stationary.
   B) What is spurious correlation?

5. A) What is "Granger causality"?
   B) What is the consequence of a dependent variable "Granger-causing" an independent variable in the regression?

6. A) What is the permanent income hypothesis?
   B) Write the Koyck model that was used to test the permanent income hypothesis and explain why this regression is a test of the hypothesis.

7. A) Explain why two nonstationary time-series are likely to be spuriously correlated.
   B) What is the consequence of using nonstationary variables in a regression?

8. A) Write the Granger regression to determine if changes in A precede changes in B. Assume lags of 2 periods.
   B) Why is it important to do the reverse Granger test before concluding that changes in A precede changes in B?

9. A) Draw the correlogram (autocorrelation function) of a stationary variable. (Be sure to label the axes of your drawing.)
   B) Draw the correlogram (autocorrelation function) of a nonstationary variable.

10. A) What is cointegration?
    B) Given $Y_t = Bo + B1 \, X_t + e_t$ describe how to determine if Y and X are cointegrated. Spell out the Dickey-Fuller regression involved.

Chapter 13

Forecasting with Regression Models

13.1 Making a Point Forecast with a Regression Model

Regression models easily lend themselves to making predictions. Suppose we have established that a good model for explaining the differences in average starting salaries of MBA students from various business schools is:

$$MBAPAY_i = \hat{\beta}_0 + \hat{\beta}_1 AVGMAT_i + \hat{\beta}_2 ACRATE_i + e_i$$

where $MBAPAY_i$ = average starting salary of MBA students from school i
$AVGMAT_i$ = average GMAT score at school i
$ACRATE_i$ = acceptance rate at school i

Ordinary least-squares is applied to estimate the structural parameters of the model:

$$MBAPAY_i = 679.83 + 146.12 AVGMAT_i - 489.53 ACRATE_i + e_i$$
$$\quad\quad (0.01) \quad (2.08) \quad\quad\quad (-3.30)$$

$$SER = 6383.53 \quad R^2 = 0.66 \quad n = 46$$

With this regression in hand we can make a forecast of the average salary of newly minted MBAs from Harvard if we have the average GMAT score for this particular class (AVGMAT = 708) and the acceptance rate (ACRATE = 11). The model predicts that the average starting salary for MBAs out of this class at Harvard is:

$$FORE(MBAPAY_i) = 679.83 + 146.12 AVGMAT_i - 489.53 ACRATE_i$$

$$FORE(MBAPAY_{Harvard}) = 679.83 + 146.12\,(708) + - 489.53\,(11) = \$98,454$$

It turns out this forecast is low since actual average starting salary for this MBA class at Harvard was $105,896. The forecast error is:

$$e_i = Y_i - \hat{Y}_i$$

$$\$7,442 = \$105,896 - \$98,454$$

A couple of things to know about this forecast:

1) This is a "point" forecast since it is a specific value as opposed to a range of values.
2) This is an "out-of-sample" forecast because the data from Harvard were not used to estimate the structural parameters of the model.

13.2 Making an Interval Forecast with a Regression Model

To forecast a range of values for the average starting salary of MBA students from this class at Harvard, we would form a confidence interval around our point forecast:

FORE -/+ SERF(t^c)

where FORE is the point forecast
SERF is the standard error of the forecast
t^c is the critical t value (d.f. = n – k = 46 – 3 = 43)

For forecasts made from simple regressions (one explanatory variable), the standard error of the forecast is given by:

$$SERF = SER\sqrt{1 + \frac{1}{n} + \frac{(X_f - \overline{X})}{\Sigma(X_i - \overline{X})^2}}$$

where SER is the standard error of the regression
and X$_f$ is the value of X used to make the forecast

For forecasts made from multiple regressions (more than one explanatory variable), the formula for the standard error of the forecast is considerably more complicated and depends on the number of explanatory variables.

In order to calculate forecast intervals, the standard error of the regression (SER) is often substituted for the standard error of the forecast (SERF) since it is a close approximation in many instances.

The 95% confidence interval for our prediction using the exact SERF is:

$98,454 -/+ 6661.56 (2.017) $85,018 - $111,890

The 90% confidence interval for our prediction using the exact SERF is:

$98,454 -/+ 6661.56 (1.681) $87,256 - $109,652

If we had not already seen that the actual value is $105,896, then we would be 95 percent confident that the average starting salary of the MBA students in this class at Harvard is between $86,163 and $111,961. We are 90 percent confident that the actual value is between $88,308 and $109,817.

More technically, if we formed an infinite number of such intervals, 95 (or 90) percent would contain the true value of the average starting salary.

For comparison, here are the same confidence intervals using the SER instead of the SERF:

The 95% confidence interval for our prediction using the SER is:
$98,454 -/+ 6383.58 (2.017) $85,578 - $111,330

The 90% confidence interval for our prediction using the SER is:

$98,454 -/+ 6383.58 (1.681) $87,723 - $109,185

On all these confidence intervals, the amount that is added and subtracted from the point forecasts can be referred to as the "margin of error." Using the 95 percent confidence interval calculated with the exact SERF for the average starting salary of Harvard MBAs:

$98,454 -/+ 6661.56 (2.017) $85,018 - $111,890

The product of 6661.56 (2.017) is the margin of error. So we may report that the predicted average starting salary for this class of Harvard MBAs is $98,454 with a margin of error of $13,436 (= 6661.56 x 2.017). The margin of error represents the amount a forecast can be in error without being considered unusual.

13.3 In-Sample Forecasts

Things would be only slightly different if we had included the data for Harvard when we estimated our regression model:

$$MBAPAY_i = \hat{\beta}_0 + \hat{\beta}_1 AVGMAT_i + \hat{\beta}_2 ACRATE_i + e_i$$

where: $MBAPAY_i$ = average starting salary of MBA students from school i
$AVGMAT_i$ = average GMAT score at school i
$ACRATE_i$ = acceptance rate at school i

Ordinary least-squares is applied to estimate the structural parameters of the model:

with Harvard
$$MBAPAY_i = -296.16 + 148.67 AVGMAT_i -508.38 ACRATE_i + e_i$$
$$(-0.01) \quad (2.12) \quad\quad\quad (-3.44)$$

$$SER = 6401.49 \quad R^2 = 0.68 \quad n = 47$$

without Harvard
$$MBAPAY_i = 679.83 + 146.12 AVGMAT_i - 489.53 ACRATE_i + e_i$$
$$(0.01) \quad (2.08) \quad\quad\quad (-3.30)$$

$$SER = 6383.53 \quad R^2 = 0.66 \quad n = 46$$

The previous sections looked at point and interval forecasts using the "without Harvard" results. Those forecasts were "out-of-sample." If we make a point prediction using the "with Harvard" regression results, then we have an "in-sample" forecast:

$$FORE(MBAPAY_i) = -296.16 + 148.67 AVGMAT_i + -508.38 ACRATE_i$$
$$FORE(MBAPAY_{Harvard}) = -296.16 + 148.67\,(708) + -508.38\,(11) = \$99,062$$

Like the out-of-sample prediction, this forecast is low since actual average starting salary for this MBA class at Harvard was $105,896. The forecast error is:

$$e_i = Y_i - \hat{Y}_i$$

$$\$6,834 = \$105,896 - \$99,062$$

The confidence intervals are formed in the exact same manner as before, only some details are different:

$$FORE\ -/+\ SERF(t^c)$$

where FORE is the point forecast
      SERF is the standard error of the forecast
      t^c is the critical t value (d.f. $= n - k = 47 - 3 = 44$)

The 95% confidence interval for our prediction using the exact SERF is:

$$\$99,062\ -/+\ 6657.96\,(2.015) \qquad \$85,646 - \$112,478$$

The 90% confidence interval is:

$$\$99,062\ -/+\ 6657.96\,(1.680) \qquad \$88,308 - \$109,817$$

The 95% confidence interval for our prediction using the SER is:

$$\$99,062\ -/+\ 6401.49\,(2.015) \qquad \$86,163 - \$111,961$$

The 90% confidence interval is:

$$\$99,062\ -/+\ 6401.49\,(1.680) \qquad \$88,308 - \$109,817$$

If we had not already seen that the actual value is $105,896, then we would be 95 percent confident that the average starting salary of the MBA students in this class at Harvard is between $86,163 and $111,961. We are 90 percent confident that the actual value is between $88,308 and $109,817.

More technically, if we formed an infinite number of such intervals, 95 (or 90) percent would contain the true value of the average starting salary.

13.4 Measuring Forecast Accuracy

A variety of statistics are available to measure forecast accuracy.

Root Mean Squared Error

$$RMSE = \sqrt{\frac{1}{n}\Sigma(Y_t - \hat{Y}_t)^2}$$

where Y is the actual value of Y

$\hat{Y}$ is the forecast of Y

n is the number of values being forecasted

This may be the most popular measure of forecast accuracy. The forecast errors are squared to make them all positive and then they are averaged. Finally, the square root is taken to put the value back in its original scale. It is hoped that the RMSE will be small, but small is a relative term. Typically, the size of the RMSE is gauged against the mean of Y.

Mean Absolute Deviation

$$MAD = \frac{1}{n}\Sigma|Y_t - \hat{Y}_t|$$

This is similar to the RMSE except absolute values of the forecast errors are taken rather than squaring. And like the RMSE, it is hoped that the MAD will be low relative to the mean of Y.

Mean Absolute Percentage Deviation

$$MAPE = \frac{1}{n}\Sigma\frac{|Y_t - \hat{Y}_t|}{|Y_t|}$$

The advantage of the MAPE is that it need not be compared to anything. It expresses the average error in percentage terms. If the MAPE = 7, it means on average the forecasts are off by 7 percent.

Theil's Inequality Coefficient

$$U = \frac{\sqrt{\frac{1}{n}\Sigma(Y_t - \hat{Y}_t)^2}}{\sqrt{\frac{1}{n}\Sigma\hat{Y}_t^2} + \sqrt{\frac{1}{n}\Sigma Y_t^2}}$$

There are several variations on the exact formula used to calculate Theil's U, but everything said here applies regardless of which version is used. Theil's U will always lie between 0 and 1. If U = 0, then $Y = \hat{Y}$ for every forecast and there are no forecast errors. If U = 1, the forecasts are no better than simply guessing the average of Y.

Theil's U statistic can be decomposed into three proportions of inequality: bias, variance, and covariance. These proportions can be interpreted as follows:

> **Bias** -- The bias proportion indicates the degree of systematic error. Forecasts that are consistently too high (or too low) will be indicated by the bias proportion being greater than zero. The closer to one, the greater the consistency of the bias.

> **Variance** -- The variance proportion measures the degree to which the variance of the forecasts matches the variance of the actual values of Y. A large variance proportion indicates that the actual series has a much higher variance than the forecasts.

> **Covariance** -- This covariance proportion measures the degree to which the forecast errors can be attributed to the random nature of the phenomenon being predicted.

The bias, variance, and covariance proportions of Theil's U range from zero to one and always sum to one. A good set of forecasts will have almost no bias proportion and little or no variance proportion. That means the covariance proportion will be close to unity.

13.5 Projecting Trends

In this section we will see how to project trend lines into the future. We will use regression analysis where the dependent variable is the forecast variable and the independent variable is "time." Time is a ticker that increases by 1 unit each period. As our example, let's look at real GDP in the United States from 1948 through 2007:

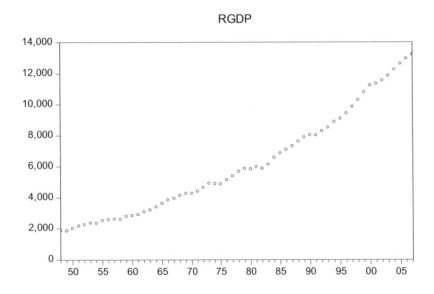

Linear Trend

To fit a linear trend line to the RGDP data, run the following regression:

$$RGDP = 433.24 + 186.95 \text{ time} + e \qquad r^2 = .956$$
$$\quad (.023) \quad (.000) \leftarrow \text{ p-values} \qquad n = 60$$

where RGDP is annual real GDP
time = 1, 2, 3, ..., 60

Here is the fitted trend line extended through 2016:

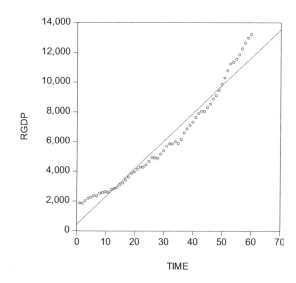

Along the horizontal axis, the years have been replaced with their number: 1948 =1; 1949 = 2, ..., 2016 = 69. We can plug the number for any year into the regression model and obtain a trend forecast for that year:

RGDP(hat) = 433.24 + 186.95 time	fore	year	actual
61	11,837	2008	13,162
62	12,024	2009	12,757
63	12,211	2010	13,063
64	12,398	2011	13,299
65	12,585	2012	13,589

These forecasts are out-of-sample since we only used data from 1948 through 2007 to estimate the trend regression. Yet we can measure the accuracy of these five point forecasts since they are ex poste:

RMSE = 984   MAE = 963 MAPE = 7.3%
Theil U = .04 Bias = .96   Variance = .00   Covariance = .04

Although the measures of accuracy are encouraging, all five forecasts are lower than the actual values, resulting in a bias proportion of 0.96. Looking at the scattergram with the linear regression line drawn in makes it clear that this model will most likely continue to underestimate RGDP going forward. Nevertheless, here are the trend projections for the future:

RGDP(hat) = 433.24 + 186.95 time

	fore	year
66	12,772	2013
67	12,959	2014
68	13,146	2015
69	13,333	2016

Lin-Log Trend

To fit a trend line that assumes a diminishing growth rate to the RGDP data, run the following regression:

$$RGDP = -3405.7 + 3034.8 \log(time) + e \qquad r^2 = .670$$
$$(.000) \quad (.000) \leftarrow \text{p-values} \qquad n = 60$$

where RGDP is annual real GDP
log(time) = the natural log of 1, 2, 3, …

This is sometimes referred to as a "lin-log" regression. Here is the regression line extended out to 2016:

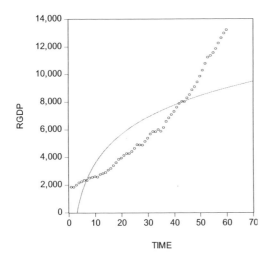

Ex poste, out-of-sample forecasts for 2008 through 2012:

RGDP(hat) = 3405.7 + 3034.8 log(time)

	fore	year	actual
61	9,070	2008	13,162
62	9,119	2009	12,757
63	9,168	2010	13,063
64	9,216	2011	13,299
65	9,263	2012	13,589

Measures of accuracy:

RMSE = 4013   MAE = 4007 MAPE = 30.4%
Theil U = .18   Bias = .99   Variance = .00   Covariance = .00

The measures of accuracy are all worse than the linear trend forecasts. Also, the r-squared from this regression was much worse than the linear regression. Looking at the scattergram with the diminishing growth trend regression line drawn in makes it clear that this model is a poor choice for the actual data on RGDP. Nevertheless, here are the trend projections for the future:

RGDP(hat) = 3405.7 + 3034.8 log(time)	fore	year
66	9,309	2013
67	9,355	2014
68	9,400	2015
69	9,444	2016

Log-Lin Trend

To fit a trend line that assumes an exponential growth rate to the RGDP data run the following regression:

$$log(RGDP) = 7.56 + .033 \text{ time} + e \qquad r^2 = .995$$
$$(.000) \ (.000) \leftarrow \text{p-values} \qquad n = 60$$

where log(RGDP) is the natural log of annual real GDP
time = 1, 2, 3, …

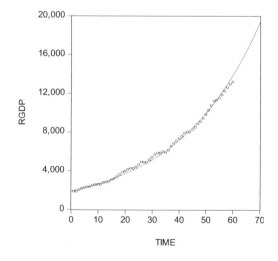

Ex poste, out-of-sample forecasts for 2008 through 2012:

log(RGDP)(hat) = 7.56 + .033 time

time	fore	year	actual
61	14,397	2008	13,162
62	14,881	2009	12,757
63	15,382	2010	13,063
64	15,899	2011	13,299
65	16,434	2012	13,589

RMSE = 2292   MAE = 2224 MAPE = 16.9%
Theil U = .08   Bias = .94   Variance = .04   Covariance = .02

Comparing these measures of accuracy with the previous two trend forecasts shows the linear trend to be most accurate with these from the exponential model next best. The diminishing trend model is least accurate for the 2008 through 2012 period.
Here are the ex ante exponential trend projections:

log(RGDP)(hat) = 7.56 + .033 time

time	fore	year
66	16,987	2013
67	17,558	2014
68	18,149	2015
69	18,760	2016

Polynomial Trend
To fit a trend line that assumes a quadratic growth rate to the RGDP data run the following regression:

$$RGDP = 2014.68 + 33.91 \text{ time} + 2.51 \text{ time}^2 + e \qquad r^2 = .997$$
$$\quad (.000) \quad\quad (.000) \quad\quad\quad (.000) \; \leftarrow \text{p-values} \qquad n = 60$$

where RGDP is annual real GDP
time = 1, 2, 3, …
$time^2$ = 2, 4, 9, …

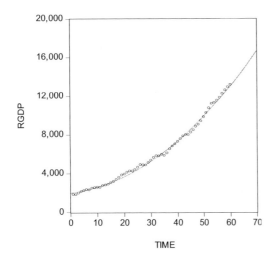

Ex poste, out-of-sample forecasts for 2008 through 2012:

RGDP(hat) = 2014.68+ 33.91 time + 2.51 time²		fore	year	actual
61	61²	13,419	2008	13,162
62	62²	13,716	2009	12,757
63	63²	14,109	2010	13,063
64	64²	14,461	2011	13,299
65	65²	14,819	2012	13,589

RMSE = 1002 MAE = 940 MAPE = 7.12%
Theil U = .04   Bias = .88   Variance = .05 Covariance = .07

The forecast accuracy of the quadratic trend compares favorably with the linear trend. The accuracy of these two models is far superior to the diminishing trend and exponential trend models. It is difficult to choose one of the two best models as superior. The linear trend underestimates RGDP 2008 through 2012:

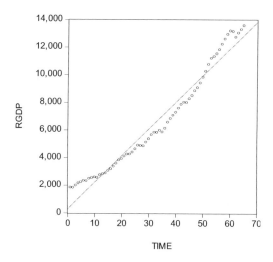

Whereas the quadratic trend overestimates RGDP over the same time frame:

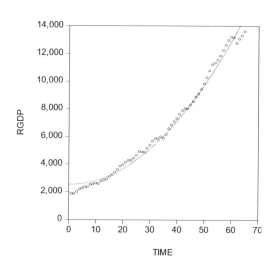

The quadratic trend would have been the better extrapolation had the United States not experienced a severe recession during the forecast period. For this reason, the ex ante forecasts from the quadratic trend are most reliable. Here they are:

$$\text{RGDP(hat)} = 2014.68 + 33.91 \text{ time} + 2.51 \text{ time}^2$$

time	time^2	fore	year
66	66^2	15,181	2013
67	67^2	15,549	2014
68	68^2	15,922	2015
69	69^2	16,299	2016

13.6 Summary

In this chapter we have shown how to make forecasts with regression models. Point and interval forecasts are possible, as are ex ante, ex poste, in-sample, and out-of-sample forecasts. The emphasis was on projecting trend lines with regression models, but our first example showed that almost any regression can be used to make forecasts.

An important point was overlooked in all our examples: If a regression suffers from serial correlation, it should be remedied with generalized least-squares (GLS) before making any forecasts. Remember that serial correlation means the error terms from a regression are related to one another. This relationship could be exploited to improve forecasts from the model.

Consider the case of positive autocorrelation in a regression model that severely overestimated the forecast for last period. In other words, our regression model exhibited a large negative error: ($e_t = Y_t - \hat{Y}_t$). The forecast ($\hat{Y}_t$) was much higher than the actual value (Y_t). It is likely that the same regression will make another negative error next period because positive serial correlation is present. Therefore, we would adjust the forecast for next period downward.

Exactly how much should the forecast be adjusted? There is no need to worry about that. Simply correct for serial correlation with GLS and use the corrected model to make the forecast.

In the previous chapter we pointed out the importance of working with stationary data. Forecasts made from regressions using nonstationary time-series data are unlikely to perform well. The better the regression model, the better the forecasts. Be sure to check that your regression uses stationary data and is not suffering from autocorrelation.

One form of nonstationary data is a random walk. Time-series follow a random walk when the change in the series from one period to the next is random. Consider the following time-series:

$$Y_t = \beta_0 + \beta_1 Y_{t-1} + \varepsilon_t$$

Moving terms, we have:

$$Y_t - \beta_0 - \beta_1 Y_{t-1} = \varepsilon_t$$

If β_0 and $\beta_1 = 0$, then:

$$Y_t - Y_{t-1} = \varepsilon_t$$

This is the definition of a random walk. The change in $Y_t = \varepsilon_t$; where ε_t is a random error term. Thus, the change in Y_t is random. Do not look foolish and use a regression equation to forecast a random time-series. Any forecast in this case is precarious. The appropriate forecast for a random walk is its value in the last period. Indeed, this value would be the forecasts for every period into the future.

To test if a time-series Y_t is a random walk, you can run the regression $Y_t = \hat{\beta}_0 + \hat{\beta}_1 Y_{t-1} + e_t$. If $\hat{\beta}_0 = 0$ and $\hat{\beta}_1 = 1$, then Y_t follows a random walk. Also, random walks have no trend. Therefore, another way to test for a random walk is to run a regression like $Y_t = \hat{\beta}_0 + \hat{\beta}_1 t + e_t$; where t is time. If $\hat{\beta}_1 = 0$, then Y_t may be a random walk.

A random walk with drift occurs when $Y_t = \beta_0 + \beta_1 Y_{t-1} + \varepsilon_t$ and $\beta_1 = 0$ but $\beta_0 \neq 0$. In this case, the expected change in the time-series going forward is $\beta_0 + \varepsilon_t$. The change is random with the addition of the constant β_0. The appropriate forecast of a random walk with drift is its value last period plus the constant $\hat{\beta}_0$. $\hat{\beta}_0$ is added each succeeding period to obtain forecasts into the future.

Terms

Ex ante forecast – A forecast made before the fact, so its accuracy cannot be checked.

Exponential trend – A trend line fitted assuming an exponential growth rate.

Ex poste forecast – A forecast made after the fact, so that its accuracy can be checked.

In-sample forecast – A forecast made for an observation that was used to estimate the forecasting model.

Interval forecast – A prediction that is a range of values, as opposed to one value.

Lin-log trend – A trend line fit assuming a diminishing growth rate.

Log-lin trend – A trend line fit assuming an increasing growth rate.

Margin of error – The SERF times t^c for a confidence interval. The amount a point forecast can be off and not be considered unusual.

Mean absolute deviation – A measure of forecast accuracy given by:

$$MAD = \frac{1}{n} \Sigma \left| Y_t - \hat{Y}_t \right|$$

Mean absolute percentage deviation – A measure of forecast accuracy given by:

$$MAPE = \frac{1}{n} \Sigma \frac{\left|Y_t - \hat{Y}_t\right|}{\left|Y_t\right|}$$

Out-of-sample forecast – A forecast made for an observation not used to estimate the forecasting model.

Point forecast – A prediction that is one value, as opposed to a range of values.

Polynomial trend – A trend line fit assuming a quadratic growth rate.

Random walk – A series of sequential movements in which the magnitude of each move is determined randomly.

Random walk with drift – A series of sequential movements in which the magnitude of each move is some constant amount plus a random amount.

Root mean squared error– A measure of forecast accuracy given by:

$$RMSE = \sqrt{\frac{1}{n} \Sigma (Y_t - \hat{Y}_t)^2}$$

Standard error of the forecast (SERF) – How much a forecast for a specific observation typically varies in repeated sampling.

Theil's inequality coefficient– A measure of forecast accuracy given by:

$$U = \frac{\sqrt{\frac{1}{n} \Sigma (Y_t - \hat{Y}_t)^2}}{\sqrt{\frac{1}{n} \Sigma \hat{Y}_t^2} + \sqrt{\frac{1}{n} \Sigma Y_t^2}}$$

Chapter 13 Problems

1. Using Eviews and the data in QUALLCOMM.XLS, make in-sample forecasts of the price of quallcomm stock for each of the four weeks subsequent to 11/22/1999 (11/29/1999, 12/06/1999, 12/13/1999, and 12/20/1999) using a:

A) linear trend
B) lin-log trend
C) log-lin trend
D) polynomial trend
E) polynomial to the sixth order

(qualprice$_t$ = $\hat{\beta}_0$ + $\hat{\beta}_1$ time$_t$ + $\hat{\beta}_2$ time^2_t + $\hat{\beta}_3$ time^3_t + $\hat{\beta}_4$ time^4_t + $\hat{\beta}_5$ time^5_t + $\hat{\beta}_6$ time^6_t + e$_t$)

F) Which trend provides the least accurate forecasts? Based on …?

qualprice – the closing price of quallcomm stock that week
time – 1, 2, 3, …

2. Using Eviews and the data in MATISSE.XLS, predict the price of a 1,500-square-inch Mattisse painting based on its size using a:

A) linear model
B) lin-log model
C) log-lin model
D) polynomial model
E) Which model provides the least accurate forecasts over all the observations? Based on …?

price – the price of a Matisse painting at auction
size – the size of the painting

3. Using Eviews and the data in RUPT1.XLS:

A) Find the best model you can to explain cor.
B) Is multicollinearity mild, moderate, or severe in your model? Explain.
C) Did multicollinearlity affect your model selection? Explain.
D) Use your model to predict cor for Argentina.
E) Form a 95% confidence interval around your prediction.
F) The average cor for all 48 countries = 5.135. Certainly, it would have been better to rely on this "naïve" forecast than our regression model in the case of Argentina. Would it have been better to forecast this value for all 48 nations instead of relying on our regression model? Explain.

cor – the corruption level in a country 0 lowest to 10 highest
country – country name

ecfree – measure of economic freedom 0 lowest to 5 highest
fines – unpaid traffic fines per diplomat of the nation
indy – year of independence
mil – number of military personnel per 1,000 population
over 65 – percent of the population older than 65
popsq – population per square mile

4. Using Eviews and the data in QSP500.XLS:

A) Run the regression: $\text{dsp500}_t = \hat{\beta}_0 + \hat{\beta}_1 \text{time}_t + e_t$ The results indicate dsp500

    i) has a trend
    ii) does not have a trend

B) Run the regression: $\text{sp500}_t = \hat{\beta}_0 + \hat{\beta}_1 \text{sp500}_{t-1} + e_t$ The results indicate dsp500 is

    i) a random walk
    ii) a random walk with drift
    iii) not a random walk

C) Given the two regressions above and your responses in A) and B), a valid forecast of dsp500 in 1998Q4 is:

    i) 0
    ii) ∞
    iii) -2.2 (its value in 1998Q3)
    iv) 3.4
    v) 2.950129

dsp500 – the quarterly change in the S&P500
time = 1, 2, 3, …

Chapter 14

Forecasting with ARIMA Models

14.1 ARIMA Models

Autoregressive integrated moving average (ARIMA) models, or ARIMA forecasting, are sometimes referred to as the Box-Jenkins approach after the authors of the seminal and authoritative work on the topic (Box and Jenkins 1970). Like trend extrapolation and exponential smoothing, ARIMA models "look back" at past values of the series to be forecasted in order to determine if there are any patterns or consistencies to be exploited. Indeed, ARIMA models are a generalization of exponential smoothing models. The Box-Jenkins approach to forecasting is popular enough so that we will want to consider it in some detail.

ARIMA models attempt to exploit patterns and trends in the past values of a data series to make forecasts of future values. This approach will be fruitless if there are no patterns and trends to exploit. Recent developments in trend analysis with economic data suggest that there may be patterns, but these patterns are continually changing in an unpredictable way. This section considers these developments and their implications for time-series forecasting.

14.2 Autoregressive Models

Let us begin by looking at a simple autoregressive model, the "AR" portion of an ARIMA model. An autoregressive model stipulates that the current value of a data series is a linear function of its past values. Thus, the inflation rate (INFL) might depend on its own values in the previous three years:

$$\text{INFL}_t = \hat{\beta}_0 + \hat{\beta}_1 \text{INFL}_{t-1} + \hat{\beta}_2 \text{INFL}_{t-2} + \hat{\beta}_3 \text{INFL}_{t-3} + e_t$$

where $\hat{\beta}_0$ is a constant term; $\hat{\beta}_1$, $\hat{\beta}_2$, and $\hat{\beta}_3$ are weights given to the three previous values of INFL; e_t is an error term that will be discussed shortly. $\hat{\beta}_0$, $\hat{\beta}_1$, $\hat{\beta}_2$, and $\hat{\beta}_3$ are called the parameters of the model. In order to use the autoregressive equation to make predictions, these parameter values must be determined. Several techniques are applicable for determining these values including ordinary least-squares. More information concerning parameter determination will be given below.

Ignoring the error term, e_t, for the moment, and assuming parameter values have been obtained, one simply plugs in the three past values for INFL to come up with a forecast for current INFL. Or one could plug in the current value of INFL (into INFL_{t-1}) and its two prior values to obtain a forecast for next period's INFL. Astute readers may notice that autoregressive forecasts are very similar to exponentially smoothed forecasts. Both use weighted averages of past values to formulate predictions. In fact, it can be shown that exponential smoothing is just a specific case of autoregressive forecasting. With exponential smoothing the weights are forced to be geometrically declining, while autoregressive models are not restricted in this manner.

The error term in the autoregressive formulation denotes the fact that the relationship between INFL and its past values is not exact. There is some randomness. The difference between what we would expect INFL to be, based on its past values, and its actual value is e_t. Hopefully, these error terms (there is one for each time period) are relatively small. Large error terms would indicate that the autoregressive model is not working well or, in econometric jargon, does not have a good fit. A model that does not fit well will probably, but not necessarily, forecast poorly.

Perhaps a better fit can be achieved if more previous values of INFL are included in the equation. Techniques have been developed to help determine the appropriate number of lagged values to include in an autoregressive model. Even if these are employed, trial and error is typically a part of the determination process. If more past values of INFL improve the performance of the model, they are included.

Let us say that we have annual data for INFL from 1952 to 2012 and that the values of the parameters for our autoregressive model were determined to be:

$$\hat{\beta}_0 = 3.28; \ \hat{\beta}_1 = 0.92; \ \hat{\beta}_2 = -0.34; \ \hat{\beta}_3 = 0.24.$$

We are then in a position to derive a "forecast" for 2012:

$$INFL_t = \hat{\beta}_0 + \hat{\beta}_1 INFL_{t-1} + \hat{\beta}_2 INFL_{t-2} + \hat{\beta}_3 INFL_{t-3} + e_t$$

$$FORE(INFL_{2012}) = 3.28 + 0.92 \ INFL_{2011} - 0.34 \ INFL_{2010} + 0.24 \ INFL_{2009}$$

$$FORE(INFL_{2012}) = 3.28 + 0.92 \ (3.14) \quad - 0.34 \ (1.64) \quad + 0.24 \ (-0.32) = 2.83$$

This is known as an "in-sample" forecast since 2012 was one of the years used to estimate the model. In addition, this is an "ex poste" forecast since 2012 has already passed and our forecast can be checked against the actual value of INFL 2012, which was 2.08. The difference between actual INFL and the forecast, $2.08 - 2.83 = -0.75$, is the value of e_t, the error term for 2012.

A prediction for INFL in 2013 (1.82) is obtained in a similar fashion since we have data for INFL in 2012, 2011, and 2010:

$$FORE(INFL_{2013}) = 3.28 + 0.92 \ INFL_{2012} - 0.34 \ INFL_{2011} + 0.24 \ INFL_{2010}$$

$$FORE(INFL_{2013}) = 3.28 + 0.92 \ (2.08) \quad - 0.34 \ (3.14) \quad + 0.24 \ (1.64) = 1.82$$

Forecasts for 2014 and beyond can be made by employing a "dynamic" procedure. To formulate a forecast for 2014 we need the three previous values for INFL. We do not, however, have a value for INFL in 2013 (assuming our data set only runs through 2012), unless we use our forecasted value of 1.82:

$$FORE(INFL_{2014}) = 3.28 + 0.92 \ INFL_{2013} - 0.34 \ INFL_{2012} + 0.24 \ INFL_{2011}$$

$$FORE(INFL_{2014}) = 3.28 + 0.92 \ (1.82) \quad - 0.34 \ (2.08) \quad + 0.24 \ (3.14) = 2.32$$

Thus we obtain a forecast for 2014 (2.32). To get a prediction for 2015 we may use the two forecasted of values of INFL in 2014 and 2013 along with the actual value from 2012:

$$\text{FORE(INFL}_{2015}) = 3.28 + 0.92 \text{ INFL}_{2014} - 0.34 \text{ INFL}_{2013} + 0.24 \text{ INFL}_{2012}$$

$$\text{FORE(INFL}_{2015}) = 3.28 + 0.92\,(2.32) \quad - 0.34\,(1.82) \quad + 0.24\,(2.08) = 2.60$$

This dynamic process can be carried on ad infinitum, but the accuracy of the forecasts may degenerate as we use forecasts to obtain more forecasts. On the other hand, it is possible for the forecast errors of successive periods to cancel each other out. More typically, the forecast errors tend to accumulate.

14.3 Autoregressive Moving Average Models

But the fun is just beginning. We may add some moving average terms (MA) to the autoregressive (AR) equation to obtain an autoregressive moving average (ARMA) model.

Moving average terms are nothing more than the previous forecast errors. Remember that each time a forecast is made, there will be an error term, e_t. These errors may help to improve subsequent forecasts. For instance, if an autoregressive model gave a large overestimate of INFL last period, perhaps next period's forecast should be adjusted downward. In fact, it might pay to consider not only the previous forecast error, but errors going back several periods. There may be some sort of pattern in the previous forecast errors that can be exploited to improve the next forecast.

ARMA models create forecasts based on the past values of the data series and the past forecast errors. By including moving average terms in the analysis, we are attempting to improve forecast accuracy by taking into account previous forecast errors.

$$\text{INFL}_t = \hat{\beta}_0 + \hat{\beta}_1 \text{ INFL}_{t-1} + \hat{\beta}_2 \text{ INFL}_{t-2} + \hat{\beta}_3 \text{ INFL}_{t-3} + \hat{\gamma}_1 e_{t-1} + \hat{\gamma}_2 e_{t-2} + e_t$$

The moving average terms are represented by e_{t-1} and e_{t-2}. Each moving average term has a parameter attached to it -- $\hat{\gamma}_1$ and $\hat{\gamma}_2$. The values of the moving average terms, as discussed, are the forecast errors generated by the equation in the past. For instance, if the ARMA equation overestimated INFL by 0.75 in 2012, then -0.75 would be plugged in for e_{t-1} when t is 2013. The forecast error in 2011 would be the value substituted in for e_{t-2}.

The values of the parameters attached to the moving average terms need to be determined. The determination procedure will be described a bit later. For now it is enough to understand that $\hat{\gamma}_1$ and $\hat{\gamma}_2$ represent weights attached to the prior forecast errors.

An ARMA model may have one or a few moving average terms. The example under consideration here has two: e_{t-1} and e_{t-2}. The optimal number of moving average terms to include in any given model is not always easily determined. There are some procedures that will help, but, as with the number of autoregressive terms, trial and error is necessary. If the forecast error from two periods ago improves the current forecast, include it in the model. In essence, one needs to figure out how far to look back. How many previous forecast errors should be considered? It is unusual for ARMA models to contain more than two or three moving average terms.

Despite the inclusion of the moving average terms, the ARMA model is still not perfectly accurate. It will have its own forecast errors--the ε_t's. Ideally, these will be smaller than the forecast errors from the autoregressive model. If not, it would be better to stick with the simple autoregressive model since the inclusion of the moving average terms is not reducing the size of the forecast errors.

14.4 Integration

Statistical theory indicates that ARMA models will not provide accurate forecasts unless the data series being forecasted has some special characteristics. Specifically, the time-series under consideration should be "stationary." It will pay to develop an intuitive grasp of this concept because it sheds light on how ARMA models work.

In the best circumstances, time-series regressions will use only stationary data -- time-series whose basic properties do not change over time. Specifically, a time-series, X, is said to be stationary if:

1) the mean of X is constant over time
2) the variance of X is constant over time
3) the correlation between X_t and X_{t-k} (for all k) is constant.

If one or more of these properties is not met, then X is nonstationary. The use of nonstationary time-series in regressions may result in spurious correlation and that means biased estimates of the structural parameters.

The graph below shows real GDP (RGDP) over the years since 1948. This time-series exhibits a pronounced upward trend and therefore cannot have a constant mean.

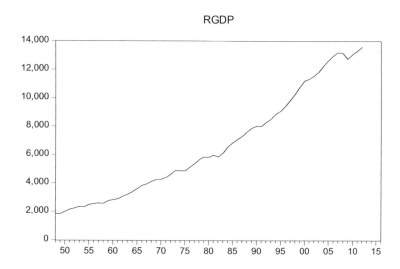

Whether or not the variance of RGDP is constant over time is difficult to tell from visual inspection. We could take the variance of the first half of the time-series and compare it to the variance of the second half.

There is no way to tell from visual inspection whether or not observations a given distance apart have a constant correlation. Checking the correlation between X_t and X_{t-k}

requires a correlogram -- a chart that shows the degree to which observations k spaces apart are correlated. Correlograms that do not approach zero quickly indicate nonstationary data.

It is quite tedious to obtain a correlogram by hand and we are glad to have computers do this for us. Given time-series data such as RGDP, take each pair of observations that are adjacent. This means taking the first and second observation, the second and third, the third and fourth, and so on. Now calculate the correlation coefficient (r) between all these pairs.

We are just getting started. Now take observations of RGDP that are a space apart. These are observations one and three, two and four, three, and five, and so on. Now calculate the correlation coefficient (r) between all these pairs. Repeat this for all pairs of observations up to 12 spaces apart (k = 12).

k	r
1	0.99
2	0.97
3	0.96
4	0.94
5	0.93
6	0.91
7	0.90
8	0.89
9	0.87
10	0.86
11	0.85
12	0.83

The table above indicates that adjacent observations in RGDP are highly correlated (r = 0.99). Even observations twelve years ago are highly correlated with this year's level of RGDP (r = 0.83).

If we make a chart from the table above, we have a correlogram:

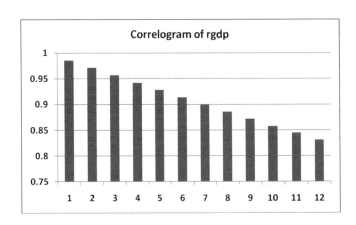

The vertical axis of the correlogram reports the correlation coefficients from the table, while the horizontal axis measures k. Correlograms that do not quickly decay toward r = 0, such as the one above, are typical of nonstationary time-series. Regressions that use nonstationary data will probably suffer from spurious correlation and yield biased results.

The Q statistic, developed by Ljung and Box (1978), can be used to determine if a time-series is autocorrelated up to lag k:

$$Q = n(n = 2)\Sigma \frac{r_k^2}{n-k} \text{ ; where } r_k^2 \text{ is the correlation between observation k spaces apart.}$$

The hypothesis test using the Q statistic is sometimes referred to as a "portmanteau" test, since the null hypothesis is that there is no autocorrelation in the time-series up to and including lag k.

1) Ho: There is no autocorrelation through lag k
   Ha: There is at least one significant autocorrelation through lag k
2) 5%
3) If $Q > \chi^{2c}$, then reject Ho
4) Obtain Q and χ^{2c}
5) Reject or Do Not Reject Ho

If a time-series is nonstationary, then it may be best to work with the first differences of the data. First differences are the change from one period to the next in the data series. The graphs below depict the first differences in RGDP (FD1RGDP):

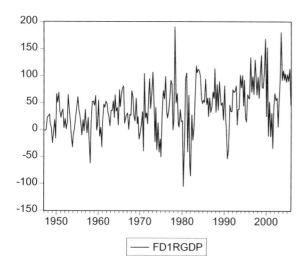

Visual inspection suggests a constant mean (perhaps), but it appears as if the latter half of the line has a larger variance than the first half. It is a tough call. The correlogram suggests significant correlations between observations at k =1 through 4. In other words, the first differences in RGDP may be stationary since the correlations become insignificant after four lags.

k	r
1	0.42
2	0.38
3	0.21
4	0.20
5	0.11
6	0.13
7	0.07
8	0.02
9	0.14
10	0.11
11	0.10
12	-0.04

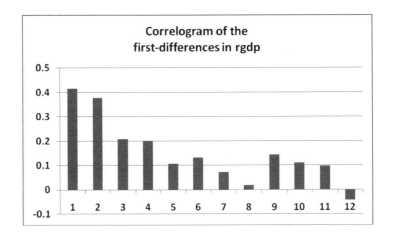

The second differences in RGDP (FD2RGDP) are the differences in the first differences, or the change in the change, in RGDP.

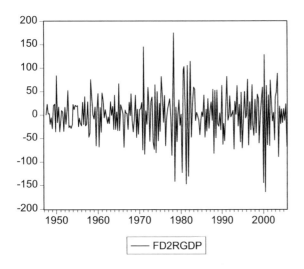

The correlogram suggests that the second differences are stationary since they become insignificant after $k = 1$.

k	r
1	-0.47
2	0.12
3	-0.14
4	0.08
5	-0.11
6	0.07
7	-0.01
8	-0.15
9	0.14
10	-0.02
11	0.12
12	-0.18

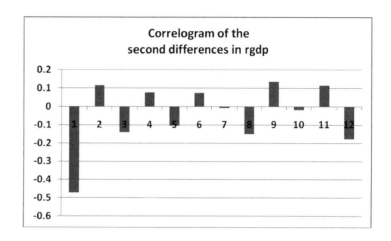

It appears as if any regressions that use RGDP are using a nonstationary variable. This is a serious allegation because the results of any such regressions may be biased. It would be better to use the first differences in RGDP since they appear to be stationary according to a check of the correlogram.

The premier test for stationarity is the Dickey-Fuller, or unit root, test (Dickey and Fuller 1979). To test if a time-series, X_t, is stationary:

A) run $(X_t - X_{t-1}) = \hat{\beta}_0 + \hat{\beta}_1 X_{t-1} + e_t$

B) perform a negative sign test on $\hat{\beta}_1$

    1) Ho: $\beta_1 = 0$ (X is nonstationary)   Ha: $\beta_1 < 0$ (X is stationary)
    2) 5%
    3) If t-ratio $< -t^c*$, reject Ho
    4) The t-ratio is the usual one, but t^c* is about 60% higher than tc from the usual t table. As n approaches infinity, t^c* approaches 2.86 from higher levels.
    5) State the results of the test

Using the data on RGDP as an example, we have:

A) $(RGDP_t - RGDP_{t-1}) = 91.97 + 0.01\ RGDP_{t-1} + e_t$
                                  (2.70) ←t-ratio

B) negative sign test on $\hat{\beta}_1$:

1) Ho: $\beta_1 = 0$ (X is nonstationary)   Ha: $\beta_1 < 0$ (X is stationary)
2) 5%
3) If $2.70 < -2.91^*$, reject Ho
4) Eviews gives the t-ratio and t^c for the Dickey-Fuller test
5) Do Not Reject Ho; RGDP is nonstationary

Now let's test if the first differences in RGDP are stationary:

A) $(d(RGDP_t) - d(RGDP)_{t-1}) = 114.53 - 0.60\ d(RGDP)_{t-1} + e_t$
$\qquad\qquad\qquad\qquad\qquad\qquad$ (-5.19)   ←t-ratio

B) negative sign test on $\hat{\beta}_1$:

1) Ho: $\hat{\beta}_1 = 0$ (X is nonstationary)   Ha: $\hat{\beta}_1 < 0$ (X is stationary)
2) 5%
3) If $-5.19 < -2.91^*$, reject Ho
4) Eviews gives the t-ratio and t^c for the Dickey-Fuller test
5) Reject Ho; the first differences in RGDP are stationary

The augmented Dickey-Fuller test for a unit root (i.e., nonstationarity) adds a lagged dependent variable to the right-hand side:

$$(X_t - X_{t-1}) = \hat{\beta}_0 + \hat{\beta}_1 X_{t-1} + \hat{\beta}_2 (X_{t-1} - X_{t-2}) + e_t$$

It is left to the reader as an exercise to determine if the augmented Dickey-Fuller test gives the same results concerning the stationarity of RGDP and the first differences of RGDP.

ARMA models perform poorly when applied to nonstationary time-series. Most economic data exhibit trends and are therefore nonstationary. This, as it turns out, is not an impediment to the use of ARMA models in economic forecasting because it is a simple matter to take first differences to obtain a stationary time-series. Occasionally, the first differences of a time-series will continue to exhibit a trend. Then the differences of the differences, what is known as second differences, may be taken. Indeed, a data series may be differenced any number of times until a constant mean is achieved. Economic data rarely require third differences.

It is somewhat of a misnomer, but taking differences to attain stationarity is known as "integration" in time-series forecasting. Thus an autoregressive moving average (ARMA) model becomes an autoregressive integrated moving average (ARIMA) model when the data series to be forecasted is differenced.

To summarize this section to this point, ARMA models are not applicable to time-series that are not stationary. Stationary time-series meet three requirements: they have a constant (1) mean, (2) variance, and (3) correlation between observations a given number of periods apart. One can consider correlograms or apply a Dickey-Fuller test to determine if a time-series is stationary. If a time-series is not stationary, it should be differenced one or more times until stationarity is achieved. In ARMA modeling, this differencing process is called "integration."

Finally, correlograms and their cousins, partial correlograms, can suggest how many autoregressive and moving average terms are appropriate for a given time-series. Partial correlations are the degree to which observations k spaces apart are linearly correlated, net of the correlation explained by the intervening k-1 observations. If a time-series is stationary, then the patterns displayed by the correlogram and partial correlogram can be interpreted according to the table below:

Correlogram/Partial correlogram	Interpretation
Decays/ Cuts off abruptly	AR terms only
Decays/ Decays	AR and MA terms
Cuts off abruptly/Decays	MA terms only
Cuts off abruptly/Cuts off abruptly	White noise

14.5 A Complete Example

Let us employ an ARIMA model to forecast INFL. To do so, all that is required are the past values of INFL. The more past data available for the modeling procedure, the better. ARIMA forecasters prefer using at least fifty observations covering an uninterrupted sample period of the immediate past. This is necessary to firmly establish the correlations between observations. Also, the favored procedure for estimating the parameters of an ARIMA model is more reliable the greater the number of past observations. The economic literature is sprinkled with examples of ARIMA models that are estimated with fewer than fifty observations, but these typically include a caution regarding the paucity of data.

Say we have 64 annual observations of INFL from 1949 to 2012. The first task is to discern if these data are stationary. Here is the augmented Dickey-Fuller test:

A) $(INFL_t - INFL_{t-1}) = 1.12 - 0.30\ INFL_{t-1} + 1.12\ (INFL_{t-1} - INFL_{t-2}) + e_t$
$\qquad\qquad\qquad (-3.35)\quad \leftarrow \text{t-ratio}$

B) negative sign test on $\hat{\beta}_1$:

1) Ho: $\beta_1 = 0$ (INFL is nonstationary)   Ha: $\beta_1 < 0$ (INFL is stationary)
2) 5%
3) If t-ratio < -t^c*, reject Ho
4)   -2.06 > -2.91
5) Do Not Reject Ho; INFL is nonstationary

Perhaps the first differences are stationary:

1) Ho: $\beta_1 = 0$ (D(INFL) is nonstationary)   Ha: $\beta_1 < 0$ (D(INFL) is stationary)
2) 5%
3) If t-ratio < -t^c*, reject Ho
4)   -8.75 < -2.91
5) Reject Ho; D(INFL) is stationary

So we will work with the first differences of INFL. The next step is to determine how many autoregressive and how many moving average terms to include in the model. There are several procedures that can help with this determination, such as considering the patterns of the correlogram and partial correlogram:

Autocorrelation	Partial Correlation		AC	PAC	Q-Stat	Prob
		1	0.050	0.050	0.1642	0.685
		2	-0.328	-0.331	7.3749	0.025
		3	-0.194	-0.175	9.9435	0.019
		4	-0.112	-0.240	10.822	0.029
		5	0.138	0.015	12.164	0.033
		6	0.197	0.055	14.943	0.021
		7	0.006	0.009	14.945	0.037
		8	-0.182	-0.110	17.423	0.026
		9	-0.072	-0.002	17.815	0.037
		10	0.109	0.066	18.726	0.044
		11	0.101	0.036	19.534	0.052
		12	-0.039	-0.058	19.654	0.074
		13	-0.064	0.002	19.995	0.095
		14	-0.068	-0.033	20.383	0.119
		15	0.008	-0.007	20.389	0.158
		16	0.021	-0.091	20.427	0.202
		17	0.049	0.011	20.643	0.243
		18	-0.007	-0.018	20.647	0.298
		19	-0.029	0.015	20.727	0.352
		20	-0.058	-0.087	21.043	0.395
		21	-0.081	-0.112	21.681	0.418
		22	-0.011	-0.084	21.693	0.478
		23	0.272	0.251	29.289	0.171
		24	0.047	-0.020	29.525	0.201
		25	-0.231	-0.127	35.287	0.083
		26	0.004	0.112	35.289	0.106
		27	0.012	0.037	35.306	0.131
		28	0.031	-0.015	35.416	0.158

The second and third autocorrelations appear to be significant while the second and fourth partial autocorrelations appear significant. The Q statistics, and their p-values in the last column, indicate that autocorrelations in the first differences of INFL are significant beginning at k = 2. It is hard to say whether the autocorrelations cut off abruptly or fade. The same goes for the partial autocorrelations. From this we learned that the first differences in INFL are autocorrelated beginning at lag 2, but not much more. It looks like trial and error will have to be our main model determination technique.

If adding an extra autoregressive or moving average term improves the forecast accuracy of the model it should be included. Once we settle on a model, we can see if the residuals are white noise and check forecast accuracy by having the model generate ex poste forecasts for previous years.

For first differences in annual INFL, the model below appeared to work well:

$$INFL_t = \hat{\beta}_0 + \hat{\beta}_1 INFL_{t-1} + \hat{\beta}_2 INFL_{t-2} + \hat{\gamma}_1 e_{t-1} + \varepsilon_t$$

The model above can be referred to as an ARIMA(2,1,1): there are 2 autoregressive terms, first differences were taken, and there is 1 moving average term. In-sample, ex poste forecasts were made for each year from 2000 to 2012. Here are the summary statistics from those forecasts:

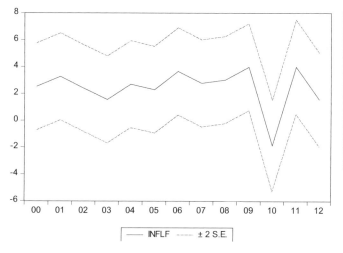

Forecast: INFLF	
Actual: INFL	
Forecast sample: 2000 2012	
Included observations: 13	
Root Mean Squared Error	1.664095
Mean Absolute Error	1.113577
Mean Abs. Percent Error	139.3412
Theil Inequality Coefficient	0.298793
Bias Proportion	0.000882
Variance Proportion	0.062806
Covariance Proportion	0.936312

The root mean squared error and mean absolute error indicate that our forecasts are typically off the mark by about 1.1 to 1.7 percent. This is nothing to brag about since the absolute value of the differences in INFL average 1.44. Theil's inequality coefficient is not encouraging either. However, Theil's proportions are good and the residuals of the model are not autocorrelated according to a Lagrange multiplier test:

     1) Ho: no serial correlation   Ha: serial correlation exists
     2) 5%
     3) If nR2 > χc, then reject Ho (d.f. = # of lagged residual terms = 1)
     4) 0.023 < 3.84
     5) Do Not Reject Ho; there is no serial correlation

We will re-estimate our ARIMA(2,1,1) model from 1949 to 1999 and then consider out-of-sample, dynamic forecasts for 2000 to 2013. These forecasts are dynamic in the sense that we will only use actual data for INFL up to 1999. After that, we will use our forecasts of INFL in the model. For example, to forecast INFL in 2010 we will need INFL in 2009 and 2008. Instead of using the actual values of INFL for those years, we will our forecasted values. In this way, our forecast of INFL in 2013 will be made 13 years ahead.

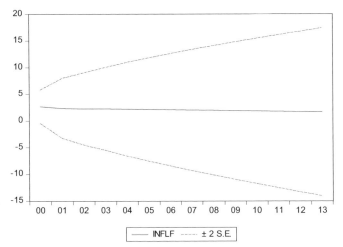

Forecast: INFLF	
Actual: INFL	
Forecast sample: 2000 2013	
Included observations: 13	
Root Mean Squared Error	1.081313
Mean Absolute Error	0.882391
Mean Abs. Percent Error	78.16469
Theil Inequality Coefficient	0.223936
Bias Proportion	0.139677
Variance Proportion	0.529827
Covariance Proportion	0.330496

Interestingly enough, our out-of-sample dynamic forecasts turn out to be more accurate than the in-sample static forecasts. All of the measures of accuracy are better, although Theil's proportions are slightly worse for the dynamic forecasts.

14.6 The Maximum Likelihood Procedure

We have ignored exactly how the values for the structural parameters are obtained in ARIMA models. Our usual approach, ordinary least-squares (OLS), will not work. OLS minimizes the sum of the error terms squared. This is because the values to use for the moving average terms (the lagged e_t's) are determined simultaneously with the error terms for the ARIMA model (the e_t's).

Fortunately, readily available computer software handles the number-crunching. The predominant technique for parameter determination in ARIMA models is known as the "maximum likelihood" procedure. This procedure selects parameter values that minimize the Σe_t^2. This is a complicated task since Σe_t^2 depends on the e_t's, whose values depend on the values of $\hat{\beta}_0$, $\hat{\beta}_1$, $\hat{\beta}_2$, and $\hat{\gamma}_1$. And these values, in turn, depend on the e_t's. Therefore, all these values ($\hat{\beta}_0$, $\hat{\beta}_1$, $\hat{\beta}_2$, $\hat{\gamma}_1$ and the e_t's) must be estimated simultaneously. Here is how the maximum likelihood procedure accomplishes that:

1) Initial values for $\hat{\beta}_0$, $\hat{\beta}_1$, $\hat{\beta}_2$, and $\hat{\gamma}_1$ are selected. Usually the forecaster has no clue as to what the appropriate values might be so they are all set equal to 0.5 to begin with. In any case, the selection of initial values is arbitrary.

2) The initial values are used to generate "forecasts" for the sample period. Since we have the actual INFL data for the sample period, these forecasts can be checked for accuracy.

3) The values of the parameters are revised in accordance with the maximum likelihood algorithm, which reduces the sum of the squared forecast errors.

4) Return to step (2) with the revised parameter estimates.

5) The procedure stops when the revisions made to the parameter values in step (3) are insignificant.

The maximum likelihood procedure yields values for $\hat{\beta}_0$, $\hat{\beta}_1$, $\hat{\beta}_2$, and $\hat{\gamma}_1$ that are most probable given the values of INFL and the model.

14.7 Final Thoughts

ARIMA forecasts of economic and financial time-series perform well relative to regression analysis and even large-scale econometric models. Since these models look to the past to predict the future, sharp turning points are hardly ever foreseen. However, regression analysis and large-scale econometric models do not predict turning points well either.

Notice that ARIMA forecasts require no data except for the time-series to be forecasted. This is a major advantage of this technique and allows to make forecasts into the indefinite future. We only have data to 2012 for INFL, but we can use the forecasted future values to extend the data set. Here are forecasts for INFL to 2016:

2013	2.419623
2014	2.446868
2015	2.297717
2016	2.278627

Terms

ARIMA model – A time-series model that may employ autoregressive and moving average terms in addition to being differenced any number of times.

Autoregressive model – A time-series model with the lagged dependent variable as an explanatory variable.

Correlation – The degree to which two variables are linearly related.

Correlogram – A chart showing the correlations between observations in a time-series any given number of spaces apart.

First differences – The change from period to period in a time-series.

Integration – When a time-series is differenced one or more times to make it stationary.

Maximum likelihood procedure – A procedure for estimating the parameters of a regression model.

Moving average term – The lagged error term of a regression used as an explanatory variable.

Partial autocorrelation – The degree to which observations in a time-series any given number of spaces apart are correlated net of the correlation of the intervening observations.

Partial correlogram – A chart showing the partial autocorrelations of a time-series for observations any number of spaces apart.

Q statistic – A test used to determine if a time-series is autocorrelated up to a specified number of lags.

Second differences – The change from period to period of the first differences of a time-series.

Stationary time-series – A time-series with constant mean, variance, and correlation between observations k spaces apart; where k is any integer.

Chapter 14 Problems

1. Use Eviews and the data in RGDP.XLS to answer the following:

A) Produce a correlogram of SP500. Does it suggest the levels of SP500 are stationary? Explain.
B) Produce a correlogram of the first differences of SP500. Does it suggest the first differences of SP500 are stationary? Explain.
C) Do an augmented Dickey-Fuller test on the levels of SP500. Show the 5-step procedure.
D) Do an augmented Dickey-Fuller test on the first differences of SP500. Show the 5-step procedure.
E) Working with the first differences in SP500, what sort of model is suggested by the pattern of the correlogram and partial correlogram?
      i) purely autoregressive
      ii) purely moving average
      iii) autoregressive and moving average
      iv) neither autoregressive nor moving average since the time-series is white noise
F) Find an appropriately specified ARIMA model for the first differences of SP500 and fill in your result here: ARIMA(?,1,?)
G) Use the model you found to make an in-sample, ex poste forecast of SP500 (not the first differences) for 2012. Fill in the values below:

   Forecast of SP500 in 2012 = _____

   Standard error of this forecast = _____

   Forecast error = _____

H) Make out-of-sample forecasts for SP500 from 2013 to 2016 and paste those here:

I) How confident are you in these forecasts? Explain.

2. Use Eviews and the data in RGDP.XLS to answer the following:

A) Produce a correlogram of cpi. Does it suggest the levels of cpi are stationary? Explain.
B) Produce a correlogram of the first differences of cpi. Does it suggest the first differences of cpi are stationary? Explain.
C) Do an augmented Dickey-Fuller test on the levels of cpi. Show the 5-step procedure.
D) Do an augmented Dickey-Fuller test on the first differences of cpi. Show the 5-step procedure.
E) Working with the second differences in cpi, what sort of model is suggested by the pattern of the correlogram and partial correlogram?

       i) Purely autoregressive
       ii) Purely moving average
       iii) Putoregressive and moving average
       iv) Neither autoregressive nor moving average since the time-series is white noise

F) Find an appropriately specified ARIMA model for the second differences of cpi and fill in your result here: ARIMA(?,2,?)
G) Use the model you found to make an in-sample, ex poste forecast of cpi (not the second differences) for 2012. Fill in the values below:

Forecast of cpi in 2012 = _____

Standard error of this forecast = _____

Forecast error = _____

H) Make out-of-sample forecasts for cpi from 2013 to 2016 and paste those here:

I) How confident are you in these forecasts? Explain.

Test Yourself on Chapters 13 and 14

1. Label each statement below TRUE or FALSE.

A) To calculate the standard error of an in-sample, point forecast made from a multiple regression, use:

$$SERF = SER\sqrt{1 + \frac{1}{n} + \frac{(X_f - \overline{X})}{\Sigma(X_i - \overline{X})^2}}$$

B) Theil's bias proportion will always be zero for in-sample regression forecasts over the entire sample period.
C) An ex ante forecast cannot be in-sample.
D) It is possible to estimate an ARIMA(2,1,0) with OLS.

E) An ARIMA(3,1,2) model will yield different dynamic forecasts if the forecast period is 2010 to 2015 rather than 2011 to 2015.

F) To make ex ante, out-of-sample, point forecasts for periods t+1 and t+2 using a large-scale econometric model with data through time t, one must assume values for the exogenous variables in periods t+1 and t+2.

G) If a regression suffers from serial correlation, then forecasts based on this regression can be improved by exploiting the relationship between the error terms.

H) To develop an ARIMA model and make forecasts from it, no data are required other than the time-series to be forecasted.

I) Once a time-series has been established to be a random walk, it is pointless to develop a regression model to make forecasts of the time-series.

J) A random walk with drift is a time-series with a trend.

2. Use Eviews and the data in TC.XLS to answer the following:

A) Fit a linear trend to TC using all but the last 5 months of data. Make ex poste, out-of-sample forecasts for the last 5 months of data. For just those 5 forecasts:
   - i) RMSE =
   - ii) MAD =
   - iii) MAPE =
   - iv) Theil's U =
   - v) Point forecast of TC in DEC 2012 =
   - vi) The forecast error =
   - vii) The standard error of this forecast (SERF) =
   - viii) 95% confidence interval for point forecast =

B) Fit an increasing growth rate trend line to TC using all but the last 5 months of data. Make ex poste, out-of-sample forecasts for the last 5 months of data. For just those 5 forecasts:
   - i) RMSE =
   - ii) MAD =
   - iii) MAPE =
   - iv) Theil's U =
   - v) Point forecast of TC in DEC 2012 =
   - vi) The forecast error =
   - vii) The standard error of this forecast (SERF) =
   - viii) 95% confidence interval for point forecast =

C) If you had to make ex ante, out-of-sample, point forecasts, which of the two models above would you choose? Explain why.

D) Re-estimate the model you selected in part C) above using data from JAN 1985 through DEC 2012. Use this model to make out-of-sample, point forecasts for the 12 months of 2013 and paste those forecasts here:

3. Use Eviews and the data in WHYZEE.XLS to answer the following:

A) Does WHY follow a random walk, a random walk with drift, or neither? Explain how you reached your conclusion.

B) Based on your response above, make forecasts of WHY for 2013 through 2020.

C) Does ZEE follow a random walk, a random walk with drift, or neither? Explain how you reached your conclusion.

D) Based on your response above, make forecasts of ZEE for 2013 through 2020.

References

Andersen, Leonall C., and Jordan, Jerry L. 1969. "Monetary and Fiscal Actions: A Test of Their Relative Importance in Economic Stabilization." *Federal Reserve Bank of St. Louis Review* 51(4): 12–16.

Box, George, and Jenkins, Gwilym. 1970. *Time Series Analysis: Forecasting and Control*. San Francisco: Holden-Day.

Breusch, T. S. 1978. "Testing for Autocorrelation in Dynamic Linear Models." *Australian Economic Papers* 17:334–355.

Caudill, Steven. 1990. "Econometrics in Theory and Practice." *Eastern Economic Journal* 16(3): 249–256.

Dasgupta, S., Laplante, B., Wang, H., and Wheeler, D. 2002. "Confronting the Environmental Kuznets Curve."*Journal of Economic Perspectives* 16(1): 147–168.

Dickey, D. A., and Fuller, W. A. 1979. "Distribution of the Estimators for Autoregressive Time Series with a Unit Root." *Journal of the American Statistical Association* 74:427–431.

Durbin, J. 1970. "Testing for Serial Correlation in Least-Squares Regression When Some of the Regressors Are Lagged Dependent Variables." *Econometrica* 38:410–421.

Durbin, J., and Watson, G. S. 1951. "Testing for Serial Correlation in Least-Squares Regression." *Biometrika* 38:159–177.

Godfrey, L. G. 1978. "Testing against General Autoregressive and Moving Average Error Models When the Regressors Include Lagged Dependent Variables." *Econometrica* 46:1293–1302.

Granger, C. W. J. 1969. "Investigating Causal Relations by Econometric Models and Cross-Spectral Methods." *Econometrica* 37:24–36.

Keynes, John Maynard. 1936. *The General Theory of Employment, Interest, and Money*. New York: Macmillan.

Koyck, L. M. 1954. *Distributed Lags and Investment Analysis*. Amsterdam: North-Holland Publishing Company.

Leamer, Edward. 1983. "Let's Take the Con Out of Econometrics." *American Economic Review* 73(1): 31–43.

Levitt, Steven D., and Dubner, Stephen J. 2009. *Freakonomics: A Rogue Economist Explores the Hidden Side of Everything*. New York: Harper Perennial.

Ljung, G. M., and Box, G. E. P. 1978. "On a Measure of a Lack of Fit in Time Series Models." *Biometrika* 65(2): 297–303.

Marshall, Alfred. 1890. *Principles of Economics*. London: Macmillan.

Newey, W. K., and West, K. D. 1987. "A Simple, Positive Semi-Definite Heteroskedasticity and Autocorrelation Consistent Covariance Matrix." *Econometrica* 55(3): 703–708.

Okun, Arthur M. 1962. "Potential GNP: Its Measurement and Significance." *Proceedings of the Business and Economic Statistics Section of the American Statistical Association*, 89–104.

Park, R. E. 1966. "Estimation with Heteroscedastic Error Terms." *Econometrica* 34(4): 888.

Ramsey, J. B. 1969. "Tests of Specification Errors in Classical Linear Least Squares Regression Analysis." *Journal of the Royal Statistical Society, Series B* 31:350–371.

Spector, Lee C., and Mazzeo, Michael. 1980. "Probit Analysis and Economic Education." *Journal of Economic Education* 11(2): 37–44.

Theil, Henri. 1971. *Principles of Econometrics*. New York: Wiley.

White, H. 1980. "A Heteroskedasticity Consistent Covariance Matrix Estimator and a Direct Test of Heteroskedasticity." *Econometrica* 48(4): 817–818.

Solutions to Odd End-of-Chapter Problems

Chapter 1 Odd Problem Solutions

1. The hours of study (per weekday) and GPA of three students are given below:

hours	GPA
2	2
4	3
2	3

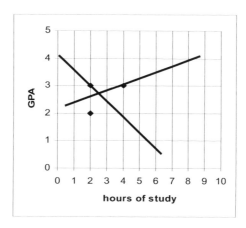

A) Draw a line through these dots so that the sum of the vertical distances from the dots to the line equals zero. When the dot lies above the line the distance is positive. When the dot lies below the line the distance is negative. Can you draw another line that meets this criterion? **Any line (except perfectly vertical) passing through hours = 2.67 and GPA = 2.67 works. Two such lines are pictured above.**

B) Now draw a line through the dots so that the sum of the absolute value of the vertical distances between the dots and the line is minimized. Can you draw another line that meets this criterion? **The minimum is one. Any line passing thru GPA = 3 and study hours = 4 and in between the two lines shown will yield this minimum.**

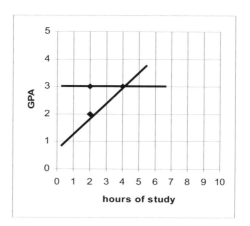

3. Suppose we estimate the following regression: CONS = -1218 + 0.97 INC + u

    A) What is the predicted value of CONS in 1960 given INC = $9,735 in 1960?

CONS = -1218 + 0.97 (9,735) = $8,224.95

    B) Actual CONS in 1960 equals $8,837. Give several reasons why the forecast may
        be off from the actual.

1) Important explanatory variables may be excluded from the analysis.
2) The relationship between CONS and INC may have some randomness.
3) The data may contain errors.
4) Minor or immeasurable variables may be excluded from the analysis.
5) The relationship between CONS and INC may be non-linear.

5. A) Specify an econometric model to test the theory that an increase in the money
        supply has no effect on real GDP.

    RealGDP = β_0 + β_1 MS + u

    B) What does this theory imply about the value of β_1?

    β_1 **= 0.**

7. A professor gathers data on student performance in college and the number of
alcoholic drinks students consume to determine if alcohol consumption affects
performance in college. Can this research be classified as econometrics? Explain why or
why not. **It can be classified as econometrics because it considers how student
choices affect student achievement. Do students sacrifice academic performance
when they drink? The research could also be considered ""Sociometrics."**

Chapter 2   Odd Problem Solutions

1. Which of the following is (are) NOT correct?

A) $Y_i = \beta_0 + \beta_1 X_i + e_i$ D) $Y_i = \hat{\beta}_0 + \hat{\beta}_1 X_i + e_i$ G) $Y_i = \beta_0 + \beta_1 X_i$

B) $\hat{Y}_i = \beta_0 + \beta_1 X_i + e_i$ E) $\hat{Y}_i = \hat{\beta}_0 + \hat{\beta}_1 X_i + e_i$ H) $\hat{Y}_i = \beta_0 + \beta_1 X_i + u_i$

C) $Y_i = \beta_0 + \beta_1 X_i + u_i$ F) $Y_i = \hat{\beta}_0 + \hat{\beta}_1 X_i + u_i$ I) $E(Y_i|X_i) = \hat{\beta}_0 + \hat{\beta}_1 X_i + e_i$

ABEFGHI

3. The savings and number of children of four families are given below:

sav	child
0.03	2
0.874	2
0.374	0
1.2	1

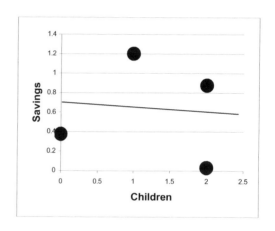

a) Calculate the values of $\hat{\beta}_0$ and $\hat{\beta}_1$ so that Σe_i^2 is minimized for

$sav_i = \hat{\beta}_0 + \hat{\beta}_1 \, child_i + e_i$

b) Interpret the values you obtained.
c) Sketch your line in the graph.

SAVING	CHILD		Xi - X	(Xi - X) Yi	(Xi - X)2			
0.03	2		0.75	0.02	0.56		B1 =	-0.03
0.874	2		0.75	0.66	0.56			
0.374	0		-1.25	-0.47	1.56			
1.2	1		-0.25	-0.30	0.06		B0 =	0.66
0.62	1.25			-0.09	2.75			

Xi squared	Yi hat	Yi - Y hat	ei squared	(Yi - Y)2
4.00	0.60	-0.57	0.32	0.35
4.00	0.60	0.28	0.08	0.06
0.00	0.66	-0.29	0.08	0.06
1.00	0.63	0.57	0.33	0.34
9		0	0.81	0.81

C) Bo: If CHILD = 0, then SAV is expected to be 0.66 units.
   B1: If CHILD increases by 1 unit, then SAV is expected to decrease by .03 units.

5. A) Calculate the values of the structural parameters for a regression of X on Y given:

Y	X
1.8	2
1.7	5
1.5	-2
0.6	5
25.4	6

$\beta_0 = 1.32$

$\beta_1 = 1.53$

B) Show that the $\Sigma e_i = 0$ in this case.

$e_1 = -2.57$

$e_2 = -7.25$

$e_3 = 3.24$

$e_4 = -8.35$

$e_5 = \underline{14.93}$

sum to 0

7. Prove $\dfrac{\Sigma Y_i X_i - \bar{Y}\Sigma X_i}{\Sigma X_i^2 - \bar{X}\Sigma X_i} = \dfrac{\Sigma(X_i - \bar{X})(Y_i - \bar{Y})}{\Sigma(X_i - \bar{X})^2}$

Starting with the numerator of the second term, foil it out:

$\Sigma(X_i - \bar{X})(Y_i - \bar{Y}) = \Sigma(X_i Y_i - X_i \bar{Y} - \bar{X}Y_i + \bar{X}\bar{Y}) = \Sigma X_i Y_i - \bar{Y}\Sigma X_i - \bar{X}\Sigma Y_i + n\bar{X}\bar{Y}$

The last two terms are equivalent and will cancel since one is negative and one is positive, leaving:

$\Sigma X_i Y_i - \bar{Y}\Sigma X_i$

To prove that the two denominators are equal, foil out the denominator of the second term:

$\Sigma(X_i - \bar{X})(X_i - \bar{X}) = \Sigma(X_i X_i - X_i \bar{X} - \bar{X}X_i + \bar{X}\bar{X}) = \Sigma X_i^2 - \bar{X}\Sigma X_i - \bar{X}\Sigma X_i + n\bar{X}\bar{X}$

The last two terms are equivalent and will cancel since one is negative and one is positive, leaving:

$\Sigma X_i^2 - \bar{X}\Sigma X_i$

9. Prove that $\Sigma e_i X_i = 0$ for the ordinary least-squares regression line.

Substitute in for the e_i and foil:

$\Sigma e_i = \Sigma(Y_i - \hat{\beta}_0 - \hat{\beta}_1 X_i)X_i = \Sigma Y_i X_i - \hat{\beta}_0 \Sigma X_i - \hat{\beta}_1 \Sigma X_i^2$

Sustitute in for $\hat{\beta}_0$ **and distribute:**

$$\Sigma Y_i X_i - (\overline{Y} - \hat{\beta}_1 \overline{X})\Sigma X_i - \hat{\beta}_1 \Sigma X_i^2 = \Sigma Y_i X_i - \overline{Y}\Sigma X_i - \hat{\beta}_1 \overline{X}\Sigma X_i - \hat{\beta}_1 \Sigma X_i^2$$

Combine the last two terms:

$$\Sigma Y_i X_i - \overline{Y}\Sigma X_i - \hat{\beta}_1 (\Sigma X_i^2 - \overline{X}\Sigma X_i)$$

Divide through by $(\Sigma X_i^2 - \overline{X}\Sigma X_i)$:

$$\frac{\Sigma Y_i X_i - \overline{Y}\Sigma X_i - \hat{\beta}_1 (\Sigma X_i^2 - \overline{X}\Sigma X_i)}{\Sigma X_i^2 - \overline{X}\Sigma X_i}$$

Notice that the first two terms in the numerator over the denominator $= \hat{\beta}_1$.

And the last term in the numerator over the denominator $= -\hat{\beta}_1$. **So this entire expression** $= 0$.

Chapter 3   Odd Problem Solutions

1. A) Calculate the values of the structural parameters for a regression of X on Y given:

Y	X
1.8	2
1.7	5
1.5	-2
0.6	5
25.4	6

$\hat{\beta}_1 = 1.5$

$\hat{\beta}_0 = 1.3$

B) Interpret the value you obtained for the intercept.
   If X = 0, then Y is expected to equal 1.3

C) Interpret the value you obtained for the slope coefficient.
   If X increases 1 unit, then Y is expected to increase by 1.5 units

D) Calculate r^2 for this regression. **$r^2 = .22$**

$$r^2 = = 1 - \frac{\Sigma e_i^2}{\Sigma(Y_i - \bar{Y})^2} = 1 - \frac{362.0}{461.7} = .22$$

E) Interpret the value of r^2 for this regression.
   22 percent of the variation in Y is explained by X.

F) Calculate the SER for this regression. **SER = 10.99**

$$SER = \sqrt{\frac{362.0}{3}} = 10.99$$

G) Interpret the value of the SER for this regression.
   The typical distance of an observation from the regression line = 10.99.

H) Calculate the standard error of the intercept term. **SE($\hat{\beta}_0$) = 7.3**

$$SE(\hat{\beta}_0) = = \sqrt{\frac{\hat{\sigma}^2 \Sigma X_i^2}{n\Sigma(X_i - \bar{X})^2}} = \sqrt{\frac{11353.3}{213.0}} = 7.3$$

I) Interpret the standard error of the intercept term.
   In repeated sampling, $\hat{\beta}_0$ typically varies by 7.3.

J) Calculate the standard error of the slope coefficient. **SE($\hat{\beta}_1$) = 1.7**

$$SE(\hat{\beta}_1) = = \sqrt{\frac{\hat{\sigma}^2}{\sum(X_i - \bar{X})^2}} = \sqrt{\frac{120.8}{42.6}} = 1.7$$

K) Interpret the standard error of the slope coefficient.

In repeated sampling, $\hat{\beta}_1$ typically varies by 1.7.

3. Given the following: $GDP_i = \hat{\beta}_0 + \hat{\beta}_1 COR_i + e_i$

Nation	COR	GDP
Ukraine	7.4	2200
UK	1.4	21200
USA	2.5	31500
Vietnam	7.4	1770

Where COR measures corruption in a nation on a scale of 0 (least) to 10 (most) and GDP measures output in dollars per capita.

A) Calculate the values of the structural parameters for the regression above.

$$\hat{\beta}_1 = \textbf{-4194.5} \quad \hat{\beta}_0 = \textbf{33,776.7}$$

$$\hat{\beta}_1 = -127124.25/30.31 = \textbf{--4194.5} \quad \hat{\beta}_0 = 14167.5 - (-4195.5 \times 4.68) = \textbf{33,776.7}$$

B) Interpret the values of the structural parameters.

If COR = 0, then GDP is expected to equal 33,776.7.
If COR increases 1 unit, then GDP is expected to decrease by 4194.5 units.

C) Calculate r^2 for this regression. r^2 **= .82**

$$r^2 = = 1 - \frac{\Sigma e_i^2}{\Sigma(Y_i - \bar{Y})^2} = = 1 - \frac{113570352}{646790675} = .82$$

D) Interpret the value of r^2 for this regression.

82 percent of the variation in GDP is explained by COR.

E) Calculate the SER for this regression. **SER = 7535.6**

$$SER = \sqrt{\frac{113570352}{2}} = 7535.6$$

F) Interpret the value of the SER for this regression.

The typical distance of an observation from the regression line is 7535.6.

G) Does this regression have a good fit? Explain.

No because SER > ½ the mean of GDP
or
Yes because r^2 = .82

H) Calculate the standard error of the intercept term. $SE(\hat{\beta}_0)$ **= 7425.0.**

$$SE(\hat{\beta}_0) = = \sqrt{\frac{\hat{\sigma}^2 \Sigma X_i^2}{n\Sigma(X_i - \overline{X})^2}} = \sqrt{\frac{117.73 \times 56785267}{121.24}} = \mathbf{7425.0}$$

I) Interpret the standard error of the intercept term.

In repeated sampling, $\hat{\beta}_0$ typically varies by 7425.0

J) Would you be surprised if the intercept term equaled 26776.70 if you re-ran this regression with data on four different countries? Explain.

No, because $\hat{\beta}_0$ typically varies by 7425.0, and 26776.70 is within range.

Chapter 4 Odd Problem Solutions

1. A professor has polled 25 students and asked them about their seat belt use (Do you wear your seat belt regularly?) and smoking (Do you smoke cigarettes?).

A) The correlation coefficient (r) between seat belt use and cigarette smoking is -.034. Are you surprised that the correlation is negative? Explain.

No, people who smoke are more likely to go without a seat belt because they are risk takers or don't value their lives as highly.

B) Do a test to determine if r is different than zero. Show the 5-step procedure.

1. Ho: r = 0   Ha: r $\neq$ 0
2. 5%
3. If | t-ratio | > t^c, then reject Ho
4. 0.163 < 2.069 (d.f. = n - 2 = 25 – 2 = 23)
5. Do Not Reject Ho; r is not statistically different from zero.

$$t-ratio = \frac{r\sqrt{n-2}}{\sqrt{(1-r^2)}} = \frac{-0.034\sqrt{25-2}}{\sqrt{1-.1156}} = \frac{-0.163}{.99} = -0.163$$

C) Do a test to determine if r is less than zero. Show the 5-step procedure.

1. Ho: r = 0   Ha: r < 0
2. 5%
3. If t-ratio < -t^c, then reject Ho
4. – 0.163 > -1.714 (d.f. = n - 2 = 25 – 2 = 23)
5. Do Not Reject Ho; r is not statistically less from zero.

D) Explain why seat belt use and smoking may be correlated despite the tests above.

There is some probability that we are making a TYPE II error.

3. Given the following regression results:

$$CORUPT_i = 5.47 - 0.05\ MIL_i + e_i$$
(0.49) (0.05)   ← standard errors
(0.00) (0.34)   ← P-values

SER = 2.35 $\overline{CORUPT}$ = 5.14 r^2 = 0.02   n = 48

CORUPT$_i$ is the corruption level of the country
(1 is low; 10 is high)
MIL$_i$ is military presence in the country
(military personnel per 1000 citizens)

A) Do a test of significance on the coefficient on MIL. Show the 5-step procedure.

1. Ho: $\beta_1 = 0$ Ha: $\beta_1 \neq 0$
2. 5%
3. If $|$ t-ratio $| > t^c$, then reject Ho
4. 1.00 < 2.021 (using 40d.f.) (d.f. = n - k = 48 – 2 = 46)
5. Do Not Reject Ho; β_1 is not statistically different from zero.

B) Would the results of your test turn out differently if the critical level of the test was 40% instead of 5%? Explain.

Yes, we would reject Ho at the 40% critical level because the P-value is .34.

C) Is the constant term significant at the 1% critical level? Answer this question without doing a test of significance. Just explain.

Yes, the constant term is significant at the 1% critical level because the P-value is 0.00.

D) Form a 90% confidence interval around the coefficient on MIL.

90% CI for $\hat{\beta}_1$ = -0.05: $\hat{\beta}_1$ +/- se($\hat{\beta}_1$)(t^c)

-0.05 +/- 0.05 (1.684)   →   -0.13 to 0.034

E) Determine if $r^2 = 0$ for this regression. (The F-statistic = 0.95.) Show the 5-step procedure.

1. Ho: $r^2 = 0$ Ha: $r^2 > 0$
2. 5%
3. If F > Fc, then reject Ho
4. 0.95 < 4.08 (d.f. = k-1 in the numerator and n-k in the denominator) (1&46 using 1&40)
5. Do Not Reject Ho; r^2 is not statistically greater than zero

F) Would your results for E) be different if the critical level of the test was 33%? Explain.
    (P-value for this test is 0.34.)

No, since the P-value > critical level of the test, we still say do not reject Ho.

G) Do a test to determine if the coefficient on MIL equals zero or if it is greater than zero. Show the 5-step procedure.

1) Ho: $\beta_1 = 0$ **Ha:** $\beta_1 > 0$

2) 5%

3) If t-ratio > t^c, then reject Ho

4)   -1.00 < 1.684 (d.f. = n- k = 48 – 2 =46) (using 40d.f.)

5) Do Not Reject Ho; β_1 **is not significantly positive**

H) Do a test to determine if the coefficient on MIL equals - 0.1 or not. Show the 5-step procedure.

1) Ho: $\beta_1 = -0.1$ **Ha:** $\beta_1 \neq -0.1$

2) 5%

3) If $|$ **t-ratio** $| > t^c$**, then reject Ho**

4) 1 < 2.021   **(d.f. = n - k = 48 – 2 =46) (using 40d.f.)**

5) Do Not Reject Ho; β_1 **is not statistically different from -0.1**

$$t - ratio = \frac{\hat{\beta}_0 - \beta_{Ho}}{SE(\hat{\beta}_0)} = \frac{-0.05 - (-0.1)}{0.05} = 1$$

Chapter 5 Odd Problem Solutions

1. Use the data in SDATA.XLS and statistical software to run the following regression:
$$GPA_i = \hat{\beta}_0 + \hat{\beta}_1 \, ST_i + e_i$$

where GPA = grade point average
and ST = study time per day

Dependent Variable: GPA
Method: Least Squares
Sample: 1 100
Included observations: 100

Variable	Coefficient	Std. Error	t-Statistic	Prob.
C	3.273582	0.057858	56.57915	0.0000
ST	0.026922	0.015906	1.692630	0.0937

R-squared	0.028404	Mean dependent var	3.347000
Adjusted R-squared	0.018490	S.D. dependent var	0.386503
S.E. of regression	0.382913	Akaike info criterion	0.937782
Sum squared resid	14.36903	Schwarz criterion	0.989885
Log likelihood	-44.88909	F-statistic	2.864998
Durbin-Watson stat	1.833710	Prob(F-statistic)	0.093703

A) Interpret the value you obtained for $\hat{\beta}_0$.

If ST = 0 , then GPA = 3.273582.

B) Interpret the value you obtained for $\hat{\beta}_1$.

If ST increases 1 unit, then GPA is expected to increase 0.026922 units.

C) How much does $\hat{\beta}_1$ typically vary in repeated sampling? **0.015906**

D) Perform a test of significance on $\hat{\beta}_1$. Show the 5-step procedure.
   1) Ho: $\beta_1 = 0$ Ha: $\beta_1 \neq 0$
   2) 5%
   3) If |t-ratio| tc, then reject Ho
   4) 1.692630 < 1.984 (d.f. = n-k = 100–2 = 98)
   5) Do Not Reject Ho; β_1 is not statistically different from zero

E) What percent of the variation in GPA is explained by study time? **2.8404%**

F) Perform a test to determine if $r^2 = 0$. Show the 5-step procedure.
   1) Ho: $r^2 = 0$ Ha: $r^2 > 0$
   2) 5%
   3) If F > Fc, then reject Ho
   4) 2.864998 < 3.938 (d.f.: N=k-1; D=n-k = 98)
   5) Do Not Reject Ho; R^2 is not statistically greater than zero

G) According to these results, how many hours per day would your study time have to increase in order to raise your GPA by 0.1? **? x 0.026922 = 0.1; 3.7 hours (per day)**

H) Plot the scattergram between GPA and ST with the estimated regression line drawn in. **Be sure to put ST on the X-axis and GPA on the Y-axis.**

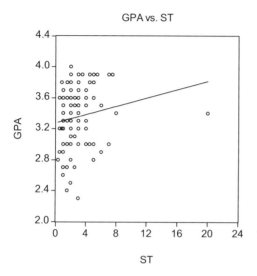

I) What is the average distance of an observation from the regression line? **0.382913**

J) Will you cut back on your study time now that you have seen these results? Explain why.

Yes, these results indicate study time does not affect GPA.
or
No, these results may be biased due to missing explanatory variables or the data may be corrupt because students exaggerated their study time or I am not typical.

3. Use the data in CONSUMP.XLS and statistical software to run the following regression:

$$RCONPC_t = \hat{\beta}_0 + \hat{\beta}_1 REALYDPC_t + \hat{\beta}_2 REALR_t + e_t$$

where RCONPC = real consumer spending in the USA per capita
REALYDPC = real disposable income per capita
REALR = real interest rate on 1 year Treasury Bonds
CC = University of Michigan Index of Consumer Confidence

A) Do all the explanatory variables attain their expected signs? **Yes**

B) Aside from CC, what explanatory variables might be missing from this regression?
Wealth and age distribution of population, among other things.

C) Perform Ramsey's Reset test. Show the 5-step procedure. Are variables missing from the model according to this test?

1) Ho: $\beta_3 = \beta_4 = 0$ Ha: β_3 and/or $\beta_4 \neq 0$
    (No variables excluded)   **(Variables excluded)**
2) **5%**
3) **If F > F^c, then reject Ho**
4) **70.51342 > 3.226; where F^c has d.f. NUM = 2 ; d.f. DEN = n-k = 46-5=41**
5) **Reject Ho; Variables are excluded from this regression**

5. Use the data in CONSUMP.XLS and statistical software to run the following regression:

$$RCONPC_t = \hat{\beta}_0 + \hat{\beta}_1 REALYDPC_t + \hat{\beta}_2 REALR_t + \hat{\beta}_3 CC_t + e_t$$

where RCONPC = real consumer spending in the USA per capita
            REALYDPC = real disposable income per capita
            REALR = real interest rate on one-year Treasury Bonds
            CC = University of Michigan Index of Consumer Confidence

A) Does CC attain its expected sign? Explain. **Yes, we would expect consumers to spend more when they are more confident, because there is no need to save for future emergencies.**

B) Does a test of significance on CC justify its presence in the regression? **Yes.**

C) Does CC belong in the regression according to Adjusted R^2? Explain. **Yes, it rises to 0.996646 from 0.993901.**

D) Does CC belong in the regression according to the Akaike information criterion? Explain. **Yes, it falls to 14.27868 from 14.85672.**

E) Does CC belong in the regression according to the Schwarz criterion? Explain. **Yes, it falls to 14.43769 from 14.97598.**

F) Does this regression fit better than the regression from question 3 above? Explain. **Yes, based on adjusted r-squared, Akaike, and Schwarz.**

G) Perform Ramsey's Reset test. Show the 5-step procedure. Are variables missing from the model according to this test?

1) Ho: $\beta_4 = \beta_5 = 0$ Ha: β_4 and/or $\beta_5 \neq 0$
    (No variables excluded)   **(Variables excluded)**
2) **5%**
3) **If F > F^c, then reject Ho**

4) 37.97626 > 3.232; where F^c has d.f. NUM = 2 ; d.f. DEN = n-k = 46-6=40
5) Reject Ho: Variables are excluded from this regression

H) Do you think the estimators in $RCONPC_t = \hat{\beta}_0 + \hat{\beta}_1 REALYDPC_t + \hat{\beta}_2 REALR_t + e_t$ are biased? Inefficient? Neither? Explain. **Biased, because at least one important explanatory variable is missing -- CC.**

I) Do you think the estimators in $RCONPC_t = \hat{\beta}_0 + \hat{\beta}_1 REALYDPC_t + \hat{\beta}_2 REALR_t + \hat{\beta}_3 CC_t + e_t$ are biased? Inefficient? Neither? Explain. **Biased, because Ramsey's suggests at least one variable is missing and theory points to wealth as being important for consumer spending.**

Chapter 6 Odd Problem Solutions

1. Derive the formula for $\hat{\beta}_1$ in $Y_i = \hat{\beta}_1 X_i + e_i$ that minimizes Σe_i^2.

We have $Y_i = \hat{\beta}_1 X_i + e_i$

We want to min Σe_i^2; or min $\Sigma(Y_i - \hat{\beta}_1 X_i)^2$

To find the equation for $\hat{\beta}_0$ that minimizes this expression, take the derivative with respect to $\hat{\beta}_0$ and set it equal to zero:

$$\frac{d\Sigma(Y_i - \hat{\beta}_1 X_i)^2}{d\hat{\beta}_1} = 2\Sigma(Y_i - \hat{\beta}_1 X_i)(-X_i) = 0$$

Dividing both sides of this equation by -2 leaves $\Sigma(Y_i - \hat{\beta}_1 X_i)(X_i) = 0$

Now distribute the summation sign: $\Sigma Y_i X_i - \hat{\beta}_1 \Sigma X_i^2 = 0$;

Moving the second term to the other side gives: $\Sigma Y_i X_i = \hat{\beta}_1 \Sigma X_i^2$

The result is known as a "normal equation."

Rearranging terms and dividing through by ΣX_i^2 gives:

$$\hat{\beta}_1 = \frac{\Sigma X_i Y_i}{\Sigma X_i^2}$$

3. In the regression below, what would be the new values of $\hat{\beta}_0$, $\hat{\beta}_1$, their t-ratios, SER, r^2, and the mean of WEIGHT if WEIGHT was measured in ounces instead of pounds?

$\text{WEIGHT}_i = 51.12 + 1.85 \text{ HEIGHT}_i + e_i$ (4.72) (9.85) ← t-ratios SER = 20.38 $\overline{\text{WEIGHT}}$ = 156.78 $r^2 = 0.49$ n = 4800	$\text{WEIGHT}_i = \mathbf{817.92} + \mathbf{29.6} \text{ HEIGHT}_i + e_i$ **(4.72) (9.85)** ← t-ratios SER = **326.08** $\overline{\text{WEIGHT}}$ = **2508.48** $r^2 = \mathbf{0.49}$ n = **4800**

5. Use the data in EGG.XLS and statistical software to do the following problems:
   Run the following regression: $QEGG_t = \hat{\beta}_0 + \hat{\beta}_1 PEGG_t + e_t$

   where QEGG is per capita egg consumption each year 1973–1997
   PEGG is the average price of a dozen eggs in the USA

A) i) Interpret the value you obtained for $\hat{\beta}_0$.
   If PEGG = 0, then QEGG = 341.1228
   ii) Interpret the value you obtained for $\hat{\beta}_1$.
   If PEGG ↑ 1 unit, then QEGG ↓ 83.70535 units
   iii) If the price of eggs goes up $1 per dozen, what is the expected change in egg consumption according to this regression? **↓ 83.70535 units**

B) Run the regression in the double-log form.
   i) Interpret the value you obtained for $\hat{\beta}_0$.
   If PEGG = 1, then LNQEGG = 5.544318 (or QEGG = 255.78)
   ii) Interpret the value you obtained for $\hat{\beta}_1$.
   If PEGG ↑ 1 %, then QEGG ↓ 0.361304 %
   iii) If the price of eggs goes up 1 percent, what is the expected percentage change in egg consumption according to this regression? **↓ 0.361304 %**

C) Run the regression in the semi-log form (where the natural log of PEGG is taken).
   i) Interpret the value you obtained for $\hat{\beta}_0$.
   If PEGG = 1, then QEGG = 256.3509
   ii) Interpret the value you obtained for $\hat{\beta}_1$.
   If PEGG ↑ 1 %, then QEGG ↓ 0.9196824 units
   iii) If the price of eggs goes up 1 percent, what is the expected change in egg consumption according to this regression? **↓ 0.9196824 units**

D) Run the regression in the semi-log form (where the natural log of QEGG is taken).
   i) Interpret the value you obtained for $\hat{\beta}_0$.
   If PEGG = 0, then LNQEGG = 5.877692 (or QEGG = 356.98)
   ii) Interpret the value you obtained for $\hat{\beta}_1$.
   If PEGG ↑ 1 unit, then QEGG ↓ 32.9175 %
   iii) If the price of eggs goes up $1 per dozen, what is the expected percentage change in egg consumption according to this regression? **↓ 32.9175 %**

E) Run the regression in the reciprocal form.
   i) Interpret the value you obtained for $\hat{\beta}_0$.
   As PEGG → ∞, QEGG → 157.0288
   ii) Interpret the value you obtained for $\hat{\beta}_1$.
   If PEGG ↑, QEGG ↓

iii) If the price of eggs goes up $1 per dozen, will egg consumption increase or decrease according to this regression? **decrease**

F) Run the regression in the polynomial form.

i) Interpret the value you obtained for $\hat{\beta}_0$.

If PEGG = 0, then QEGG = 567.0630.

ii) Interpret the values you obtained for $\hat{\beta}_1$ and $\hat{\beta}_2$.

As PEGG ↑, QEGG ↓ to a point and then QEGG ↑ with further increases in PEGG.

G) i) Do you think the data in this study require an alternate functional form or is the linear form satisfactory? Explain. **Theory is not helpful in this case. Ramsey's Reset Test says nonlinear since it flunks the linear form and passes the nonlinear forms. The scattergram suggests a curvilinear shape. Therefore, an alternate form is recommended.**

ii) Which of the six regressions fits the data best? **One cannot say since all six cannot be compared. However, of those having QEGG as the dependent variable, the polynomial fits best with an adjusted r-squared of 0.813771. Of those having LNQEGG as the dependent variable, the double-log fits best with an r-squared = 0.766749.**

7. Use the data in SDATA.XLS and statistical software to do the following problem:

Which functional form do you think is appropriate for the regression below:

$$GPA_i = \hat{\beta}_0 + \hat{\beta}_1 ST_i + e_i$$

Explain your response.

A scattergram does not suggest the need for an alternate functional form. Ramsey's reset test is no help since all the functional forms pass the test. However, lin-log and reciprocal regressions fit the data slightly better than a linear regression. Perhaps the reciprocal specification is best since it fits better than the linear and theory suggests an asymptotic relationship (the more you study the closer your GPA comes to 4.0).

9. Interpret every structural parameter in each of the following regressions considering:

WAGES = pay per hour of work
LNWAGES = natural log of WAGES
EXP = years of experience
EXPSQ = EXP squared

A) LNWAGES = 2.1 + 1.3 EXP + e
If EXP = 0, then LNWAGES = 2.1 (or WAGES = 8.17)

If EXP ↑ 1 unit, then WAGES ↑ 130%

B) WAGES = 2.1 + 1.3 EXP - 2.3 EXPSQ + e

If EXP = 0, then WAGES = 2.1

As EXP increases so do WAGES, up to a point, then WAGES decline with further EXP

C) WAGES = 2.5 - 0.1 (1/EXP)

As EXP → ∞, WAGES → 2.5

As EXP ↑, WAGES ↑

Chapter 7   Odd Problem Solutions

1. A) Interpret every structural parameter in the following regression:

$$PROFSAL_i = 17.969 + 1.3707\ EXP_i + 3.3336\ DUM_i + e_i$$

> where PROFSAL is the professor's salary
> EXP is the professor's experience in years
> DUM = 1 if the professor is male; 0 otherwise

A female with no experience is expected to have PROFSAL = 17.969.
If EXP increases 1 unit, then PROFSAL is expected to increase 1.3707 units for males and females.
A male is expected to earn 3.3336 more than a female, holding EXP constant.

>   B) Draw a diagram reflecting the regression results with PROFSAL on the vertical axis and EXP on the horizontal axis.

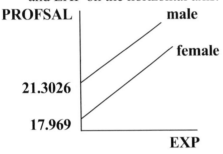

>   C) A male professor with 10 years' experience is expected to make how much in salary?
>   **PROFSAL= 17.969 + 1.3707(10) +3.3336(1) = 35.0096**
>   D) A female professor with 10 years' experience is expected to make how much in salary?
>   **PROFSAL= 17.969 +1.3707(10) + 3.3336(0) = 31.676**
>   E) What would be the new values of the structural parameters if the dummy was flip-flopped?
>   **$PROFSAL_i = 21.3026 + 1.3707\ EXP_i - 3.3336\ DUM_i + e_i$**
>   F) Using the flip-flopped results, how much would a male professor with 10 years' experience make in salary? **35.0096**

3. A) Interpret every structural parameter in the following regression:

$$PROFSAL_i = 16.1718 + 1.2016\ EXP_i + 3.2245\ DUM_i - 1.0001\ DUM*EXP_i + e_i$$

> where PROFSAL is the professor's salary
> EXP is the professor's experience in years
> DUM = 1 if the professor is male; 0 otherwise

A female with no EXP is expected to make 16.1718.
For every unit increase in EXP, PROFSAL is expected to increase by 1.2016 for females.

A male with 0 EXP will earn 3.2245 more than a female with 0 EXP.
If EXP increase 1 unit, then PROFSAL for a male will increase 1.0001 less than the 1.2016 for a female.

B) Draw a diagram reflecting the regression results with PROFSAL on the vertical axis and EXP on the horizontal axis.

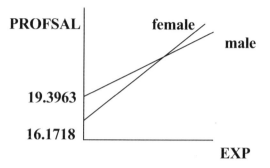

C) What would be the new values of the structural parameters if the dummy was flip-flopped?

PROFSAL$_i$ = 19.3963 + 0.2015 EXP$_i$ - 3.2245 DUM$_i$ + 1.0001 DUM*EXP$_i$ + e$_i$

5. A) Interpret every structural parameter in the following regression:

$$GPA_i = 0.37 + 0.81\ HSGPA_i + 0.00001\ SAT_i - 0.38\ GREEK_i + e_i$$

where GPA is grade point average in college
HSGPS is high school GPA
SAT is SAT score
GREEK = 1 if student is a member of a sorority or fraternity;
0 otherwise

If HSGPA and SAT = 0 and the student is not Greek, then GPA = 0.37.
If HSGPA increases 1 unit, then GPA increases 0.81 units, holding SAT constant.
If SAT increases 1 unit, then GPA increases 0.00001 units, holding HSGPA constant.
A Greek student is expected to have a GPA 0.38 lower than a non-Greek with the same HSGPA and SAT.

B) Draw a diagram reflecting the regression results with GPA on the vertical axis and SAT on the horizontal axis.

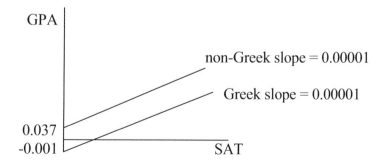

7. Use the data in WAGES.XLS and statistical software run to run a regression where wages are explained by a constant term, education, experience, and a dummy variable for gender.

NAME	VARIABLE
WAGES	wages
LNWAGES	the natural logarithm of wages
ED	education in years
NONWH	1 if nonwhite; 0 otherwise
FEM	1 if female; 0 otherwise
MARRIED	1 if married; 0 otherwise
EXPER	experience in years
EXPSQ	experience squared
UNION	1 if union member; 0 otherwise
PRO	1 if employed in a profession; 0 otherwise

A) Interpret the coefficient on education.

If ED increases 1 unit, then WAGES increases 0.940489 units, holding EXPER constant.

B) Interpret the coefficient on the dummy variable.

A female's wages are 2.337621 less than a male's with the same ED and EXPER.

Dependent Variable: WAGES
Method: Least Squares
Date: 12/05/07   Time: 13:49
Sample: 1 534
Included observations: 534

Variable	Coefficient	Std. Error	t-Statistic	Prob.
C	-4.166703	1.186608	-3.511439	0.0005
ED	0.940489	0.078859	11.92616	0.0000
EXPER	0.113297	0.016707	6.781255	0.0000
FEM	-2.337621	0.388042	-6.024141	0.0000
R-squared	0.253171	Mean dependent var	9.023947
Adjusted R-squared	0.248944	S.D. dependent var	5.138874
S.E. of regression	4.453528	Akaike info criterion	5.832733
Sum squared resid	10511.97	Schwarz criterion	5.864796
Log likelihood	-1553.340	F-statistic	59.88904
Durbin-Watson stat	1.857160	Prob(F-statistic)	0.000000

9. Use the data in WAGES.XLS and statistical software to run a regression where the natural logarithm of wages is explained by a constant term, education, experience, and dummy variables for marital status, gender, race, union membership, and professional status.

A) Interpret the coefficient on education.

If ED increases 1 unit, then WAGES increase 8.4356%, holding experience constant.

B) Interpret the coefficient on marital status.

A married person is expected to have WAGES 7.1460% higher than an unmarried person, holding ED and EXPER constant.

C) Interpret the coefficient on union membership.

A union member is expected to have WAGES 20.2786% higher than a nonunion person, holding ED and EXPER constant.

D) Does this regression provide evidence of racial and gender discrimination? Explain.

Definitely, gender discrimination-- the coefficient on FEM is negative and significant. For racial discrimination the evidence is not so strong -- the coefficient on nonwhite is negative, but only significant at the 10.47% level.

11. Use the data in EXTRAMARITAL.XLS and statistical software to estimate a linear probability model where EXTRA is explained by a constant term, AGE, HPPYM, RELIG, and YRSMAR.

EXTRA = 1 if person participated in an extramarital affair in the past year; 0 otherwise
AGE = the age of the person
HPPYM = person's perception of their marital happiness (1 = very unhappy; 5 = very happy)
RELIG = person's perception of their religiousness (1 = very unreligious; 5 = very religious)
YRSMAR = years married

A) Interpret all five structural parameters.

A person with AGE = HPPYM = RELIG = YRSMAR = 0, has an 81.8833 % chance of an affair in the past year.

As AGE ↑ 1 unit, the chance of having had an affair in the past year ↓ 0.5948%, holding the other variables (HPPYM, RELIG, YRSMAR) constant.

As HPPYM ↑ 1 unit, the chance of having had an affair in the past year ↓ 8.7451%, holding the other variables (AGE, RELIG, YRSMAR) constant.

As RELIG ↑ 1 unit, the chance of having had an affair in the past year ↓ 5.4697%, holding the other variables (AGE, HPPYM, YRSMAR) constant.

As YRSMAR ↑ 1 unit, the chance of having had an affair in the past year ↑ 1.6910%, holding the other variables (AGE, HPPYM, RELIG) constant.

B) What is the probability that a 52-year-old person married for 27 years had an extramarital affair last year? Assume the person's RELIG = 2 and HAPPYM = 3.

EXTRA = 0.81883 – 0.005948 (52) – 0.087451 (3) – 0.054697 (2) + 0.016910 (27) = 0.594

59.4%

Chapter 8 Odd Problem Solutions

1. Prove $\Sigma w_i = 0$ and $\Sigma w_i X_i = 1$.

$$\Sigma w_i = \frac{\Sigma(X_i - \overline{X})}{\Sigma(X_i - \overline{X})^2} = \frac{\Sigma X_i - n\overline{X}}{\Sigma(X_i - \overline{X})^2} = \frac{0}{\Sigma(X_i - \overline{X})^2}$$

$$\Sigma w_i X_i = \frac{\Sigma(X_i - \overline{X})X_i}{\Sigma(X_i - \overline{X})^2} = \frac{\Sigma X_i^2 - \overline{X}\Sigma X_i}{\Sigma X_i^2 - \overline{X}\Sigma X_i} = 1$$

3. Suppose $u_i \sim N(0, \sigma^2)$ for all i. Why can't we guarantee $\hat{\beta}_1$ will be efficient? **Because maybe $E[u_i u_j] \neq 0$ for all $i \neq j$**

5. From the article "Econometrics in Theory and Practice" by Steven Caudill, *Eastern Economic Journal* 16(3): 249–256.

http://college.holycross.edu/eej/Volume16/V16N3P249_256.pdf

A) What is the "Axiom of Specification"?

The Axiom of Specification is a set of criteria beyond the assumptions of the classic linear regression model that a regression must meet if the estimators are to be BLUE.

B) Is the Axiom of Specification an assumption of the Classical Linear Regression Model? If not, then should it be? If so, then which one corresponds to it?
The Axiom of Specification is an implicit assumption of the CLRM. Most econometricians would put it under assumption 2: $E[u_i] = 0$ since this assumption will be violated if the set of dependent variables is not unique, complete, small in number, observable, or unknown parameters are not constant.

C) What is the difference between "applied econometricians" and "econometric theorists"?
Applied econometricians are interested in testing theories and not so interested in Classical assumptions. They are more likely to data mine. Econometric theorists are concerned with adhering to the Classical assumptions and not so concerned with testing any particular economic theory. They are more likely to do proofs.

D) What is "data mining"?

Some would say data mining is torturing the data until they scream the results you want, but that is unfair. When theory is no guide to what variables belong in a regression, mining the data can help determine if a particular variable belongs and the correct functional form. Because many regressions are run in the data mining process, variables get more than one chance to be significant. This violates the axioms of the Classical Linear Regression Model.

Chapter 9 Odd Problem Solutions

1. Use the data in CONSUMP.XLS and statistical software to run the following regression:

$$RCONPC_t = \hat{\beta}_0 + \hat{\beta}_1 REALYDPC_t + \hat{\beta}_2 REALR_t + \hat{\beta}_3 CC_t + e_t$$

where RCONPC = real consumer spending in the USA per capita
       REALYDPC = real disposable income per capita
       REALR = real interest rate on one-year Treasury Bonds
       CC = University of Michigan Index of Consumer Confidence

A) Which explanatory variables do not obtain their expected signs?
They all obtain their expected signs.

B) According to the correlation coefficients between the explanatory variables, would you classify the multicollinearity in this regression as severe, moderate, mild, or non-existent? Explain. **Mild to non-existent with r's of 0.016, 0.135, and 0.276**

C) According to the correlation coefficients between the explanatory variables, which two variables are most collinear? **REALR and CC**

D) Calculate the three VIFs for this regression. Would you classify the multicollinearity in this regression as severe, moderate, mild, or non-existent? Explain.
VIF = 1.02; 1.08; 1.10 >>>>non-existent to mild

E) Run the regression in first difference form. Which explanatory variables do not obtain their expected signs? **They all obtain their expected signs.**

F) According to the correlation coefficients between the explanatory variables, would you classify the multicollinearity in this regression as severe, moderate, mild, or non-existent? Explain. **Mild with r's of 0.26, 0.28, and 0.34**

G) Calculate the three VIFs for this regression. Would you classify the multicollinearity in this regression as severe, moderate, mild, or non-existent? Explain.
Non-existent to mild with VIFs of 1.124, 1.176, and 1.176

H) Based on your look into this matter, what do you recommend doing about the multicollinearity in the original regression? Explain.
There was no or very little multicollinearity in the original regression.

Chapter 10   Odd Problem Solutions

1. Given $Y_i = \hat{\beta}_0 + \hat{\beta}_1 X1_i + \hat{\beta}_2 X2_i + e_i$

A) Write the auxiliary regression required for the Park test assuming X2 is the "culprit" variable. $\ln(e_i^2) = \alpha_0 + \alpha_1 \ln(X2_i) + \varepsilon_i$

B) Suppose n = 23 and the t-ratio on X2 in the auxiliary regression is –2.222. Is heteroskedasticity present? Show the 5-step procedure for the Park test.

1) Ho: $\alpha_2 = 0$ (no hetero)   Ha: $\alpha_2 \neq 0$ (hetero exists)
2) 5%
3) If |t-ratio| > tc, reject Ho
4) 2.222 > 2.080 (d.f.= n-k)
5) Reject Ho; heteroskedasticity is present in the original regression

C) Write the auxiliary regression required for the White test.
$e_i^2 = \alpha_0 + \alpha_1 X1_i + \alpha_2 X1_i^2 + \alpha_3 X2_i + \alpha_4 X2_i^2 + \alpha_5 (X1_i)(X2_i) + \varepsilon_i$

D) Suppose n = 23 and the R-squared on the auxiliary regression is 0.55. Is heteroskedasticity present? Show the 5-step procedure for the White test.

1) Ho: no hetero   Ha: hetero exists
2) 5%
3) If $nR^2 > \chi c$, then reject Ho
4) 23(.55) = 12.65 ; $\chi c = 11.07$ (d.f. = k-1 from the auxiliary regression = 5)
5) Reject Ho; heteroskedasticity is present in the original regression

E) Write the weighted least-squares regression that would remedy the heteroskedasticity if it were proportional to X2.

$$\frac{Y_i}{\sqrt{X2_i}} = \beta_0 \left[\frac{1}{\sqrt{X2_i}}\right] + \beta_1 \left[\frac{X1_i}{\sqrt{X2_i}}\right] + \beta_2 \left[\frac{X2_i}{\sqrt{X2_i}}\right] + \frac{u_i}{\sqrt{X2_i}}$$

3. Use the data in ALCO5.XLS and statistical software to run a regression where drink is explained by a constant term, gpa, male, ofage, cig, pot, intra, and white.

VARIABLE	DESCRIPTION
drink	number of alcoholic drinks consumed per week
gpa	grade point average 0–4 scale
male	1 if the student is male; 0 otherwise
ofage	1 if the student is 21 or older; 0 otherwise
cig	1 if the student uses tobacco; 0 otherwise
pot	1 if the student uses marijuana: 0 otherwise
intra	1 if the student participates in intramural athletics; 0 otherwise
white	1 if the student is white; 0 otherwise

A) Which variables do not attain their expected signs? **Perhaps intra; otherwise the signs are correct.**

B) Which variables are not significant at the 5% critical level? **white**

C) Plot the squared residuals from the regression against gpa. Does the plot show evidence of heteroskedasticity? Explain. **Yes, higher gpa yields wider variance on the squared errors.**

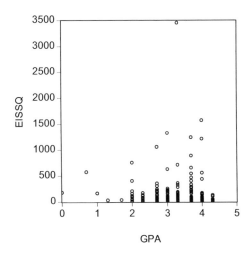

D) Do a Park test for heteroskedasticity assuming gpa is the "culprit" variable. Show the 5-step procedure.
      1) Ho: $\alpha_2 = 0$ (no hetero)   Ha: $\alpha_2 \neq 0$ (hetero exists)
      2) 5%
      3) If |t-ratio| > tc, reject Ho
      4) 6.376729 > 1.984 (d.f.= n-k=694-2=692)
      5) Reject Ho; heteroskedasticity is present in the original regression

E) Perform White's test for heteroskedasticity. Show the 5-step procedure.
      1) Ho: no hetero   Ha: hetero exists
      2) 5%
      3) If nR^2 > χc, then reject Ho
      4) 89.95281 ;χc = 43.77 (d.f. = k-1 from the auxiliary regression = 31 – 1 = 30)
      5) Reject Ho; heteroskedasticity is present in the original regression

F) Run the original regression using weighted least-squares. Assume 1/gpa is the correct weight. Then apply White's test for heteroskedasticity to the errors from this weighted regression. Show the 5-step procedure.
      1) Ho: no hetero   Ha: hetero exists
      2) 5%
      3) If nR^2 > χc, then reject Ho
      4) 209.4133;χc = 43.77 (d.f. = k-1 from the auxiliary regression = 31 – 1 = 30)
      5) Reject Ho; heteroskedasticity is present in the WLS regression

G) Run the original regression using weighted least-squares. Assume $1/\sqrt{gpa}$ is the correct weight. Then apply White's test for heteroskedasticity to the errors from this weighted regression. Show the 5-step procedure.

1) Ho: no hetero   Ha: hetero exists
2) 5%
3) If $nR^2 > \chi c$, then reject Ho
4) 125.3590; χc = 43.77 (d.f. = k-1 from the auxiliary regression = 31 – 1 = 30)
5) Reject Ho; heteroskedasticity is present in the WLS regression

H) Use the Newey-West technique to obtain heteroskedasticity-corrected standard errors with the original regression. Did heteroskedasticity appear to biasing the standard errors of the structural parameters very much? Explain. **The heteroskedasticity appears to be biasing the SEs of the structural parameters a moderate to minor amount. They are all slightly higher in the Newey-West regression except for the SE on white, which is slightly lower.**

Dependent Variable: DRINK
Method: Least Squares
Date: 02/22/08   Time: 14:39
Sample: 1 699
Included observations: 695
Excluded observations: 4
Newey-West HAC Standard Errors & Covariance (lag truncation=6)

Variable	Coefficient	Std. Error	t-Statistic	Prob.
C	8.951717	2.463179	3.634213	0.0003
GPA	-2.705399	0.705993	-3.832049	0.0001
MALE	4.538337	0.674783	6.725629	0.0000
OFAGE	1.799706	0.638602	2.818198	0.0050
CIG	3.045336	0.833358	3.654294	0.0003
POT	4.579583	0.780064	5.870777	0.0000
INTRA	2.990046	1.619902	1.845819	0.0653
WHITE	1.839064	0.897039	2.050149	0.0407

R-squared	0.278284	Mean dependent var	7.589928
Adjusted R-squared	0.270930	S.D. dependent var	9.241721
S.E. of regression	7.891096	Akaike info criterion	6.980791
Sum squared resid	42779.07	Schwarz criterion	7.033095
Log likelihood	-2417.825	F-statistic	37.84261
Durbin-Watson stat	2.009937	Prob(F-statistic)	0.000000

Chapter 11   Odd Problem Solutions

1. Complete the following table:

Sample Size	k	d stat	Autocorrelation present?
20	2	0.83	Yes
32	3	1.24	Yes
45	4	1.98	No
100	5	3.72	Yes
150	7	1.71	Inconclusive

3. Use the data in CONSUMP.XLS and statistical software to run the following regression:

$$RCONPC_t = \hat{\beta}_0 + \hat{\beta}_1 REALYDPC_t + e_t$$

A) Plot the error terms over time. Do you suspect serial correlation? Explain.

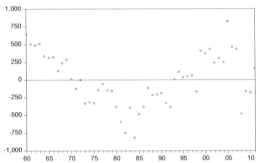

Obvious pattern of positive serial correlation with runs of + and then − errors

B) Plot the error terms against their lagged values. Do you suspect serial correlation? Explain.

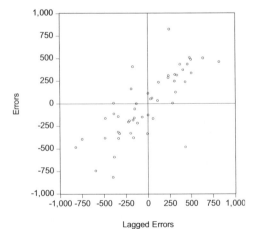

Obvious + auto with observations splayed mainly in I and III quadrants

---

C) Perform a Durbin-Watson test. Show the 5-step procedure.

1) Ho: no positive auto   Ha: positive auto
2) 5%
3) If $0 < d < d_L$, then reject Ho
  If $d_L < d < d_U$, then inconclusive
4) d= 0.460249; d_L = 1.50; d_U =1.59 (using k = 2 and n = 50)
5) Reject Ho; positive auto is present

5. Use the data in CONSUMP.XLS and statistical software to run the following regression:

$$RCONPC_t = \hat{\beta}_0 + \hat{\beta}_1 REALYDPC_t + \hat{\beta}_2 REALR_t + \hat{\beta}_3 CC_t + e_t$$

where RCONPC = real consumer spending in the USA per capita
       REALYDPC = real disposable income per capita
       REALR = real interest rate on one-year Treasury Bonds
       CC = University of Michigan Index of Consumer Confidence

A) Plot the residuals from the regression over time. Does this plot suggest serial correlation is present? Positive or negative? Explain.

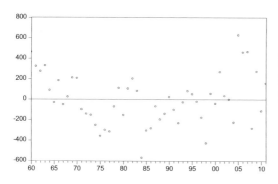

Positive autocorrealtion is suggested since there are long runs of positive and negative errors.

B) Plot the residuals from the regression against their lagged values. Does this plot suggest serial correlation is present? Positive or negative? Explain.

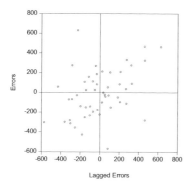

An upward splay of observations indicates positive serial correlation.

C) Does the regression suffer from serial correlation? Show the 5-step procedure of the Durbin-Watson test.

1) Ho: no positive auto   Ha: positive auto
2) 5%
3) If $0 < d < d_L$, then reject Ho
  If $d_L < d < d_U$, then inconclusive
4) d=1.162141 ; d_L= 1.42 ; d_U= 1.67 (n = 52 (using 50); k = 4)
5) Reject Ho; positive serial correlation is present

1) Ho: no serial correlation   Ha: serial correlation exists
2) 5%
3) If $nR^2 > \chi c$, then reject Ho (d.f. = # of lagged residual terms = 1)
    7.63 > 3.84
4) Calculate nR^2 and find χc
5) Reject Ho; serial correlation is present

D) Estimate ρ by regressing the residuals on their lagged values (no constant term). What is the estimate of ρ? **0.74**

E) Check for second-order serial correlation. Do you think it is present? Explain. **No, because the second lag of the errors is not significant in**
$eis_t = \rho_1 eis_{t-1} + \rho_2 eis_{t-2} + \varepsilon_t$

F) Estimate ρ and correct for first-order serial correlation using GLS with maximum likelihood estimation. What is this estimate of ρ? **0.57**

G) Did GLS remedy the serial correlation? Show the 5-step procedure.

1) Ho: no negative auto   Ha: negative auto
2) 5%
3) If $4 - d_L < d < 4$, then reject Ho
  If $4 - d_U < d < 4 - d_L$, then inconclusive
4) d= 2.359058; d_L= 1.38 ; d_U= 1.72 (n = 51 (using 50); k = 5);
5) Inconclusive; GLS may have remedied the negative autocorrelation

1) Ho: no serial correlation   Ha: serial correlation exists
2) 5%
3) If $nR^2 > \chi c$, then reject Ho (d.f. = # of lagged residual terms = 1)
4) 5.31 > 3.84
5) Reject Ho; serial correlation is present

H) Compare the t-ratios from the original regression and the GLS regression. Are you surprised by which ones turn out to be larger? Explain. **The absolute values of the t-stats are lower after correcting for serial correlation, and that is to be expected since they were biased to look better than they actually were in the original regression.**

I) Apply the Newey-West technique to the original regression. Are you surprised at the new standard errors of the estimators? Explain. **The SEs on realydpc and realr rise after applying the Newey-West technique as expected since they were biased downward in the original regression. But the the standard errors on c and cc rise unexpectedly.**

Chapter 12   Odd Problem Solutions

1. Consider the following regression:

$$M_t = 2.00 - 0.10\ R_t + 0.70\ Y_t + 0.60\ M_{t-1} + e_t$$
$$\quad\quad (0.10)\quad (0.35)\quad (0.10)\quad \leftarrow \text{standard errors}$$

$$R^2 = .9 \qquad\qquad DW = 1.80 \qquad\qquad n = 26$$

  where M is the demand for M1
  R is the interest rate on 10-year Treasuries
  Y is national income

A) Do the variables attain their expected signs? **Yes**
B) Test for serial correlation in this regression. Show the 5-step procedure.

Durbin's h- test
1) **Ho: no autocorrelation Ha: auto present**
2) **5%**
3) **If $|\,h\,| > t^c$, then reject Ho (d.f. = n-k)**
4) **$h = (.1)(5.93) = 0.59$; $t^c = 2.074$**
5) **Do Not Reject Ho; auto is not present**

C) What is the short-run impact of a change in the interest rate on money demand?
   -0.10
D) What is the long-run impact? **Is equal to $\beta_1/(1-\lambda) = -0.10/(1-.60) = -0.25$**

3. Use the data in QLEISCOIN and statistical software to do the following problems.

   COIN = percentage change in the composite index of coincident economic indicators
   LEIS = percentage change in the composite index of leading economic indicators

A) Run a regression to determine if COIN is affected by LEIS and LEIS lagged 1
    through 8 quarters. Do you think LEIS 8 quarters ago helps predict COIN this
    quarter? Explain. **No, the sign on LEIS(-8) is negative and it is insignificant.**
B) How many lags of the LEIS should be used to explain COIN? Explain how you
    came to this conclusion. **Lag length 7 works well (all correct signs and only
    lags 6 and 5 are insignificant); 6 works well (all correct signs and only lag 5 is
    insignificant); 5 is not an improvement over 6 (all correct signs with lag 2
    insignificant); 4 and 3 are same as 5; finally, 2 has all correct signs and
    statistical significance. So, 7, 6, and 5 are good responses.**
C) Does the regression you settled on in B) above suffer from serial correlation
    according to the Durbin-Watson test? Show the 5-step procedure.

Working with a lag of 6:
1) Ho: no positive auto   Ha: positive auto
2) 5%
3) If $0 < d < d_L$, then reject Ho
  If $d_L < d < d_U$, then inconclusive
4) d=1.239550; d_L= 1.64 ; d_U = 1.83 (n=173; k=8)
5) Reject Ho; positive serial correlation is present

D) Does the regression you settled on in B) above suffer from serial correlation according to the Lagrange multiplier test? Show the 5-step procedure.

  Lagrange Multiplier test (lag of 6)
  1) Ho: no serial correlation   Ha: serial correlation exists
  2) 5%
  3) If $nR^2 > \chi c$, then reject Ho (d.f. = # of lagged residual terms = 1)
  4) 30.19793 > 3.84, reject Ho
  5) Reject Ho; auto is present

E) Does the regression you settled on in B) above suffer from multicollinearity? On what do you base your response? **Not very much, mild to moderate -- the VIF = 1.37.**

F) Employ a Koyck lag structure in the COIN/LEIS regression. Does this regression suffer from serial correlation according to the h test? Show the 5-step procedure.

A) Ho: no autocorrelation Ha: auto present

$$h = (1 - \frac{d}{2})\sqrt{\frac{n}{1 - n(\text{var}(\hat{\beta}))}} \qquad h = (1 - \frac{2.13}{2})\sqrt{\frac{178}{1 - 178(0.05^2)}} = -1.16$$

B) 5%
C) If $|h| > t^c$, then reject Ho (d.f. = n-k)
D) $|h|$ = 1.16 ; t^c = 1.984 (d.f.=178-3; using d.f.=100)
E) Do Not Reject Ho; auto is not present

G) Employ a Koyck lag structure in the COIN/LEIS regression. Does this regression suffer from serial correlation according to the Lagrange multiplier test? Show the 5-step procedure.

  1) Ho: no serial correlation   Ha: serial correlation exists
  2) 5%
  3) If $nR^2 > \chi c$, then reject Ho (d.f. = # of lagged residual terms = 1)
  4) 5.808074 < 3.84,
  5) Do Not Reject Ho; auto is not present

H) Employ a Koyck lag structure in the COIN/LEIS regression. Does this regression suffer from multicollinearity? On what do you base your response? **Not very much; the VIF = 1.01.**

I) According to the Koyck model, a 1-unit increase in LEIS implies COIN will be how much higher or lower in the short run? **0.327359 higher**

J) In the long run, the 1-unit increase in LEIS implies COIN will eventually change how much? $\beta_1/(1-\lambda) = 0.33/(1- 0.603959) = 0.83$

5. Use the data in QLEISCOIN and statistical software to do Granger tests to determine if changes in the leading economic indicators (LEIS) precede changes in the coincident indicators (COIN).

A) Using lag lengths of 6, show the 5-step procedure for the Granger test that changes in LEIS do not precede changes in COIN.

Pairwise Granger Causality Tests
Sample: 1959:1 2003:4
Lags: 6

Null Hypothesis:	Obs	F-Statistic	Probability
COIN does not Granger Cause LEIS	173	8.00292	1.5E-07
LEIS does not Granger Cause COIN		15.6394	4.4E-14

1) Ho: LEIS does not Granger Cause COIN
   Ha: LEIS do Granger Cause COIN
2) 5%
3) If F > F^C, reject Ho
4) 15.6394 vs 2.18 (d.f. num. = R = 6; d.f. den. = n-k = 173-13=160; using 120)
5) Reject Ho; changes in LEIS precede changes in COIN

B) Using lag lengths of 6, show the 5-step procedure for the Granger test that changes in COIN do not precede changes in LEIS.

1) Ho: COIN does not Granger Cause LEIS
   Ha: COIN does Granger Cause LEIS
2) 5%
3) If F > F^C, reject Ho
4) 8.00292 vs 2.18 (d.f. num. = R = 6; d.f. den. = n-k = 173-13=160; using 120)
5) Reject Ho; changes in COIN precede changes in LEIS

Dependent Variable: LEIS
Method: Least Squares
Date: 04/16/10   Time: 08:47
Sample(adjusted): 1960:4 2003:4
Included observations: 173 after adjusting endpoints

Variable	Coefficient	Std. Error	t-Statistic	Prob.
C	0.523021	0.131798	3.968344	0.0001
COIN(-1)	-0.990878	0.175292	-5.652734	0.0000
COIN(-2)	-0.051971	0.200176	-0.259625	0.7955
COIN(-3)	-0.119829	0.189817	-0.631286	0.5288
COIN(-4)	0.098743	0.178740	0.552438	0.5814
COIN(-5)	-0.052785	0.165461	-0.319020	0.7501
COIN(-6)	0.179148	0.144364	1.240950	0.2164
LEIS(-1)	0.653975	0.092049	7.104657	0.0000
LEIS(-2)	0.176288	0.109281	1.613163	0.1087
LEIS(-3)	0.277366	0.109328	2.537014	0.0121
LEIS(-4)	-0.019450	0.105757	-0.183911	0.8543
LEIS(-5)	0.125042	0.102509	1.219815	0.2243
LEIS(-6)	0.024625	0.085896	0.286678	0.7747

R-squared	0.438093	Mean dependent var	0.394833
Adjusted R-squared	0.395950	S.D. dependent var	1.183041
S.E. of regression	0.919467	Akaike info criterion	2.742126
Sum squared resid	135.2672	Schwarz criterion	2.979079
Log likelihood	-224.1939	F-statistic	10.39538
Durbin-Watson stat	1.975072	Prob(F-statistic)	0.000000

Dependent Variable: LEIS
Method: Least Squares
Date: 04/16/10   Time: 08:49
Sample(adjusted): 1960:4 2003:4
Included observations: 173 after adjusting endpoints

Variable	Coefficient	Std. Error	t-Statistic	Prob.
C	0.250640	0.089861	2.789191	0.0059
LEIS(-1)	0.508384	0.077577	6.553257	0.0000
LEIS(-2)	-0.068384	0.087131	-0.784839	0.4337
LEIS(-3)	0.140603	0.085915	1.636523	0.1036
LEIS(-4)	-0.196359	0.085897	-2.285992	0.0235
LEIS(-5)	-0.011192	0.086981	-0.128668	0.8978
LEIS(-6)	-0.013386	0.077324	-0.173115	0.8628

R-squared	0.269459	Mean dependent var	0.394833
Adjusted R-squared	0.243054	S.D. dependent var	1.183041
S.E. of regression	1.029277	Akaike info criterion	2.935211
Sum squared resid	175.8621	Schwarz criterion	3.062800
Log likelihood	-246.8957	F-statistic	10.20483
Durbin-Watson stat	1.993804	Prob(F-statistic)	0.000000

$$F = \frac{(SSR_R - SSR)/R}{SSR/(n-k)} = \frac{(175.8621 - 135.2672)/6}{135.2672/(173-13)} = \frac{6.7658}{.84542} = 8.0029059$$

C) Given your results in A) and B) above, can you unequivocally conclude that changes in LEIS precede changes in COIN? **No**

D) Does your answer to C) above change when lag lengths of 10 are used? **No**

Pairwise Granger Causality Tests
Sample: 1959:1 2003:4
Lags: 10

Null Hypothesis:	Obs	F-Statistic	Probability
COIN does not Granger Cause LEIS	169	4.36968	2.3E-05
LEIS does not Granger Cause COIN		10.9508	8.0E-14

E) Does your answer to C) above change when lag lengths of 12 are used? **No**

Pairwise Granger Causality Tests
Sample: 1959:1 2003:4
Lags: 12

Null Hypothesis:	Obs	F-Statistic	Probability
COIN does not Granger Cause LEIS	167	4.01460	2.4E-05
LEIS does not Granger Cause COIN		9.44066	2.8E-13

7. Use the data in MACRO.XLS and statistical software to run Granger tests to determine if changes in M2 Granger-cause INFL or vice-versa.

   A) What are the appropriate lag lengths? Explain. **Lower lags (2-4) are closer to showing some significance, but no hypothesis is rejected for any lags up to at least 12.**
   B) What do you conclude? Explain. **Since no hypothesis is rejected at almost all lag lengths, it appears as if changes in M2 do not Granger-cause INFL and vice-versa.**

9. Using the data in MACRO.XLS and statistical software, which of the following variables appear to be nonstationary because of nonconstant means or nonconstant variances? Produce the graph for each variable and say if the problem is a nonconstant mean or variance, both, or neither.

A) Real investment (rinv)
Nonstationary– Nonconstant mean; variance?

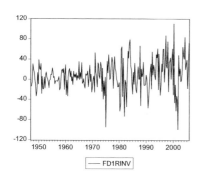

B) The first-difference in real investment
Stationary or not due to nonconstant variance

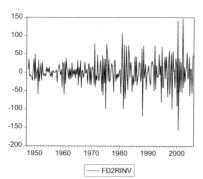

C) The second-difference in real investment
Stationary or not due to nonconstant variance

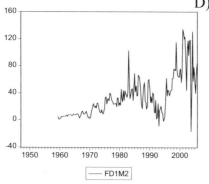

D) The first difference in the money supply (m2)
Nonstationary– nonconstant variance & mean

E) Interest rate on AAA corporate bonds (aaa)
Nonstationary– nonconstant mean

11. Which variables from the list above are nonstationary according to the Dickey-Fuller test? Show the 5-step procedure for each variable.

A) Real investment (rinv)

ADF Test Statistic	2.548323	1% Critical Value*	-3.4597
		5% Critical Value	-2.8739
		10% Critical Value	-2.5733

1) Ho: B1 = 0 (X is nonstationary)   Ha: B1 < 0 (X is stationary)
2) 5%
3) If t-ratio < -tc*, reject Ho
4) 2.548323 < -2.8739 ???
5) Do Not Reject Ho; rinv is nonstationary

B) The first difference in real investment

ADF Test Statistic	-12.72571	1% Critical Value*	-3.4598
		5% Critical Value	-2.8740
		10% Critical Value	-2.5733

1) Ho: B1 = 0 (X is nonstationary)   Ha: B1 < 0 (X is stationary)
2) 5%
3) If t-ratio < -tc*, reject Ho
4) -12.72571 < -2.8740 ???
5) Reject Ho; fd1rinv is stationary

C) The second difference in real investment

ADF Test Statistic	-26.49940	1% Critical Value*	-3.4599
		5% Critical Value	-2.8740
		10% Critical Value	-2.5734

1) Ho: B1 = 0 (X is nonstationary)   Ha: B1 < 0 (X is stationary)
2) 5%
3) If t-ratio < -tc*, reject Ho
4) -26.49940 < -2.8740 ???
5) Reject Ho; fd2rinv is stationary

D) The first difference in the money supply (m2)

ADF Test Statistic	-4.709242	1% Critical Value*	-3.4667
		5% Critical Value	-2.8771
		10% Critical Value	-2.5750

1) Ho: B1 = 0 (X is nonstationary)   Ha: B1 < 0 (X is stationary)
2) 5%
3) If t-ratio < -tc*, reject Ho
4) -4.709242 < -2.8771 ???
5) Reject Ho; fd1m2 is stationary

E) Interest rate on AAA corporate bonds (aaa)

ADF Test Statistic	-1.432218	1% Critical Value*	-3.4597
		5% Critical Value	-2.8739
		10% Critical Value	-2.5733

1) Ho: B1 = 0 (X is nonstationary)   Ha: B1 < 0 (X is stationary)
2) 5%
3) If t-ratio < -tc*, reject Ho
4) -1.432218 < -2.8739 ???
5) Do Not Reject Ho; AAA is nonstationary

13. Use the data in AJ.XLS to replicate the famous Andersen-Jordan study by regressing a constant term, lagged money supply (m2), and the lagged standardized federal deficit (fp) on nominal GDP (ngdp): $\text{ngdp}_t = \hat{\beta}_0 + \hat{\beta}_1 \text{m2}_{t-1} + \hat{\beta}_2 \text{fp}_{t-1} + e_t$

A) Which explanatory variable has the more profound impact on nominal GDP? Explain your response. **Only m2 is statistically significant.**

B) Which variables in the regression are nonstationary? Explain. **Line graphs are inconclusive. Correlograms suggest that the first differences in M2 and NGDP are nonstationary. Dickey-Fuller tests indicate that the first-differences of M2, and NGDP are nonstationary.**

C) Check for cointegration among the variables in the regression. Show the 5-step Dickey-Fuller procedure.

1) Ho: $\beta_1 = 0$ (e_t is nonstationary)   Ha: $\beta_1 < 0$ (e_t is stationary)
   (X and Y are not cointegrated)   (X and Y are cointegrated)
2) 5%
3) If t-ratio < -tc*, reject Ho
4) -3.11 < -2.9350
5) Reject Ho; The regression is cointegrated

Chapter 13   Odd Problem Solutions

1. Using Eviews and the data in QUALLCOMM.XLS, make in-sample forecasts of the price of quallcomm stock for each of the four weeks subsequent to 11/22/1999 (11/29/1999, 12/06/1999, 12/13/1999, and 12/20/1999) using a:

A) linear trend

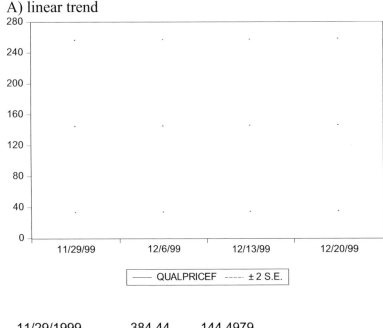

Forecast: QUALPRICEF
Actual: QUALPRICE
Forecast sample: 11/29/1999 12/20/...
Included observations: 4
Root Mean Squared Error   281.3159
Mean Absolute Error   278.9913
Mean Abs. Percent Error   65.49879
Theil Inequality Coefficient 0.492401
   Bias Proportion   0.983542
   Variance Proportion   0.016424
   Covariance Proportion   0.000034

11/29/1999	384.44	144.4979
12/06/1999	391.50	145.0784
12/13/1999	455.00	145.6590
12/20/1999	466.50	146.2395

B) lin-log trend

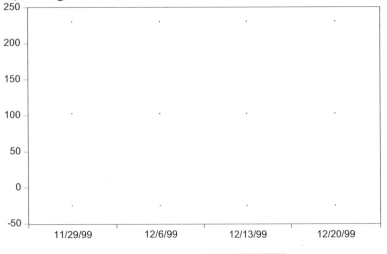

Forecast: QUALPRICEF
Actual: QUALPRICE
Forecast sample: 11/29/1999 12/20/...
Included observations: 4
Root Mean Squared Error   324.1509
Mean Absolute Error   322.0813
Mean Abs. Percent Error   75.71942
Theil Inequality Coefficient 0.613663
   Bias Proportion   0.987271
   Variance Proportion   0.012723
   Covariance Proportion   0.000005

11/29/1999	384.44	102.0936
12/06/1999	391.50	102.2174
12/13/1999	455.00	102.3406
12/20/1999	466.50	102.4633

C) log-lin trend

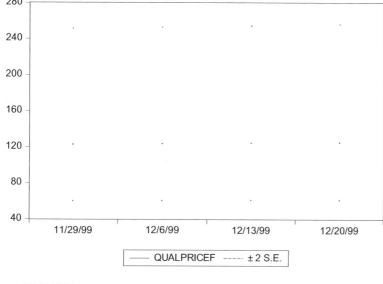

Forecast: QUALPRICEF
Actual: QUALPRICE
Forecast sample: 11/29/1999 12/20/...
Included observations: 4
Root Mean Squared Error 302.8925
Mean Absolute Error 300.7573
Mean Abs. Percent Error 70.67037
Theil Inequality Coefficient 0.551165
 Bias Proportion 0.985951
 Variance Proportion 0.014011
 Covariance Proportion 0.000038

11/29/1999	384.44	122.4666
12/06/1999	391.50	123.2209
12/13/1999	455.00	123.9799
12/20/1999	466.50	124.7436

D) polynomial trend

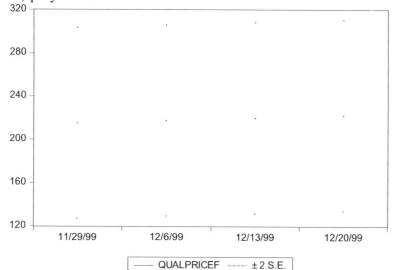

Forecast: QUALPRICEF
Actual: QUALPRICE
Forecast sample: 11/29/1999 12/20/...
Included observations: 4
Root Mean Squared Error 208.8244
Mean Absolute Error 205.9938
Mean Abs. Percent Error 48.20511
Theil Inequality Coefficient 0.324098
 Bias Proportion 0.973074
 Variance Proportion 0.026680
 Covariance Proportion 0.000247

11/29/1999	384.44	214.8952
12/06/1999	391.50	217.2002
12/13/1999	455.00	219.5187
12/20/1999	466.50	221.8509

E) polynomial to the sixth order

$$(\text{qualprice}_t = \hat{\beta}_0 + \hat{\beta}_1 \text{time}_t + \hat{\beta}_2 \text{time}^2_t + \hat{\beta}_3 \text{time}^3_t + \hat{\beta}_4 \text{time}^4_t + \hat{\beta}_5 \text{time}^5_t + \hat{\beta}_6 \text{time}^6_t + e_t)$$

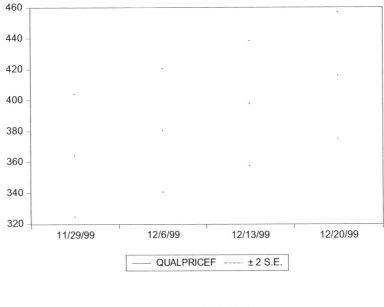

Forecast: QUALPRICEF
Actual: QUALPRICE
Forecast sample: 11/29/1999 12/20/...
Included observations: 4
Root Mean Squared Error 39.98314
Mean Absolute Error 34.85913
Mean Abs. Percent Error 7.896328
Theil Inequality Coefficient 0.049004
Bias Proportion 0.760115
Variance Proportion 0.190103
Covariance Proportion 0.049782

11/29/1999	384.44	364.0065
12/06/1999	391.50	380.5348
12/13/1999	455.00	397.7595
12/20/1999	466.50	415.7027

F) Which trend provides the least accurate forecasts? Based on …?
Lin-log trend based on RMSE, MAE, MAPE, and Theil's U

qualprice – the closing price of quallcomm stock that week
time – 1, 2, 3, …

3. Using Eviews and the data in RUPT1.XLS:

cor – the corruption level in a country 0 lowest to 10 highest
country – country name
ecfree – measure of economic freedom 0 lowest to 5 highest
fines – unpaid traffic fines per diplomat of the nation
indy – year of independence
mil – number of military personnel per 1,000 population
over 65 – percent of the population older than 65
popsq – population per square mile

A) Find the best model you can to explain cor.

ECFREE and OVER65 are the only appropriate variables to explain COR:

Dependent Variable: COR
Method: Least Squares
Date: 03/06/13   Time: 12:07
Sample: 1 48
Included observations: 48

Variable	Coefficient	Std. Error	t-Statistic	Prob.
C	11.86516	0.698706	16.98161	0.0000
ECFREE	-2.503604	0.326438	-7.669460	0.0000
OVER65	-0.116565	0.042427	-2.747461	0.0086

R-squared	0.694178	Mean dependent var	5.135417
Adjusted R-squared	0.680586	S.D. dependent var	2.343800
S.E. of regression	1.324639	Akaike info criterion	3.460618
Sum squared resid	78.96005	Schwarz criterion	3.577568
Log likelihood	-80.05483	Hannan-Quinn criter.	3.504814
F-statistic	51.07228	Durbin-Watson stat	2.204328
Prob(F-statistic)	0.000000		

B) Is multicollinearity mild, moderate, or severe in your model? Explain.

	ECFREE	FINES	INDY	MIL	OVER65	POPSQ
ECFREE	1.000000	-0.391304	-0.320851	0.074481	0.425012	0.329055
FINES	-0.391304	1.000000	0.145005	-0.102551	-0.211461	-0.078545
INDY	-0.320851	0.145005	1.000000	0.126057	-0.397867	0.033999
MIL	0.074481	-0.102551	0.126057	1.000000	0.102940	0.260075
OVER65	0.425012	-0.211461	-0.397867	0.102940	1.000000	-0.049151
POPSQ	0.329055	-0.078545	0.033999	0.260075	-0.049151	1.000000

Moderate with a .425 max r, and 3 r's above .321

C) Did multicollinearlity affect your model selection? Explain.
No, I went with two explanatory variables, both significant.
Yes, I went three explanatory variables, one not significant.

D) Use your model to predict cor for Argentina. **3.416** (actual = 7.0!)

E) Form a 95% confidence interval around your prediction.

3.416 +/- 1.325(2.014)   d.f. = 48 – 3 = 45

0.747 to 6.085

F) The average cor for all 48 countries = 5.135. Certainly, it would have been better to rely on this "naïve" forecast than our regression model in the case of Argentina. Would it have been better to forecast this value for all 48 nations instead of relying on our regression model? Explain.

The naïve forecasts:

Dependent Variable: COR
Method: Least Squares
Sample: 1 48
Included observations: 48

Variable	Coefficient	Std. Error	t-Statistic	Prob.
C	5.135417	0.338298	15.18014	0.0000

R-squared	0.000000	Mean dependent var	5.135417
Adjusted R-squared	0.000000	S.D. dependent var	2.343800
S.E. of regression	2.343800	Akaike info criterion	4.562038
Sum squared resid	258.1898	Schwarz criterion	4.601021
Log likelihood	-108.4889	Hannan-Quinn criter.	4.576770
Durbin-Watson stat	1.777375		

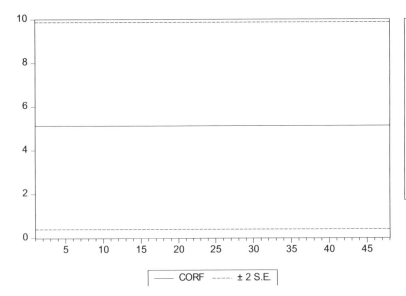

Forecast: CORF
Actual: COR
Forecast sample: 1 48
Included observations: 48

Root Mean Squared Error	2.319257
Mean Absolute Error	1.947656
Mean Abs. Percent Error	98.68947
Theil Inequality Coefficient	0.215339
Bias Proportion	0.000000
Variance Proportion	NA
Covariance Proportion	NA

The regression model forecasts:

Dependent Variable: COR
Method: Least Squares
Sample: 1 48
Included observations: 48

Variable	Coefficient	Std. Error	t-Statistic	Prob.
C	11.86516	0.698706	16.98161	0.0000
ECFREE	-2.503604	0.326438	-7.669460	0.0000
OVER65	-0.116565	0.042427	-2.747461	0.0086

R-squared	0.694178	Mean dependent var		5.135417
Adjusted R-squared	0.680586	S.D. dependent var		2.343800
S.E. of regression	1.324639	Akaike info criterion		3.460618
Sum squared resid	78.96005	Schwarz criterion		3.577568
Log likelihood	-80.05483	Hannan-Quinn criter.		3.504814
F-statistic	51.07228	Durbin-Watson stat		2.204328
Prob(F-statistic)	0.000000			

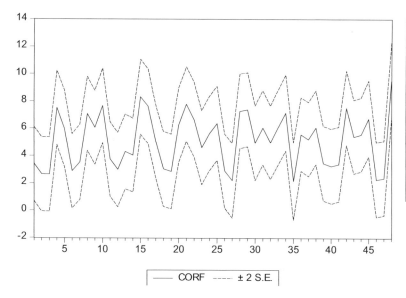

Forecast: CORF	
Actual: COR	
Forecast sample: 1 48	
Included observations: 48	
Root Mean Squared Error	1.282576
Mean Absolute Error	1.070592
Mean Abs. Percent Error	45.96385
Theil Inequality Coefficient	0.115321
Bias Proportion	0.000000
Variance Proportion	0.091004
Covariance Proportion	0.908996

—— CORF ---- ± 2 S.E.

The regression model makes better forecasts based on RMSE, MAE, MAPE, and Theil's U.
The regression model makes better forecasts since SER < S.E.(COR)
1.3246   2.3438

Chapter 14   Odd Problem Solutions

1. Use Eviews and the data in RGDP.XLS to answer the following:

A) Produce a correlogram of SP500. Does it suggest the levels of SP500 are stationary? Explain.
No, not stationary. The autocorrelations take 12 or so periods to decay to zero.
B) Produce a correlogram of the first differences of SP500. Does it suggest the first differences of SP500 are stationary? Explain.
Yes, stationary. The autocorrelations are insignificant by lag 6 plus no decay.
C) Do an augmented Dickey-Fuller test on the levels of SP500. Show the 5-step procedure.

> **1) Ho: $\beta_1 = 0$ (SP500 is nonstationary)   Ha: $\beta_1 < 0$ (SP500 is stationary)**
> **2) 5%**
> **3) If t-ratio < -t^c*, reject Ho**
> **4) -0.464290 > -2.92**
> **5) Do Not Reject Ho; SP500 is nonstationary**

D) Do an augmented Dickey-Fuller test on the first differences of SP500. Show the 5-step procedure.

> **1) Ho: $\beta_1 = 0$ (DSP500 is nonstationary)   Ha: $\beta_1 < 0$ (DSP500 is stationary)**
> **2) 5%**
> **3) If t-ratio < -t^c*, reject Ho**
> **4) -6.059915 < -2.92**
> **5) Reject Ho; The first differences of SP500 are stationary**

E) Working with the first differences in SP500, what sort of model is suggested by the pattern of the correlogram and partial correlogram?

> **i) Purely autoregressive**
> ii) Purely moving average
> **iii) Autoregressive and moving average**
> iv) Neither autoregressive nor moving average since the time-series is white noise

F) Find an appropriately specified ARIMA model for the first differences of SP500 and fill in your result here: **ARIMA(4,1,3) ARIMA(1,1,2) ARIMA(2,1,4) ARIMA(4,1,2) are all good choices.**

Dependent Variable: D(SP500)
Method: Least Squares
Date: 04/17/13   Time: 12:29
Sample (adjusted): 1962 2012
Included observations: 51 after adjustments
Convergence achieved after 25 iterations
MA Backcast: 1959 1961

Variable	Coefficient	Std. Error	t-Statistic	Prob.
C	21.62865	10.94312	1.976461	0.0545
AR(1)	0.562303	0.139624	4.027275	0.0002
AR(2)	-0.982842	0.098802	-9.947580	0.0000
AR(3)	0.188724	0.169543	1.113134	0.2718
AR(4)	-0.589554	0.128169	-4.599823	0.0000
MA(1)	-0.099959	0.165587	-0.603662	0.5492
MA(2)	0.602995	0.135616	4.446346	0.0001
MA(3)	0.582075	0.167245	3.480373	0.0012

R-squared	0.595979	Mean dependent var	25.74667
Adjusted R-squared	0.530208	S.D. dependent var	103.4175
S.E. of regression	70.88374	Akaike info criterion	11.50306
Sum squared resid	216053.7	Schwarz criterion	11.80609
Log likelihood	-285.3280	Hannan-Quinn criter.	11.61886
F-statistic	9.061452	Durbin-Watson stat	1.922143
Prob(F-statistic)	0.000001		

Inverted AR Roots	.55-.80i	.55+.80i	-.27-.75i	-.27+.75i
Inverted MA Roots	.34-.94i	.34+.94i	-.58	

G) Use the model you found to make an in-sample, ex poste forecast of SP500 (not the first differences) for 2012. Fill in the values below:

Forecast of SP500 in 2012 = _1345.760_____

Standard error of this forecast = __75.43875_____

Forecast error = _1379.350 – 1345.760 = _33.590_____

H) Make out-of-sample forecasts for SP500 from 2013 to 2016 and paste those here:

		SP500f	SERF
2013	NA	1572.204	86.17779
2014	NA	1507.856	153.7650
2015	NA	1286.888	183.6600
2016	NA	1235.811	216.1574

I) How confident are you in these forecasts? Explain.

Not very confident as they have the sp500 falling for three years and the SERF increases with time.

Dependent Variable: D(SP500)
Method: Least Squares
Date: 04/17/13   Time: 12:34
Sample (adjusted): 1959 2012
Included observations: 54 after adjustments
Convergence achieved after 21 iterations
MA Backcast: 1957 1958

Variable	Coefficient	Std. Error	t-Statistic	Prob.
C	33.45761	8.001003	4.181677	0.0001
AR(1)	0.808162	0.095152	8.493391	0.0000
MA(1)	-0.244147	0.114522	-2.131879	0.0380
MA(2)	-0.709669	0.107500	-6.601581	0.0000

R-squared	0.365131	Mean dependent var	24.68796
Adjusted R-squared	0.327039	S.D. dependent var	100.5541
S.E. of regression	82.48877	Akaike info criterion	11.73439
Sum squared resid	340219.9	Schwarz criterion	11.88172
Log likelihood	-312.8285	Hannan-Quinn criter.	11.79121
F-statistic	9.585482	Durbin-Watson stat	1.910677
Prob(F-statistic)	0.000042		

Inverted AR Roots	.81	
Inverted MA Roots	.97	-.73

G) Use the model you found to make an in-sample, ex poste forecast of SP500 (not the first differences) for 2012. Fill in the values below:

   Forecast of SP500 in 2012 = _1268.788_____

   Standard error of this forecast = __85.75823_____

   Forecast error = _1379.350 – 1268.788 = _110.552_____

H) Make out-of-sample forecasts for SP500 from 2013 to 2016 and paste those here:

	SP500f	SERF
NA	1489.380	87.77443
NA	1506.258	163.4299
NA	1526.317	205.2800
NA	1548.946	234.1602

I) How confident are you in these forecasts? Explain.
Not very confident as the SERF increases to a large value with time

Dependent Variable: D(SP500)
Method: Least Squares
Date: 04/17/13   Time: 12:45
Sample (adjusted): 1960 2012
Included observations: 53 after adjustments
Convergence achieved after 50 iterations
MA Backcast: 1956 1959

Variable	Coefficient	Std. Error	t-Statistic	Prob.
C	23.55675	11.03544	2.134647	0.0382
AR(1)	1.007930	0.097226	10.36690	0.0000
AR(2)	-0.875699	0.098685	-8.873654	0.0000
MA(1)	-0.496056	0.153019	-3.241793	0.0022
MA(2)	0.353915	0.146511	2.415619	0.0197
MA(3)	0.491186	0.137388	3.575185	0.0008
MA(4)	-0.450775	0.149264	-3.019977	0.0041

R-squared	0.495684	Mean dependent var		24.94226
Adjusted R-squared	0.429904	S.D. dependent var		101.4989
S.E. of regression	76.63644	Akaike info criterion		11.63852
Sum squared resid	270164.6	Schwarz criterion		11.89875
Log likelihood	-301.4209	Hannan-Quinn criter.		11.73859
F-statistic	7.535442	Durbin-Watson stat		2.047301
Prob(F-statistic)	0.000012			

Inverted AR Roots	.50+.79i	.50-.79i		
Inverted MA Roots	.60	.34-.91i	.34+.91i	-.78

G) Use the model you found to make an in-sample, ex poste forecast of SP500 (not the first differences) for 2012. Fill in the values below:

Forecast of SP500 in 2012 = _1388.922_____

Standard error of this forecast = __86.25280_____

Forecast error = _1379.350 – 1388.922 = _-9.572_____

H) Make out-of-sample forecasts for SP500 from 2013 to 2016 and paste those here:

		SP500f	SERF
2013	NA	1503.993	88.87085
2014	NA	1430.838	161.5567
2015	NA	1295.824	205.3845
2016	NA	1248.558	237.7782

I) How confident are you in these forecasts? Explain.
Not very confident as the SERF increases to a large value with time

Solutions to Test Yourself Problems

Chapters 1, 2, and 3   Test yourself solutions

1. Given

Yi	Xi
11.2	5.4
-27.1	6.7
33.4	7.1
0.02	-8.8

A) Calculate the values for the structural parameters of $Y_i = \hat{\beta}_0 + \hat{\beta}_1 X_i + e_i$

(Show your work making the details of your calculations apparent.)

$\hat{\beta}_1 = 0.4$ $\hat{\beta}_0 = 3.33$

B) Interpret the values you obtained for $\hat{\beta}_0$ and $\hat{\beta}_1$ above.

If X = 0, then Y is expected to equal 3.33.
If X increases 1 unit, then Y is expected to increase 0.4 units.

C) According to the SER, is the fit of the regression adequate? Explain.

No, the SER (= 30.58) is greater than ½ Y-bar (= 4.38).

D) What percent of the variation in Y is explained by X in this regression?

r2 = .015 – 1.5 percent of the variation in Y is explained by X.

E) Suppose we ran this regression again with a new set of observations on Y

and X. Would you be surprised if $\hat{\beta}_1$ turned out to be -2.0? Explain why or

why not.

SE($\hat{\beta}_1$) = 2.31. No, because -2.0 is very close to the expected variation in $\hat{\beta}_1$ in repeated
sampling.

2. Answer the following questions:

A) Distinguish between the population regression function and the sample
regression function.

The population regression function is the line that minimizes the Σe_i^2 for the entire

population of error-free observations on X and Y. The sample regression function

minimizes the Σe_i^2 for a sample from the entire population of observations of X and Y that

may contain errors.

B) Distinguish between cross-sectional and time-series data.

Cross-sectional data are observations on X and Y a given point in time. Time-series data
are observations on X and Y over time.

C) What is a normal equation?

A normal equation will be encountered when deriving formulae for structural parameters
in regression equations. Once the derivatives, or partial derivatives, of the function to be
minimized are taken and set equal to zero, the normal equation(s) can be found by
beginning to solve for the unknown(s). Normal equations have no negative terms.

D) Explain why a perfectly vertical regression line is impossible.

Any observations on a scattergram that do not lie directly on a vertical line will have an
infinite vertical distance to the line. Since regression lines minimize the sum of the squared
vertical distances to the line, a vertical line cannot provide that minimum.

3. Which of the following is (are) NOT correct? **A, E, F, H, I**

A) $Y_i = \beta_0 + \beta_1 X_i$

B) $\hat{Y}_i = \beta_0 + \beta_1 X_i$

C) $Y_i = \beta_0 + \beta_1 X_i + u_i$

D) $Y_i = \hat{\beta}_0 + \hat{\beta}_1 X_i + e_i$

E) $\hat{Y}_i = \hat{\beta}_0 + \hat{\beta}_1 X_i + e_i$

F) $Y_i = \hat{\beta}_0 + \hat{\beta}_1 X_i + u_i$

G) $E(Yi|Xi) = \beta_0 + \beta_1 X_i$

H) $\hat{Y}_i = \beta_0 + \beta_1 X_i + u_i$

I) $E(Yi|Xi) = \hat{\beta}_0 + \hat{\beta}_1 X_i + e_i$

4. Answer True or False:

A) **F** Sabermetrics is the application of statistical analysis to war.

B) **T** Unless all the observations lie on a straight line, it is impossible to fit a line such that $\Sigma |e_i| = 0$.

C) **T** When a line is fit to observations on a scattergram so that Σe_i^2 is minimized, then $\Sigma e_i = 0$.

D) **F** When a line is fit to observations on a scattergram so that Σe_i^2 is minimized, then sometimes more than one line meets this criteria.

E) **F** $\Sigma(X_i - \overline{X})(Y_i - \overline{Y}) = \overline{X}\Sigma Y_i - \overline{Y}\Sigma X_i$

F) **T** $\Sigma(X_i - \overline{X}) = 0$

G) **T** A large SER and low r^2 can be the result of the Y-variable being very random.

H) **T** If $r^2 = 0$, then β_1 must $= 0$.

I) **F** If $r^2 = 1$, then β_1 must $= 1$.

J) **T** If SER $= 0$, then r^2 must $= 1$.

Chapters 4 and 5   Test yourself solutions

Dependent Variable: WHY
Method: Least Squares
Sample: 1978 2006
Included observations: 29

Variable	Coefficient	Std. Error	t-Statistic	Prob.
C	1.997710	51.03278	0.039146	0.9691
EX1	15.81597	3.734046	4.235611	0.0003
EX2	3.046501	2.188336	1.392154	0.1761
EX3	-0.000145	0.005735	-0.025229	0.9801
R-squared	0.765250	Mean dependent var		152.0576
Adjusted R-squared	0.737080	S.D. dependent var		51.28692
S.E. of regression	26.29775	Akaike info criterion		9.504286
Sum squared resid	17289.29	Schwarz criterion		9.692879
Log likelihood	-133.8121	F-statistic		27.16539
Durbin-Watson stat	0.723982	Prob(F-statistic)		0.000000

1. Use the Eviews output above and below to help with A) through G)

    A) Interpret the coefficient on EX1. **If EX1 increases 1 unit, then WHY is expected to increase 15.81597 units, holding EX2 and EX3 constant.**

    B) Interpret the coefficient on the constant term. **If X1 = X2 = X3 = 0, then WHY is expected to equal 1.997710.**

    C) Is EX2 significant at the 17% critical level? Explain. **No, its Prob-value is greater than .17**

    D) Perform a positive sign test on the coefficient attached to EX2. Show the 5-step procedure.

        1) Ho: $\beta_2 = 0$ Ha: $\beta_2 > 0$

        2) 5%

        3) If t-ratio > t^c, then reject Ho

        4)   1.392154 > 1.708 (d.f. = n- k = 29 – 4 =25)

        5) Do Not Reject Ho; β_0 is not significantly positive

    E) Perform a test to determine if the coefficient on EX3 is greater than -1.11. Show the 5-step procedure.

        1) Ho: $\beta_3 = -1.11$ Ha: $\beta_3 > -1.11$

        2) 5%

        3) If t-ratio > t^c, then reject Ho

        4)   193.6 > 1.708 (d.f. = n- k = 29 – 4 =25)

        5) Reject Ho; β_0 is significantly greater than -1.11

$$t - ratio = \frac{\hat{\beta}_0 - \beta_{Ho}}{SE(\hat{\beta}_0)} = \frac{-0.000145 + 1.11}{0.005735} = \textbf{193.6}$$

F) Perform a test to determine if R-squared is greater than zero. Show the 5-step procedure.
1) Ho: $r^2 = 0$ Ha: $r^2 > 0$
2) 5%
3) If F > Fc, then reject Ho
4) 27.16539 > 2.99 (d.f. = k-1=3 in the numerator and n-k=25 in the denominator)
5) Reject Ho; r^2 is statistically greater than zero

G) Based on the information in the table above (and ignoring Ramsey's Reset test which we will perform in a moment), do you think the regression above is underspecified or overspecified? Explain. **Overspecified because EX2 and EX3 are insignificant**

H) Perform Ramsey's Reset test on the regression above using the Eviews printout below. Show the 5-step procedure.

Ramsey RESET Test:

F-statistic	15.32735	Probability	0.000059
Log likelihood ratio	24.56517	Probability	0.000005

Test Equation:
Dependent Variable: WHY
Method: Least Squares
Sample: 1978 2006
Included observations: 29

Variable	Coefficient	Std. Error	t-Statistic	Prob.
C	1190.553	228.1171	5.219043	0.0000
EX1	-314.2471	60.00884	-5.236679	0.0000
EX2	-62.55620	12.06659	-5.184249	0.0000
EX3	-0.013078	0.006110	-2.140328	0.0432
FITTED^2	0.119787	0.021647	5.533578	0.0000
FITTED^3	-0.000222	4.06E-05	-5.474315	0.0000

R-squared	0.899370	Mean dependent var	152.0576
Adjusted R-squared	0.877494	S.D. dependent var	51.28692
S.E. of regression	17.95084	Akaike info criterion	8.795142
Sum squared resid	7411.349	Schwarz criterion	9.078031
Log likelihood	-121.5296	F-statistic	41.11217
Durbin-Watson stat	1.018779	Prob(F-statistic)	0.000000

1) Ho: $\hat{\beta}_4 = \hat{\beta}_5 = 0$ Ha: $\hat{\beta}_4$ and/or $\hat{\beta}_5 \neq 0$
(No variables excluded)   (Variables excluded)
2) 5%
3) If F > F^c, then reject Ho
4) 15.32735 > 3.42; where F^c has d.f. NUM = 2 ; d.f. DEN = n-k=23
5) Reject Ho; variables are excluded

I) What do the terms "FITTED^2" and "FITTED^3" refer to in the
   Eviews printout above? **These terms represent possible missing variables. They are
the predicted WHY values from the original regression squared and cubed.**

2. Define the following terms:

   A) Unbiased estimator - **an estimator that averages out to the true value in repeated
sampling.** $E(\hat{\beta}_0) = \hat{\beta}_0$

   B) Best estimator – **an estimator that varies less than any other possible estimator in
repeated sampling.** $Var\ (\hat{\beta}_0) < Var\ (\tilde{\beta}_0)$ **where** $\tilde{\beta}_0$ **is any other possible estimator
of** β_0.

   C) Correlation coefficient (r) – **measures the degree of linear correlation between two
variables.**

   D) Prob-value – **the lowest level of significance that can be used in a hypothesis test
while still rejecting Ho.**

3. Mark each statement TRUE or FALSE.

   A) **F** If a regression is overspecified, then it would be surprising to see the t-ratios
   become more robust once the extraneous variables were removed.
   B) **F** If a regression is underspecified, then it would be surprising to see the estimators
   change markedly once the missing variables were included.
   C) **T** If a regression is overspecified, then it would be surprising to see the estimators
   change markedly once the extraneous variables were removed.
   D) **F** A 95% confidence interval for a coefficient will be smaller than a 90%
   confidence interval.
   E) **T** The Andersen-Jordan equation indicates that monetary policy is more effective
   than fiscal policy.
   F) **T** Deriving the estimators for $Y_i = \hat{\beta}_0 + \hat{\beta}_1 X1_i + \hat{\beta}_2 X2_i + e_i$ will yield three
   normal equations.
   G) **F** The Akaike criterion is monotonically decreasing with respect to the number of
   explanatory variables.
   H) **T** The higher the critical level of the hypothesis test, the less chance there is that the
   test will result in a TYPE II error.
   I) **F** A coefficient that is significant at the 1% critical level may not be significant at the
   2% critical level.
   J) **F** A test of significance is more likely to result in a TYPE I error in an overspecified
   model.

Chapters 6 and 7   Test yourself solutions

1. Interpret every structural parameter in each of the following regressions considering:

>WAGES = pay per hour of work
>EXP = years of experience
>EXPSQ = EXP squared
>ED = years of education
>DGEN = 1 if male; 0 otherwise
>INTACT = DGEN X EXP
>LN --- = the natural log of a variable

A) $LNWAGES_i = 2.1 + 1.3\ EXP_i + e_i$ Adjusted $R^2 = .77$
If EXP = 0, LNWAGES = 2.1 (WAGES=8.2)
If EXP ↑ 1 unit, then WAGES ↑ 130%

B) $LNWAGES_i = 2.1 + 1.3\ LNEXP_i + 2.3\ LNED_i + e_i$ Adjusted $R^2 = .79$
If EXP and ED = 1, then LNWAGES = 2.1 (WAGES=8.2)
If EXP ↑ 1%, then WAGES ↑ 1.3%, holding ED constant
If ED ↑ 1%, then WAGES ↑ 2.3%, holding EXP constant

C) $WAGES = 2.1 + 1.3\ EXP_i + 3.5\ DGEN_i + 4.2\ INTACT_i + e_i$ Adjusted $R^2 = .80$
For a female with 0 EXP, WAGES = 2.1.
For a female, if EXP ↑ 1 unit, then WAGES ↑ 1.3 units.
For a male with 0 EXP, WAGES are 3.5 units higher than a female with 0 EXP.
For a male, if EXP ↑ 1 unit, then WAGES ↑ 4.2 units more than the 1.3 units they would increase for a female.

2. Which regression of the three above fits best? On what do you base your response? **You cannot say since the regressions have different dependent variables.**

3. What would be the values for the structural parameters for the regression above, 1 C), if DGEN was defined as 0 if male ; 1 otherwise?
     WAGES = 5.6 + 5.5 EXP - 3.5 DGEN - 4.2 INTACT

4. Draw diagrams that reflect the following regressions. Put WAGES on the Y-axis and EXP on the
  X-axis in each case.

A) WAGES = 2.5 - .01 (1/EXP)
  (Also, show where 2.5 is on the Y axis.)

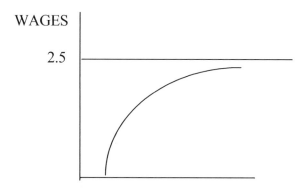

WAGES

2.5

EXP

B) WAGES = 2.5 + 1.1 EXP + 3.5 DGEN - 3.0 INTACT
(Label all intercepts and slopes with their values.)

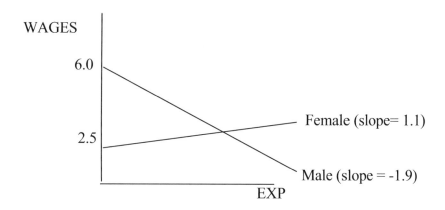

WAGES

6.0

2.5

Female (slope= 1.1)

Male (slope = -1.9)

EXP

C) WAGES = 2.5 + 1.1 EXP - 0.22 EXPSQ

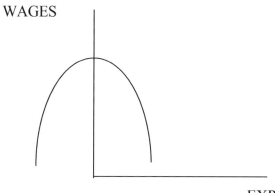

WAGES

EXP

5. Given:

Dependent Variable: BINGE
Method: Least Squares
Sample(adjusted): 1 695
Included observations: 695 after adjusting endpoints

Variable	Coefficient	Std. Error	t-Statistic	Prob.
C	0.818558	0.125126	6.541884	0.0000
GPA	-0.125652	0.033407	-3.761217	0.0002
MALE	0.135596	0.036207	3.745041	0.0002

R-squared	0.056816	Mean dependent var	0.628777
Adjusted R-squared	0.052721	S.D. dependent var	0.483480
S.E. of regression	0.470563	Akaike info criterion	1.335963
Sum squared resid	153.0075	Schwarz criterion	1.362115
Log likelihood	-460.2471	F-statistic	13.87497
Durbin-Watson stat	2.015544	Prob(F-statistic)	0.000000

where   BINGE = 1 if student is a binge drinker; 0 otherwise
            GPA = grade point average
            MALE = 1 if male; 0 otherwise

A) Interpret the constant term.
The probability of a female with 0 GPA binging is 81.8558%.
B) Interpret the coefficient on GPA.
If GPA ↑ 1 unit, then the probability of binging ↓ 12.5652% (for males and females).

6. Given the following logistic regression results:

Dependent Variable: BINGE
Method: ML - Binary Logit (Quadratic hill climbing)
Sample(adjusted): 1 695
Included observations: 695 after adjusting endpoints
Convergence achieved after 4 iterations
Covariance matrix computed using second derivatives

Variable	Coefficient	Std. Error	z-Statistic	Prob.
C	2.174010	0.565780	3.842498	0.0001
GPA	-0.552753	0.159758	-3.459934	0.0005
MALE	0.581107	0.163816	3.547312	0.0004

What is the probability that a male with a GPA = 3.2 is a binge drinker? Show your calculations.

$$\ln(\frac{BINGE_i}{1 - BINGE_i}) = 2.174010 - 0.552753(3.2) + 0.581107(1) = 0.9863074$$

$$(\frac{BINGE_i}{1 - BINGE_i}) = 2.6813; \quad BINGE = 72.84\%$$

7. Label each statement below TRUE or FALSE.

A) **T** In a regression through the origin, $\hat{\beta}_1 = \dfrac{\Sigma X_i Y_i}{\Sigma X_i^{\,2}}$.

B) **T** Altering the units that the variables in a regression are measured in may alter the values of the structural parameters, but never their t-ratios.

C) **F** If two models have the exact same dependent variable, then the one with the better fit is the better model.

D) **T** R-squared is not a good measure of fit for a linear probability model.

E) **T** The magnitude of a coefficient by itself says nothing about its significance.

F) **F** A logistic model can yield a predicted value for the dependent variable that is equal to one, but never greater than one.

G) **F** A linear probability model can yield a predicted value for the dependent variable that is equal to one, but never greater than one.

H) **F** R-squared is invalid in regressions including dummy independent variables.

I) **T** Regressions in the wrong functional form are biased.

J) **T** Ramsey's Reset test can help to determine if a regression is in the correct functional form.

Chapters 8 and 9   Test yourself solutions

1. Is a study that uses "experimental" data superior to a similar study that uses "nonexperimental" data? Explain. **Not necessarily. Experimental data has the advantage of controlling for other factors that can affect the results. However, a regression using nonexperimental data can control for other factors affecting the dependent variable by including them in the specification.**

A regression using nonexperimental data will have independent variables that are not predetermined. However, the regression may still be linear if the error terms are not correlated with the independent variables.

2. Prove that $E[\hat{\beta}_1] = \beta_1$.

Assume $\hat{\beta}_1$ is a linear estimator of β_1.

$$\hat{\beta}_1 = \frac{\Sigma(X_i - \overline{X})Y_i}{\Sigma(X_i - \overline{X})^2} = \Sigma w_i Y_i; \quad \text{where } w_i = \frac{(X_i - \overline{X})}{\Sigma(X_i - \overline{X})^2}$$

$$\hat{\beta}_1 = \Sigma w_i Y_i = \Sigma w_i (\beta_0 + \beta_1 X_i + u_i) = \beta_0 \Sigma w_i + \beta_1 \Sigma w_i X_i + \Sigma w_i u_i$$

$$\hat{\beta}_1 = \beta_1 + \Sigma w_i u_i \text{ since } \Sigma w_i = 0 \text{ and } \Sigma w_i X_i = 1$$

Then $E[\hat{\beta}_1] = E[\beta_1 + \Sigma w_i u_i] = \beta_1$ only if $E[\Sigma w_i u_i] = 0$

3. Assume $\hat{\beta}_1$ is linear and unbiased. Use that information to argue that $\hat{\beta}_0 (= \overline{Y} - \hat{\beta}_1 \overline{X})$ is unbiased as well. **If $\hat{\beta}_1$ is linear and unbiased, then so is the constant term because the constant term is a linear function of $\hat{\beta}_1$.**

4. Defend the process known as "data mining." Does this process not violate the theories of inference?
Data mining does indeed violate the the theories of inference. By running several specifications, variables are given more than one chance to be significant. This is an invalid form of hypothesis testing. However, as long as hypothesis tests are carried out with this precaution in mind, data mining can be a very useful activity. Often economic theory is not specific enough to dictate functional form or even which independent variables to include. Data mining can help make determinations of functional form and model specification.

5. Discuss the pros and cons of the following remedies for multicollinearity:
    A) Drop a variable – **This remedy is worse than the disease if it results in an underspecified model.**

B) Try first differences – **This is not possible with cross-sectional data; it often lowers r-squared; there should be a theoretical reason for using this form as well.**

C) Try an alternate functional form such as the reciprocal form – **This remedy is worse than the disease if it results in a misspecified model.**

D) Do nothing – **This is a valid response since the consequences of multicollinearity can be mild. Still, hypothesis tests should be conducted with caution.**

6. Use the following equation to argue that the $SE(\hat{\beta}_1)$ is undefined under perfect

$$multicollinearity:\ SE(\hat{\beta}_1) = \sqrt{\frac{\Sigma e_i^2/(n-k)}{\Sigma(X_{i1}-\overline{X}_1)^2(1-r^2_{12})}}\ ;\ \text{where } r^2_{12} \text{ is the square of}$$

the correlation coefficient between X1 and X2. **The square of the correlation coefficient between X1 and X2 will equal 1 under perfect multicollinearity. This makes the denominator of the formula above equal to zero, which makes the SE($\hat{\beta}_1$) undefined.**

Mark each of the following statements TRUE or FALSE.

A) **F** $\hat{\beta}_1$ is BLUE in the presence of serial correlation.

B) **F** In order to show that $\hat{\beta}_1$ is best, it must be assumed that the e_i's are not correlated with each other.

C) **F** In order to show that $\hat{\beta}_1$ is unbiased, it must be assumed that the true error terms are not correlated with each other.

D) **T** One of the conditions necessary for hypothesis testing is that the u_i's are normally distributed.

E) **F** One of the conditions necessary to prove that the OLS estimators are BLUE is that the u_i's are normally distributed.

F) **F** A regression in the incorrect functional form violates assumption 4 of the Classical Linear Regression Model (CLRM).

G) **F** In the presence of multicollinearity, the estimate of R-squared will be biased.

H) **T** $VAR(\hat{\beta}_1) = E[(\hat{\beta}_1 - \beta_1)^2] = E[(\beta_1 + \Sigma w_i u_i - \beta_1)^2] = \sigma^2 \Sigma w_i^2$

I) **T** It is possible, although unlikely, that the structural parameters in an underspecified regression are unbiased.

J) **T** With perfect multicollinearity, the OLS estimators are undefined.

K) **F** Consider $Y_i = \hat{\beta}_0 + \hat{\beta}_1 X1_i + \hat{\beta}_2 X2_i + \hat{\beta}_3 X3_i + \hat{\beta}_4 X4_i + e_i$, t. If X1 and X2 are highly collinear, then the standard errors of $\hat{\beta}_1$ and $\hat{\beta}_2$ will be bloated, but not those of $\hat{\beta}_3$ and $\hat{\beta}_4$.

L) **F** $\Sigma w_i X_i = 0$; where $w_i = \dfrac{(X_i - \bar{X})}{\Sigma(X_i - \bar{X})^2}$

M) **F** A predetermined explanatory variable is stochastic.

N) **F** A VIF (variance inflation factor) less than 5 means multicollinearity is nonexistent.

O) **T** $u_i \sim N(0, \sigma^2)$ indicates that the true error terms are normally distributed with an expected value of 0 and each true error term has a variance equal to some constant, σ^2.

P) **F** Assumptions 1 and 2 of the Classical Linear Regression Model CLRM are necessary to prove that the OLS estimators are linear.

Q) **T** Assumptions 1 and 2 of the CLRM are necessary to prove that the OLS estimators are unbiased.

R) **F** Assumptions 3 and 4 of the CLRM are necessary to prove that the OLS estimators are linear.

S) **F** Assumptions 3 and 4 of the CLRM are necessary to prove that the OLS estimators are unbiased.

T) **T** Assumptions 3 and 4 of the CLRM are necessary to prove that the OLS estimators are best.

Assumptions of the Classical Linear Regression Model

1. The independent variable(s) is (are) predetermined or at least not correlated with the error term: $E[u_i \, X_i] = 0$

2. The expected value of the error terms is zero: $E[u_i \,|\, X_i] = 0$

3. The error terms are not related to one another: $E[u_i \, u_j] = 0$ for all $i \neq j$

4. The error terms all have the same variance: $E[u_i^2] = E[u_j^2] = \sigma^2$ for all $i \neq j$

Chapters 10 and 11   Test yourself solutions

1. Describe the following procedures:

A) Park test

To test if $Y_i = \hat{\beta}_0 + \hat{\beta}_1 X_i + e_i$ suffers from heteroskedasticity, square the residuals and regress them on the explanatory variable giving rise to the heteroskedasticity. Use the double-log form if possible; if that is not possible, the semi-log form will do:

$$\ln(e_i^2) = \alpha_0 + \alpha_1 \ln(X_i) + \varepsilon_i$$

If α_1 is statistically significant, then heteroskedasticity is present.

B) Weighted least-squares

Suppose the error terms from $SAVING_i = \beta_0 + \beta_1 INCOME_i + u_i$ are heteroskedastic in that the variance of the error terms varies with INCOME. Multiply through the original regression by 1/INCOME.

$$\frac{SAVING_i}{INCOME_i} = \beta_0 \frac{1}{INCOME_i} + \beta_1 \frac{INCOME_i}{INCOME_i} + \frac{u_i}{INCOME_i}$$

Or

multiplying through by $1/\sqrt{INCOME_i}$

$$\frac{SAVING_i}{\sqrt{INCOME_i}} = \beta_0 \left[\frac{1}{\sqrt{INCOME_i}} \right] + \beta_1 \left[\frac{INCOME_i}{\sqrt{INCOME_i}} \right] + \frac{u_i}{\sqrt{INCOME_i}}$$

C) Generalized least-squares

$$Y_t - \rho Y_{t-1} = \beta_0 (1-\rho) + \beta_1 (X_t - \rho X_{t-1}) + u_t - \rho u_{t-1}$$

D) Cochrane-Orcutt iterative procedure

(A) Estimate ρ with this formula → $\rho = \dfrac{\Sigma e_t e_{t-1}}{\Sigma e_{t-1}^2}$

(B) Run GLS and obtain the new e_t's
(C) Go back to (A)
(D) Stop when sequential estimates of ρ do not vary by much.

E) Hildreth-Lu scanning procedure

Since ρ is expected to lie between plus and minus unity, a computer can easily check to see which value of ρ gives the best results in a GLS regression.
Assume $\rho = -1$; Run GLS; Assume $\rho = -.9$; Run GLS; Assume $\rho = -.8$; Run GLS; ...; Assume $\rho = +.9$; Run GLS; Assume $\rho = +1$; Run GLS. Of all these GLS regressions, use the one that has the best fit according to the R^2 or SER.

F) Maximum likelihood procedure

This procedure assigns initial values to $\hat{\beta}_0$, $\hat{\beta}_1$, and ρ, then considers the residuals from this GLS model. The pattern of the residuals indicates adjustments to the initial values of $\hat{\beta}_0$, $\hat{\beta}_1$, and ρ. The residuals from the new GLS model are again considered and used to make further adjustments to $\hat{\beta}_0$, $\hat{\beta}_1$, and ρ. The process stops when sequential estimates of $\hat{\beta}_0$, $\hat{\beta}_1$, and ρ do not vary significantly.

2. Draw a diagram indicative of heteroskedasticity. Label the horizontal axis "culprit" and be sure to correctly label the vertical axis. Draw a diagram indicative of negative serial correlation. Be sure to label the axes of your diagram.

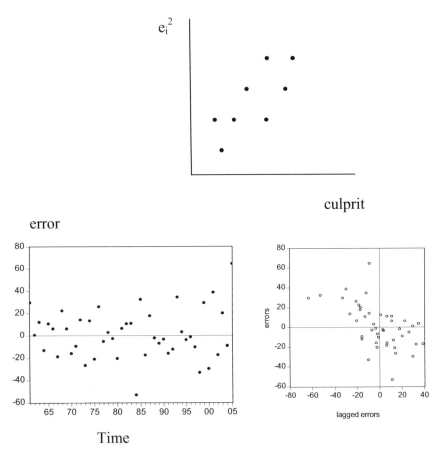

3. Describe the pros and cons of any 3 remedies for heteroskedasticity.

Use alternate functional form – simple; often effective, but may lead to biased results

Do nothing – unbiased estimators good for forecasting, but hypothesis testing is invalid.

Form ratios – simple; often effective, but not always possible
Newey-West – fixes standard errors and t-ratios, but not biased residual stats
Weighted Least-Squares – the appropriate remedy, but what weights to use?

4. What is a first-order Markov scheme? What is second-order serial correlation? What is "white noise"?

A first-order Markov scheme is when the error terms from a regression are related to one another by: $e_t = \rho\, e_{t-1} + \varepsilon_t$ where $-1 < \rho < +1$ and ε_t is white noise. (i.e. $\varepsilon_t \sim N(0, \sigma^2)$) for all t. Second order serial correlation is when the error terms from a regression are related to one another by: $e_t = \rho_1\, e_{t-1} + \rho_2\, e_{t-2}\, \varepsilon_t$

5. Does the White test below indicate heteroscedasticity? Show the 5-step procedure.

White Heteroskedasticity Test:

F-statistic	0.491592	Probability	0.780723
Obs*R-squared	2.645362	Probability	0.754462

Test Equation:
Dependent Variable: RESID^2
Method: Least Squares
Sample: 1 50
Included observations: 50

Variable	Coefficient	Std. Error	t-Statistic	Prob.
C	-275.2148	329.0460	-0.836402	0.4074
ED	18.22919	33.65147	0.541706	0.5908
ED^2	-0.211078	0.952250	-0.221662	0.8256
ED*EXPER	-0.453429	0.645192	-0.702781	0.4859
EXPER	16.12281	15.23650	1.058170	0.2958
EXPER^2	-0.236866	0.208270	-1.137306	0.2616

R-squared	0.052907	Mean dependent var	19.62276
Adjusted R-squared	-0.054717	S.D. dependent var	66.54024
S.E. of regression	68.33644	Akaike info criterion	11.39893
Sum squared resid	205474.2	Schwarz criterion	11.62837
Log likelihood	-278.9733	F-statistic	0.491592
Durbin-Watson stat	2.086374	Prob(F-statistic)	0.780723

1) **Ho: no hetero   Ha: hetero exists**
2) **5%**
3) **If $nR^2 > \chi c$, then reject Ho**
4) **50(0.052907) = 2.645362; $\chi c = 11.07$ (d.f. = k-1 from the auxiliary regr = 5)**
5) **do not Reject Ho: heteroskedasticity is not present in the original regression**

6. Does the regression featured in the Eviews printout below suffer from autocorrelation according to a Durbin-Watson test at the 5% critical level? Show the 5-step procedure.

Dependent Variable: WHY
Method: Least Squares

Sample: 1956 1980
Included observations: 25

Variable	Coefficient	Std. Error	t-Statistic	Prob.
C	-0.325482	8.371100	-0.038882	0.9693
EX1	0.913309	0.032584	28.02956	0.0000
EX2	-0.558162	2.745564	-0.203296	0.8408

R-squared	0.997461	Mean dependent var	640.6560
Adjusted R-squared	0.997230	S.D. dependent var	173.4284
S.E. of regression	9.127571	Akaike info criterion	7.372643
Sum squared resid	1832.876	Schwarz criterion	7.518908
Log likelihood	-89.15804	F-statistic	4321.229
Durbin-Watson stat	1.655326	Prob(F-statistic)	0.000000

----

1) Ho: no positive auto   Ha: positive auto
2) 5%
3) If $0 < d < d_L$, then reject Ho
   If $d_L < d < d_U$, then inconclusive
4) get the numbers
5) reject or do not reject Ho

1) Ho: no negative auto   Ha: negative auto
2) 5%
3) If $4 - d_L < d < 4$, then reject Ho
   If $4 - d_U < d < 4 - d_L$, then inconclusive
4) get the numbers
5) reject or do not reject Ho

1) Ho: no positive auto   Ha: positive auto
2) 5%
3) If $0 < d < d_L$, then reject Ho
   If $d_L < d < d_U$, then inconclusive
4) d = 1.65 d_L = 1.21 d_U = 1.55 (n = 25; k = 3)
5) Do Not Reject Ho > no auto present

Mark each of the following statements TRUE or FALSE.

1. **F** The "culprit variable" is the dependent variable in a heteroskedastic regression.
2. **F** Application of White's heteroskedasticity-corrected standard errors technique will alter the estimate of the SER.
3. **F** The standard error of the regression (SER) is biased downward in a regression suffering from heteroskedasticity.
4. **F** $E[e_i^2] = E[e_j^2] = \sigma^2$ for all $i \neq j$ is the definition of homoskedasticity.
5. **T** In the presence of heteroskedasticity, tests of significance must be carried out with caution since the T-ratios of the structural parameters are biased.
6. **T** The standard error of $\hat{B}_1$ is biased downward in the presence of serial correlation.
7. **T** The R-squared from a GLS regression is not directly comparable to the R-squared from the same regression run using OLS.
8. **T** The standard error of the regression (SER) is biased downward in a regression suffering from serial correlation.
9. **T** After correcting for autocorrelation, one would expect the standard errors of the structural parameters to increase.
10. **F** After correcting for heteroskedasticity, one would expect the standard errors of the structural parameters to increase.

Chapters 12   Test yourself solutions

1. Given:

Dependent Variable: WHY
Method: Least Squares
Date: 02/26/03   Time: 15:28
Sample(adjusted): 1960 2001
Included observations: 42 after adjusting endpoints

Variable	Coefficient	Std. Error	t-Statistic	Prob.
C	-179.2567	163.7257	-1.094860	0.2803
EX	0.259430	0.091487	2.835696	0.0072
WHY(-1)	0.739760	0.198066	3.734916	0.0034

R-squared	0.997038	Mean dependent var	14665.26
Adjusted R-squared	0.996886	S.D. dependent var	4023.018
S.E. of regression	224.5044	Akaike info criterion	13.73442
Sum squared resid	1965686.	Schwarz criterion	13.85854
Log likelihood	-285.4227	F-statistic	6563.263
Durbin-Watson stat	0.866017	Prob(F-statistic)	0.000000

A) What is the short-run impact of EX on WHY? **.259430**
B) What is the long-run impact of EX on WHY? **.259430/(1-.739760)=.99688**
C) Does this regression suffer from serial correlation according to Durbin's h-test? Show the 5-step procedure.
A) Ho: no autocorrelation Ha: auto present
B) 5%
C) If | h | > t^c, then reject Ho (d.f. = n-k)
D) h = undefined ; t^c = 2.042 (d.f.=42-3; using d.f.=30)
E) Do Not Reject Ho; no auto is present

$$h = (1 - \frac{d}{2})\sqrt{\frac{n}{1 - n(\text{var}(\hat{\beta}))}} \qquad h = (1 - \frac{0.866017}{2})\sqrt{\frac{42}{1 - 42(0.198066^2)}} = undefined$$

D) Does this regression suffer from serial correlation according to the Lagrange multiplier test? Show the 5-step procedure.
1) Ho: no serial correlation   Ha: serial correlation exists
2) 5%
3) If $nR^2 > \chi c$, then reject Ho (d.f. = k (from the auxiliary regression) - 1)
4) 14.75185 > 7.81
5) Reject Ho; serial correlation is present

Breusch-Godfrey Serial Correlation LM Test:				
F-statistic	20.57279	Probability		0.000056
Obs*R-squared	14.75185	Probability		0.000123

Test Equation:
Dependent Variable: RESID
Method: Least Squares
Date: 02/26/03   Time: 15:29
Presample missing value lagged residuals set to zero.

Variable	Coefficient	Std. Error	t-Statistic	Prob.
C	-93.87846	135.1921	-0.694408	0.4917
EX	0.104824	0.078148	1.341348	0.1878
WHY(-1)	-0.113005	0.083810	-1.348355	0.1855
RESID(-1)	0.622442	0.137231	4.535724	0.0001

E) Suppose the regression does suffer from serial correlation. What is the major consequence? **Biased estimators (and residual statistics)**

2. A) Using lags of two periods on both independent variables, write the Granger equation to test if the chicken came before the egg.
   $$EGG_t = b_0 + b_1 \, EGG_{t-1} + b_2 \, EGG_{t-2} + b_3 \, CHICK_{t-1} + b_4 \, CHICK_{t-2} + e_t$$

   B) Given the Eviews printout below, did the chicken come before the egg? Explain how you know. **Yes, because we can reject the hypothesis that CHICK does not precede EGG at the 5% critical level, but we cannot reject the hypothesis that EGG does not precede CHICK.**

Pairwise Granger Causality Tests
Date: 04/14/05   Time: 10:37
Sample: 1951 1994
Lags: 2

Null Hypothesis:	Obs	F-Statistic	Probability
CHICK does not Granger Cause EGG	42	0.09849	0.04644
EGG does not Granger Cause CHICK		12.55461	0.17900

3. Are the first differences of M1 (FDM1) stationary? Using the Eviews printout below, show the 5-step procedure.

ADF Test Statistic	-0.615077	1% Critical Value*	-3.7667
		5% Critical Value	-3.0038
		10% Critical Value	-2.6417

Unit root test on FDM1.

1) Ho: B1 = 0 (FDM1 is nonstationary)   Ha: B1 < 0 (FDM1 is stationary)
2) 5%
3) If t-ratio < -tc*, reject Ho

4) -.615077 > -3.0038
5) Do Not Reject Ho; FDM1 is nonstationary

4. A) List the three conditions for a variable to be stationary.
    1) The mean of X is constant over time.
    2) The variance of X is constant over time.
    3) The correlation between Xt and Xt-k (for all k) is constant.

    B) What is spurious correlation? **A strong relationship between variables that is the result of a statistical fluke, not of an underlying causal relationship**

5. A) What is "Granger causality"? **When changes in one times series precede the changes in another.**
    B) What is the consequence of a dependent variable "Granger-causing" an independent variable in the regression? **The estimators are biased.**

6. A) What is the permanent income hypothesis? **Consumption depends most heavily on expected future income**.
    B) Write the Koyck model that was used to test the permanent income hypothesis and explain why this regression is a test of the hypothesis.
    CONt = Bo +B1DPIt + B2CONt-1
    If B2 is positive and significant, it implies that CONt depends on DPI lagged with geometrically declining weights, which is a measure (albeit poor) of permanent income.

7. A) Explain why two nonstationary time-series are likely to be spuriously correlated. **Assume time-series A does not cause time-series B. However, if both A and B have upward trends they will have a positive correlation coefficient.**
    B) What is the consequence of using nonstationary variables in a regression? **The estimators and residual statistics are biased.**

8. A) Write the Granger regression to determine if changes in A precede changes in B. Assume lags of 2 periods. $B_t = b_1 + b_2 B_{t-1} + b_3 B_{t-2} + b_4 A_{t-1} + b_5 A_{t-2} + e_t$
    B) Why is it important to do the reverse Granger test before concluding that changes in A precede changes in B? **Because if B precedes A, then we cannot unequivocally conclude that A precedes B despite a Granger test that says so. The precedence in this case is inconclusive.**

9. A) Draw the correlogram (autocorrelation function) of a stationary variable. (Be sure to label the axes of your drawing.)

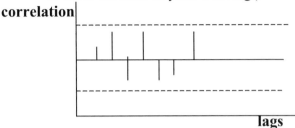

B) Draw the correlogram (autocorrelation function) of a nonstationary variable.

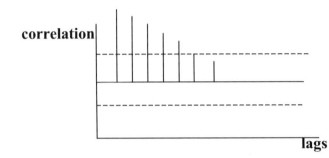

10. A) What is cointegration? **Variables that are nonstationary to the same degree**

B) Given $Y_t = Bo + B1 X_t + e_t$ describe how to determine if Y and X are cointegrated. Spell out the Dickey-Fuller regression involved.

- **Run the regression: $Y_t = Bo + B1 X_t + e_t$**
- **Run the Dickey-Fuller regression: $(e_t - e_{t-1}) = Bo + B1 e_{t-1} + z_t$**
- **Perform a negative sign test on B1**

1) Ho: B1 = 0 (e is nonstationary)   Ha: B1 < 0 (e is stationary)
   (X and Y are not cointegrated)   (X and Y are cointegrated)
2) 5%
3) If t-ratio < -tc*, reject Ho
4) The t-ratio is the usual one, but tc* is about 60% higher than tc from the usual t table. As n approaches infinity, tc* approaches 2.86 from higher levels.
5) State the results of the test

Chapters 13 and 14   Test yourself solutions

1. Label each statement below TRUE or FALSE.

A) **F** To calculate the standard error of an in-sample, point forecast made from a multiple regression, use:

$$SERF = SER\sqrt{1 + \frac{1}{n} + \frac{(X_f - \overline{X})}{\Sigma(X_i - \overline{X})^2}}$$

B) **T** Theil's bias proportion will always be zero for in-sample regression forecasts over the entire sample period.

C) **T** An ex ante forecast cannot be in-sample.

D) **T** It is possible to estimate an ARIMA(2,1,0) with OLS.

E) **T** An ARIMA(3,1,2) model will yield different dynamic forecasts if the forecast period is 2010 to 2015 rather than 2011 to 2015.

F) **T** To make ex ante, out-of-sample, point forecasts for periods t+1 and t+2 using a large-scale econometric model with data through time t, one must assume values for the exogenous variables in periods t+1 and t+2.

G) **T** If a regression suffers from serial correlation, then forecasts based on this regression can be improved by exploiting the relationship between the error terms.

H) **T** To develop an ARIMA model and make forecasts from it, no data are required other than the time-series to be forecasted.

I) **T** Once a time-series has been established to be a random walk, it is pointless to develop a regression model to make forecasts of the time-series.

J) **F** A random walk with drift is a time-series with a trend.

2. Use Eviews and the data in TC.XLS to answer the following:

A) Fit a linear trend to TC using all but the last 5 months of data. Make ex poste, out-of-sample forecasts for the last 5 months of data. For just those 5 forecasts:
    i) RMSE = **1.07**
    ii) MAD = **.926**
    iii) MAPE = **.57%**
    iv) Theil's U = **.003**
    v) Point forecast of TC in DEC 2012 = **162.76**
    vi) The forecast error = 163.28 – 162.76 = **0.52**
    vii) The standard error of this forecast (SERF) = **4.78**
    viii) 95% confidence interval for
        point forecast = **162.76 -/+ 4.78(1.97) d.f.=331–2=229**
                  153.34 to 172.18

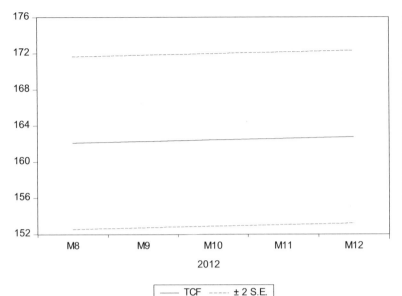

Forecast: TCF	
Actual: TC	
Forecast sample: 2012M08 2012M12	
Included observations: 5	
Root Mean Squared Error	1.071402
Mean Absolute Error	0.925672
Mean Abs. Percent Error	0.565472
Theil Inequality Coefficient	0.003289
Bias Proportion	0.746464
Variance Proportion	0.139955
Covariance Proportion	0.113580

B) Fit an increasing growth rate trend line to TC using all but the last 5 months of data. Make ex poste, out-of-sample forecasts for the last 5 months of data. For just those 5 forecasts:

      i) RMSE = **1.47**

      ii) MAD = **1.37**

      iii) MAPE = **.84%**

      iv) Theil's U = **.004**

      v) Point forecast of TC in DEC 2012 = **165.14**

      vi) The forecast error = 163.28 – 162.76 = **-1.86**

      vii) The standard error of this forecast (SERF) = **6.55**

      viii) 95% confidence interval for point forecast = **165.14 -/+ 6.55(1.97) d.f.=331–**

2=229

                                             152.24 to 178.04

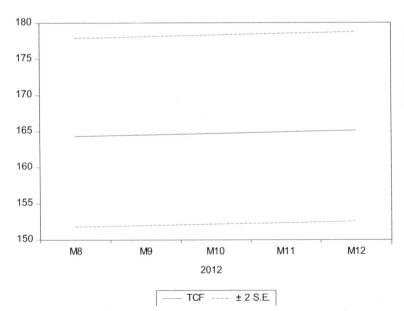

Forecast: TCF	
Actual: TC	
Forecast sample: 2012M08 2012M12	
Included observations: 5	
Root Mean Squared Error	1.472520
Mean Absolute Error	1.373920
Mean Abs. Percent Error	0.842192
Theil Inequality Coefficient	0.004488
Bias Proportion	0.870564
Variance Proportion	0.054731
Covariance Proportion	0.074705

C) If you had to make ex ante, out-of-sample, point forecasts, which of the two models above would you choose? Explain why.
The first one -- the linear trend -- because it scores better on all measures of forecasts accuracy.

D) Re-estimate the model you selected in part C) above using data from JAN 1985 through DEC 2012. Use this model to make out-of-sample, point forecasts for the 12 months of 2013 and paste those forecasts here:

2013M01	162.9801
2013M02	163.1454
2013M03	163.3107
2013M04	163.4760
2013M05	163.6413
2013M06	163.8066
2013M07	163.9719
2013M08	164.1372
2013M09	164.3025
2013M10	164.4678
2013M11	164.6331
2013M12	164.7984

3. Use Eviews and the data in WHYZEE.XLS to answer the following:

A) Does WHY follow a random walk, a random walk with drift, or neither? Explain how you reached your conclusion.
Depending on which tests are done, different conclusions will be reached.
Random walk --since β_1 is not statistically different from 1 and β_0 is not

significantly different from 0 in an autoregression: $WHY_t = \hat{\beta}_0 + \hat{\beta}_1 \, WHY_{t-1} + e_t$

1) **Ho: $\beta_1 = 1$ Ha: $\beta_1 \neq 1$**
2) **5%**
3) **If $|t\text{-ratio}| > t^c$, then reject Ho**
4) **$1.455 < 2.026$ (d.f. = n- k = 39 - 2 = 37) ; (t-ratio = $(1.016 - 1)/.011 = 1.455$)**
5) **Do Not Reject Ho; β_1 is not significantly different from 1**

Neither-- since β_1 is significantly different from 0 in a linear trend regression:
$WHY_t = \hat{\beta}_0 + \hat{\beta}_1 \, time_t + e_t$

Random walk-- since β_1 is not statistically different from 1 and β_0 and $\hat{\beta}_2$ are not
significantly different from 0 in $WHY_t = \hat{\beta}_0 + \hat{\beta}_1 \, WHY_{t-1} + \hat{\beta}_2 \, time_t + e_t$

Neither-- since $\hat{\beta}_2 \neq 0$ in $WHY_t = \hat{\beta}_0 + \hat{\beta}_1 \, WHY_{t-1} + \hat{\beta}_2 \, WHY_{t-2} + e_t$

B) Based on your response above, make forecasts of WHY for 2013 through 2020.

Random walk forecasts

2013	24.216
2014	24.216
2015	24.216
2016	24.216
2017	24.216
2018	24.216
2019	24.216
2020	24.216

Linear trend forecasts:

2013	23.30193
2014	23.66017
2015	24.01841
2016	24.37665
2017	24.73489
2018	25.09313
2019	25.45136
2020	25.80960

C) Does ZEE follow a random walk, a random walk with drift, or neither? Explain how you reached your conclusion.

Depending on which tests are done, different conclusions will be reached.

Random walk -- since β_1 is not statistically different from 1 and β_0 is not significantly different than 0 in an autoregression: $ZEE_t = \hat{\beta}_0 + \hat{\beta}_1 \, ZEE_{t-1} + e_t$

Random walk -- since β_1 is not significantly different from 0 in a linear trend regression: $ZEE_t = \hat{\beta}_0 + \hat{\beta}_1 \, time_t + e_t$

Random walk -- since β_1 is not statistically different from 1 and β_0 and $\hat{\beta}_2$ are not significantly different from 0 in $ZEE_t = \hat{\beta}_0 + \hat{\beta}_1 \, ZEE_{t-1} + \hat{\beta}_2 \, time_t + e_t$

Neither -- since $\hat{\beta}_2 \neq 0$ in $ZEE_t = \hat{\beta}_0 + \hat{\beta}_1 \, ZEE_{t-1} + \hat{\beta}_2 \, ZEE_{t-2} + e_t$

D) Based on your response above, make forecasts of ZEE for 2013 through 2020.

Random walk forecasts

2013	1.282
2014	1.282
2015	1.282
2016	1.282
2017	1.282

2018	**1.282**
2019	**1.282**
2020	**1.282**

Forecasts based on $\mathbf{ZEE_t} = \hat{\beta}_0 + \hat{\beta}_1 \ \mathbf{ZEE_{t-1}} + \hat{\beta}_2 \ \mathbf{ZEE_{t-2}} + \mathbf{e_t}$

2013	**0.027058**
2014	**0.027050**
2015	**0.027046**
2016	**0.027046**
2017	**0.027047**
2018	**0.027050**
2019	**0.027052**
2020	**0.027054**

Critical Values Tables

Critical Values of the t-Distribution

As indicated by the chart below, the areas given at the top of this table are the right tail areas for the t-value inside the table. For a one-tailed test at the 5% critical level with 6 degrees of freedom, look in the 5% column at the sixth row to get $t^c = 1.943$. For a two-tailed test at the 5% critical level with 6 degrees of freedom, look in the 2.5% column at the sixth row to get $t^c = 2.447$.

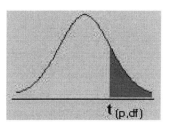

df	10%	5%	2.5%	1%
1	3.078	6.314	12.71	31.82
2	1.886	2.920	4.303	6.965
3	1.638	2.353	3.182	4.541
4	1.533	2.132	2.776	3.747
5	1.476	2.015	2.571	3.365
6	1.440	1.943	2.447	3.143
7	1.415	1.895	2.365	2.998
8	1.397	1.860	2.306	2.896
9	1.383	1.833	2.262	2.821
10	1.372	1.812	2.228	2.764
11	1.363	1.796	2.201	2.718
12	1.356	1.782	2.179	2.681
13	1.350	1.771	2.160	2.650
14	1.345	1.761	2.145	2.624
15	1.341	1.753	2.131	2.602
16	1.337	1.746	2.120	2.583
17	1.333	1.740	2.110	2.567
18	1.330	1.734	2.101	2.552
19	1.328	1.729	2.093	2.539
20	1.325	1.725	2.086	2.528
21	1.323	1.721	2.080	2.518
22	1.321	1.717	2.074	2.508
23	1.319	1.714	2.069	2.500
24	1.318	1.711	2.064	2.492
25	1.316	1.708	2.060	2.485
26	1.315	1.706	2.056	2.479
27	1.314	1.703	2.052	2.473
28	1.313	1.701	2.048	2.467
29	1.311	1.699	2.045	2.462
30	1.310	1.697	2.042	2.457
40	1.303	1.684	2.021	2.423
50	1.295	1.676	2.009	2.403
60	1.296	1.671	2.000	2.390
80	1.292	1.664	1.990	2.374
100	1.290	1.660	1.984	2.364
1000	1.282	1.646	1.962	2.330
∞	1.282	1.640	1.960	2.326

Critical Values of the F-Distribution (5%)

The table below shows critical values of the F distribution at the 5% level of significance. For example, the critical F (Fc) for 3 degrees of freedom in the numerator and 25 degrees of freedom in the denominator is 2.99.

df denom	df numerator										
	1	2	3	4	5	6	7	8	12	24	∞
5	6.61	5.79	5.41	5.19	5.05	4.95	4.88	4.82	4.68	4.53	4.37
6	5.99	5.14	4.76	4.53	4.39	4.28	4.21	4.15	4.00	3.84	3.67
7	5.59	4.74	4.35	4.12	3.97	3.87	3.79	3.73	3.57	3.41	3.23
8	5.32	4.46	4.07	3.84	3.69	3.58	3.50	3.44	3.28	3.12	2.93
9	5.12	4.26	3.86	3.63	3.48	3.37	3.29	3.23	3.07	2.90	2.71
10	4.96	4.10	3.71	3.48	3.33	3.22	3.14	3.07	2.91	2.74	2.54
11	4.84	3.98	3.59	3.36	3.20	3.09	3.01	2.95	2.79	2.61	2.41
12	4.75	3.89	3.49	3.26	3.11	3.00	2.91	2.85	2.69	2.51	2.30
13	4.67	3.81	3.41	3.18	3.03	2.92	2.83	2.77	2.60	2.42	2.21
14	4.60	3.74	3.34	3.11	2.96	2.85	2.76	2.70	2.53	2.35	2.13
15	4.54	3.68	3.29	3.06	2.90	2.79	2.71	2.64	2.48	2.29	2.07
16	4.49	3.63	3.24	3.01	2.85	2.74	2.66	2.59	2.42	2.24	2.01
17	4.45	3.59	3.20	2.96	2.81	2.70	2.61	2.55	2.38	2.19	1.96
18	4.41	3.55	3.16	2.93	2.77	2.66	2.58	2.51	2.34	2.15	1.92
19	4.38	3.52	3.13	2.90	2.74	2.63	2.54	2.48	2.31	2.11	1.88
20	4.35	3.49	3.10	2.87	2.71	2.60	2.51	2.45	2.28	2.08	1.84
21	4.32	3.47	3.07	2.84	2.68	2.57	2.49	2.42	2.25	2.05	1.81
22	4.30	3.44	3.05	2.82	2.66	2.55	2.46	2.40	2.23	2.03	1.78
23	4.28	3.42	3.03	2.80	2.64	2.53	2.44	2.37	2.20	2.01	1.76
24	4.26	3.40	3.01	2.78	2.62	2.51	2.42	2.36	2.18	1.98	1.73
25	4.24	3.39	2.99	2.76	2.60	2.49	2.40	2.34	2.16	1.96	1.71
26	4.23	3.37	2.98	2.74	2.59	2.47	2.39	2.32	2.15	1.95	1.69
27	4.21	3.35	2.96	2.73	2.57	2.46	2.37	2.31	2.13	1.93	1.67
28	4.20	3.34	2.95	2.71	2.56	2.45	2.36	2.29	2.12	1.91	1.66
29	4.18	3.33	2.93	2.70	2.55	2.43	2.35	2.28	2.10	1.90	1.64
30	4.17	3.32	2.92	2.69	2.53	2.42	2.33	2.27	2.09	1.89	1.62
40	4.08	3.23	2.84	2.61	2.45	2.34	2.25	2.18	2.00	1.79	1.51
60	4.00	3.15	2.76	2.53	2.37	2.25	2.17	2.10	1.92	1.70	1.39
80	3.96	3.11	2.72	2.49	2.33	2.21	2.13	2.06	1.88	1.65	1.33
100	3.94	3.09	2.70	2.46	2.31	2.19	2.10	2.03	1.85	1.63	1.28
120	3.92	3.07	2.68	2.45	2.29	2.18	2.09	2.02	1.83	1.61	1.26
∞	3.84	3.00	2.61	2.37	2.22	2.10	2.01	1.94	1.75	1.52	1.00

Critical Values of the χ2-Distribution

d.f.	10%	5%	1%
1	2.71	3.84	6.63
2	4.61	5.99	9.21
3	6.25	7.81	11.34
4	7.78	9.49	13.23
5	9.24	11.07	15.09
6	10.64	12.53	16.81
7	12.02	14.07	18.48
8	13.36	15.51	20.09
9	14.68	16.92	21.67
10	15.99	18.31	23.21
11	17.29	19.68	24.72
12	18.55	21.03	26.22
13	19.81	22.36	27.69
14	21.06	23.68	29.14
15	22.31	25.00	30.58
16	23.54	26.30	32.00
17	24.77	27.59	33.41
18	25.99	28.87	34.81
19	27.20	30.14	36.19
20	28.41	31.41	37.57
21	29.62	39.67	38.93
22	30.81	33.92	40.29
23	32.01	35.17	41.64
24	33.20	36.42	42.98
25	34.38	37.65	44.31
26	35.56	38.89	45.64
27	36.74	40.11	46.96
28	37.92	41.34	48.28
29	39.09	42.56	49.59
30	40.26	43.77	50.89
40	51.81	55.76	63.69
50	63.17	67.50	76.15
60	74.40	79.08	88.38
80	96.58	101.90	112.30
100	118.50	124.30	135.80

Critical Values for the Durbin-Watson Statistic
Level of Significance α = .05
k = number of structural parameters; n = number of observations

n	k = 2		k = 3		k = 4		k = 5		k = 6	
	d_L	d_U	d_L	d_U	d_L	d_U	d_L	d_U	d_L	d_U
8	0.76	1.33	0.56	1.78	0.37	2.29				
9	0.82	1.32	0.63	1.70	0.46	2.13	0.30	2.59		
10	0.88	1.32	0.70	1.64	0.53	2.02	0.38	2.41	0.24	2.82
11	0.93	1.32	0.66	1.60	0.60	1.93	0.44	2.28	0.32	2.65
12	0.97	1.33	0.81	1.58	0.66	1.86	0.51	2.18	0.38	2.51
13	1.01	1.34	0.86	1.56	0.72	1.82	0.57	2.09	0.45	2.39
14	1.05	1.35	0.91	1.55	0.77	1.78	0.63	2.03	0.51	2.30
15	1.08	1.36	0.95	1.54	0.82	1.75	0.69	1.97	0.56	2.21
16	1.10	1.37	0.98	1.54	0.86	1.73	0.74	1.93	0.62	2.15
17	1.13	1.38	1.02	1.54	0.90	1.71	0.78	1.90	0.67	2.10
18	1.16	1.39	1.05	1.53	0.93	1.69	0.92	1.87	0.71	2.06
19	1.18	1.40	1.08	1.53	0.97	1.68	0.86	1.85	0.75	2.02
20	1.20	1.41	1.10	1.54	1.00	1.68	0.90	1.83	0.79	1.99
21	1.22	1.42	1.13	1.54	1.03	1.67	0.93	1.81	0.83	1.96
22	1.24	1.43	1.15	1.54	1.05	1.66	0.96	1.80	0.96	1.94
23	1.26	1.44	1.17	1.54	1.08	1.66	0.99	1.79	0.90	1.92
24	1.27	1.45	1.19	1.55	1.10	1.66	1.01	1.78	0.93	1.90
25	1.29	1.45	1.21	1.55	1.12	1.66	1.04	1.77	0.95	1.89
26	1.30	1.46	1.22	1.55	1.14	1.65	1.06	1.76	0.98	1.88
27	1.32	1.47	1.24	1.56	1.16	1.65	1.08	1.76	1.01	1.86
28	1.33	1.48	1.26	1.56	1.18	1.65	1.10	1.75	1.03	1.85
29	1.34	1.48	1.27	1.56	1.20	1.65	1.12	1.74	1.05	1.84
30	1.35	1.49	1.28	1.57	1.21	1.65	1.14	1.74	1.07	1.83
31	1.36	1.50	1.30	1.57	1.23	1.65	1.16	1.74	1.09	1.83
32	1.37	1.50	1.31	1.57	1.24	1.65	1.18	1.73	1.11	1.82
33	1.38	1.51	1.32	1.58	1.26	1.65	1.19	1.73	1.13	1.81
34	1.39	1.51	1.33	1.58	1.27	1.65	1.21	1.73	1.15	1.81
35	1.40	1.52	1.34	1.58	1.28	1.65	1.22	1.73	1.16	1.80
36	1.41	1.52	1.35	1.59	1.29	1.65	1.24	1.73	1.18	1.80
37	1.42	1.53	1.36	1.59	1.31	1.66	1.25	1.72	1.19	1.80
38	1.43	1.54	1.37	1.59	1.32	1.66	1.26	1.72	1.21	1.79
39	1.43	1.54	1.38	1.60	1.33	1.66	1.27	1.72	1.22	1.79
40	1.44	1.54	1.39	1.60	1.34	1.66	1.29	1.72	1.23	1.79
45	1.48	1.57	1,43	1.62	1.38	1.67	1.34	1.72	1.29	1.78
50	1.50	1.59	1.46	1.63	1.42	1.67	1.38	1.72	1.34	1.77
55	1.53	1.60	1.49	1.64	1.45	1.68	1.41	1.72	1.38	1.77
60	1.55	1.62	1.51	1.65	1.48	1.69	1.44	1.73	1.41	1.77
65	1.57	1.63	1.54	1.66	1.50	1.70	1.47	1.73	1.44	1.77
70	1.58	1.64	1.55	1.67	1.52	1.70	1.49	1.74	1.46	1.77
75	1.60	1.65	1.57	1.68	1.54	1.71	1.51	1.74	1.49	1.77
80	1.61	1.66	1.59	1.69	1.56	1.72	1.53	1.74	1.51	1.77
85	1.62	1.67	1.60	1.70	1.57	1.72	1.55	1.75	1.52	1.77
90	1.63	1.68	1.61	1.70	1.59	1.73	1.57	1.75	1.54	1.78
95	1.64	1.69	1.62	1.71	1.60	1.73	1.58	1.75	1.56	1.78
100	1.65	1.69	1.63	1.72	1.61	1.74	1.59	1.76	1.57	1.78
150	1.72	1.75	1.71	1.76	1.69	1.77	1.68	1.79	1.66	1.80
200	1.76	1.78	1.75	1.79	1.74	1.80	1.73	1.81	1.72	1.82

CRITICAL VALUES TABLES

	Critical Values for the Durbin-Watson Statistic									
	Level of Significance $\alpha = .05$									
	k = number of structural parameters; n = number of observations									
	k = 7		*k* = 8		*k* = 9		*k* = 10		*k* = 11	
n	d_L	d_U	d_L	d_U	d_L	d_U	d_L	d_U	d_L	d_U
11	0.20	3.01								
12	0.27	2.83	0.17	3.15						
13	0.33	2.70	0.23	2.99	0.15	3.27				
14	0.39	2.57	0.29	2.85	0.20	3.11	0.13	3.36		
15	0.45	2.47	0.34	2.73	0.25	2.98	0.18	3.22	0.11	3.44
16	0.50	2.39	0.40	2.62	0.30	2.86	0.22	3.09	0.16	3.30
17	0.55	2.32	0.45	2.54	0.36	2.76	0.27	2.98	0.20	3.18
18	0.60	2.26	0.50	2.47	0.41	2.67	0.32	2.87	0.24	3.07
19	0.65	2.21	0.55	2.40	0.46	2.59	0.37	2.78	0.29	2.97
20	0.69	2.16	0.60	2.34	0.50	2.52	0.42	2.70	0.34	2.89
21	0.73	2.12	0.64	2.30	0.55	2.46	0.46	2.63	0.38	2.81
22	0.77	2.09	0.68	2.25	0.59	2.41	0.51	2.57	0.42	2.73
23	0.80	2.06	0.72	2.21	0.63	2.36	0.55	2.51	0.47	2.67
24	0.84	2.04	0.75	2.17	0.67	2.32	0.58	2.46	0.51	2.61
25	0.87	2.01	0.78	2.14	0.70	2.28	0.62	2.42	0.54	2.56
26	0.90	1.99	0.82	2.12	0.74	2.24	0.66	2.38	0.58	2.51
27	0.93	1.97	0.85	2.09	0.77	2.22	0.69	2.34	0.62	2.47
28	0.95	1.96	0.87	2.07	0.80	2.19	0.72	2.31	0.65	2.43
29	0.98	1.94	0.90	2.05	0.83	2.16	0.75	2.28	0.68	2.40
30	1.00	1.93	0.93	2.03	0.85	2.14	0.78	2.25	0.71	2.36
31	1.02	1.92	0.95	2.02	0.88	2.12	0.81	2.23	0.74	2.33
32	1.04	1.91	0.97	2.00	0.90	2.10	0.84	2.20	0.77	2.31
33	1.06	1.90	0.99	1.99	0.93	2.09	0.86	2.18	0.80	2.28
34	1.08	1.89	1.02	1.98	0.95	2.07	0.89	2.16	0.82	2.26
35	1.10	1.88	1.03	1.97	0.97	2.05	0.91	2.14	0.85	2.24
36	1.11	1.88	1.05	1.96	0.99	2.04	0.93	2.13	0.87	2.22
37	1.13	1.87	1.07	1.95	1.01	2.03	0.95	2.11	0.89	2.20
38	1.50	1.86	1.09	1.94	1.03	2.02	0.97	2.10	0.91	2.18
39	1.16	1.86	1.10	1.93	1.05	2.01	0.99	2.09	0.93	2.16
40	1.18	1.85	1.12	1.92	1.06	2.00	1.01	2.07	0.95	2.15
45	1.24	1.84	1.19	1.90	1.14	1.96	1.09	2.02	1.04	2.09
50	1.29	1.82	1.25	1.88	1.20	1.93	1.16	1.99	1.11	2.04
55	1.33	1.81	1.29	1.86	1.25	1.91	1.21	1.96	1.17	2.01
60	1.37	1.81	1.34	1.85	1.30	1.89	1.26	1.94	1.22	1.98
65	1.40	1.81	1.37	1.84	1.34	1.88	1.30	1.92	1.27	1.96
70	1.43	1.80	1.40	1.84	1.37	1.87	1.34	1.91	1.31	1.95
75	1.46	1.80	1.43	1.83	1.40	1.87	1.37	1.90	1.34	1.94
80	1.48	1.80	1.45	1.83	1.43	1.86	1.40	1.89	1.37	1.93
85	1.50	1.80	1.47	1.83	1.49	1.86	1.42	1.89	1.40	1.92
90	1.52	1.80	1.49	1.83	1.47	1.85	1.45	1.88	1.42	1.91
95	1.54	1.80	1.51	1.83	1.49	1.85	1.46	1.88	1.44	1.90
100	1.55	1.80	1.53	1.83	1.50	1.85	1.48	1.87	1.46	1.90
150	1.65	1.82	1.64	1.83	1.62	1.85	1.60	1.86	1.59	1.88
200	1.71	1.83	1.70	1.84	1.69	1.85	1.68	1.86	1.67	1.87

Subject and Name Index

maximum likelihood procedure, 87, 132
Mazzeo, Michael, 194
measures of goodness-of-fit, 26, 49
model specification, 52
Monte Carlo study, 96, 101
multicollinearity, 105
multiple regression, 47

negative sign test, 38
Newey, W. K., 194
Newey-West technique, 118, 120, 121, 122, 132, 134, 135, 136, 220, 224
nonstationarity, 142
normal equation, 16, 17, 33, 47, 48, 62, 209, 242, 246

Okun, Arthur M., 194
ordinary least-squares, 12
Ordinary least-squares estimators, derived, 15
out-of-sample forecast, 170
overspecification, 55

panel data, 3
Park test, 116
Park, R.E., 194
perfect multicollinearity, 105

point forecast, 157
polynomial model, 69
polynomial trend, 166
positive sign test, 39
probability values, 41
pseudoautocorrelation, 0, 130, 131, 141
psychometrics, 6

Q statistic, 179

Ramsey, J.B., 53, 194
random walk, 170
random walk with drift, 170
reciprocal model, 69
regression through the origin, 63
repeated sampling, 29
r-squared, 27

sabermetrics, 6
Schwarz criterion, 53
seasonal adjustment, 80
second difference, 181
Second differences, 149
second-order serial correlation, 125, 130, 132
serial correlation, 124
sociometrics, 6
Specific value test, 39
Spector, Lee C., 194
spurious correlation, 142, 149
standard error of the forecast, 158, 160

standard error of the regression (SER), 26
standard error, of estimator, 28, 29, 49
stationary time-series, 142, 177, 189
stochastic parameter, 30

test for r = 0, 40
test for r^2 = 0, 41
test of significance, 35
Theil, Henri., 1, 194
time-series model, 139
t-ratio, 37, 40, 42
trend variable, 71
TYPE I error, 35, 42
TYPE II error, 36, 43, 62, 107, 108, 204, 246

unbiased estimator, proof, 96
unit root test, 147, 182

variance inflation factor, 107
variance proportion, 162

Wang, H., 193
Watson, G.S., 193
weighted least-squares, 118
West, K.D., 194
white noise, 125, 130, 135, 185, 189, 190, 238
White test, 117
White, H., 194